INTOXICATING
Greater Paris

Loire, Valley of the Kings

P J A D A M S

For information: www.meanderingtrailmedia.com

Copyeditor: Lynette Smith
Senior Graphic Designer: Rachal Cox
Production Assistant: Gabrielle Désigner
Contributor: Christy Destremau

Manufactured in the United States of America
ISBN: 13-digit: 978-0-9965360-1-1 (paperback); 978-0-9965360-2-8
(ePub)

Publisher's Cataloging-in-Publication Data:
Names: Adams, P. J., 1952- author.
Title: Intoxicating greater Paris : Loire, valley of the kings / P J Adams. --
Description: Rancho Mission Viejo, California : Meandering Trail Media,
[2016] Includes index.
Identifiers: ISBN: 978-0-9965360-1-1 (paperback) | 978-0-9965360-2-
8 (ePub) | LCCN: 2016910281
Subjects: LCSH: Loire River Valley (France)--Guidebooks. | Castles--France--
Loire River Valley--Guidebooks. | Loire (France : Department)--Guidebooks. |
Loire River Valley (France)--Description and travel. | Americans--Loire River Val-
ley (France)--Guidebooks. | Loire River Valley (France)--Social life and customs. |
LCGFT: Guidebooks. | BISAC: TRAVEL / Europe / France. | BIOGRAPHY &
AUTOBIOGRAPHY / Personal Memoirs.
Classification:
LCC: DC611.L81 A33 2016 | DDC: 914.4/58104--dc23

For John, Ashley, and France lovers everywhere

TABLE OF CONTENTS

La Manche

FRANCE

Calais
Lille
Arras
Dieppe
Amiens
Le Havre
Rouen
Caen
Reims
Brest
Saint-Brieuc
Bretagne
Rennes
Quimper
Lorient
Vannes
Laval
Le Mans
Saint-Nazaire
Nantes
Cholet
Angers
Loire
Tours
Orléans
Meaux
Versailles
Paris
Melun
Châlons-en-Champagne
Metz
Nancy
Strasbourg
Troyes
Auxerre
Dijon
Mulhouse
Besançon

océan
Atlantique

La Roche-sur-Yon
Poitiers
Bourges
Nevers
La Rochelle
Montluçon
Vichy
Roanne
Limoges
Clermont-Ferrand
Lyon
Annecy
Brive-la-Gaillarde
Saint-Étienne
Golfe de
Gascogne
Bordeaux
Auvergne
Grenoble
Cévennes
Agen
Provence
Albi
Nîmes
Avignon
Nice
Bayonne
Toulouse
Béziers
Montpellier
Aix-en-Provence
Cannes
Tarbes
Narbonne
Marseille
Pyrénées
Golfe du
Lion
Toulon
Mar Ligure
Perpignan

Corse
Bastia
Ajaccio

Mar Mediterráneo

CHAPTER ONE

Introduction to the Loire, Valley of the Kings

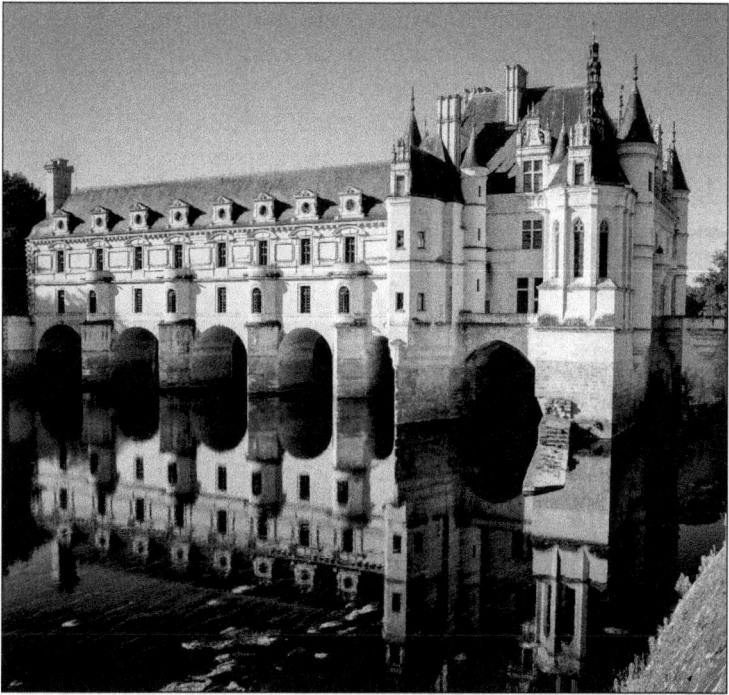

The Loire is a Queen, and Kings have loved her.
— Jules Lemaitre, French critic and dramatist

S outhwest of Paris, the pastoral Loire valley spreads across the land from Orléans in the east to the Atlantic in the west. The graceful Loire River cuts the gentle slopes and fields as it flows toward the sea. Along its pretty banks sit stately royal castles that whisper the many tales—of romance and lust, beauty and bedlam, and power and capitulation— that have shaped this storied region of France.

Lush. Majestic. Aromatic. Romantic. These are all terms

to describe the intoxications of the Valley of the Kings. Imperial history lingers in the stone and bone here. When I visit, I feel inebriated simply walking the land where so many royals and their consorts have marked the Loire.

Wily Diane de Poitiers dominated King Henri II from her pretty Chenonceau estate as his queen, Catherine de' Médici, fumed on the sidelines. Loire-bred Henry Plantagenet became King of England while married to clever Eleanor of Aquitaine; the pair came to rule much of France as well as Britain. François I fueled a Renaissance castle–building craze and along with his confidante, Leonardo da Vinci, brought artistic grace to France as well as da Vinci's Mona Lisa masterpiece that hangs in the Paris Louvre today.

The Loire's crowning glory is the 300+ aristocratic *châteaux* (castles) sprinkled like jewels across the countryside. Visiting these majestic abodes is like passing through a dreamy time capsule. Each castle has a story and a legend with a dramatic cast of characters. Unlike Versailles with its rather cold glitterati allure, the opulent Loire estates are profoundly intimate. The people who lived here—and live here now—are human and accessible. The world they inhabit pulsates with a noble zest for living still today—even at Le Mans, where "car royalty" wear fire-repellant suits to keep them safe behind the wheel of racecars. Food tastes regal in the Loire. Wines age with some kind of hereditary power. And since this resplendent lifestyle is open for viewing by the public, it's an extraordinary place to unleash one's most regal fantasies for the price of a plane or train ticket.

When I first traveled to the Loire, the smell of grapes and blossoms, coupled with the sight of the castles shimmering in the distance, made me feel like I'd entered my personal fairytale. Indeed, Sleeping Beauty's castle-twin slumbers at Château d'Ussé near Chinon. Leonardo da Vinci's flying inventions and robotic knight hint at his ability to time travel—or at least to see into the future. And when

I drifted in a hot-air balloon over Mick Jagger's Amboise castle called La e Fourchette, I grew certain that today's Loire remains a hot destination locale—whether we're rockers or ordinary fans.

Yes, the Loire Valley is a surprisingly navigable area with never-ending, affordable delights. Named a UNESCO World Heritage site, the entire area is geared to tourism. And you can visit in a variety of ways: train, car, bus, bike, balloon, canoe, boat, horse, mule, or on foot. Since the weather is pleasant April to October, you'll enjoy driving along with the windows or top down much of the time. And you can even drive parts of the Le Mans 24-hour racetrack if you like.

In springtime you'll see fire-red poppies scorching the landscape. In hot summer months you'll spy vast fields of sunflowers. In the distance, balloons drift over the castle turrets against an unbelievably blue sky. And when a combine harvester passes you on the road, you'll half expect a royal cavalcade to come charging over the hill at the mechanical beast.

Yet the Loire is not just about opulent living and royal artifice. There's modern life here too. Local towns offer today's French life pleasures coupled with Wi-Fi connectivity. The ancient cathedral town of Tours, for example, is abuzz with commerce and culture. Angers has busy nightlife. Blois, Amboise, Chinon, and Orléans offer Loire historical wonders plus fine food and wine. Saumur is the equestrian capital of France—and the handsome Cadre Noir horsemen will be glad to demonstrate their prowess to you in person. And nowhere is testosterone more evident than in Le Mans, where modern-day steeds in the form of Porsches, Audis, and Ferraris await their riders.

Top-tier restaurants and curbside cafés offer Loire specialties like tarte Tatin and tangy goat cheeses, as well as savory charcuterie and fresh seafood. Endless rows of vines zip over the hills and around the castles. From these fecund fields come the tasty Sancerre, Vouvray, and Chinon wines loved the world over. And, since the Loire has also been christened "the Garden of France," some of the country's most delectable vegetables, fruits, mushrooms, fish, and game find their way to awaiting tables all over France.

Forests dot the Loire countryside where game has run wild since the days of Good King René. Bright kitchen gardens overflow with mega-sized vegetables; succulent fruit hangs like nature's gems from the bounteous orchards. The Loire River and its tributaries teem with perch and trout. Friendly towns like Tours, Angers, and Saumur are pleasant hubs from which to tour the *châteaux*, the vineyards, the museums, the troglodyte caves, and the jovial markets. And with the establishment of the high-speed TGV train, the Loire is accessible within hours from such locations as Paris, London, and Bordeaux.

For outdoor lovers, the Loire is also rich in diversions. The river valley is a migratory corridor for many animals like heron and egrets, salmon and lamprey, and wild game. Fishing, boating, canoeing, hunting, bird watching, hiking, cycling, and hot-air ballooning all are memorable fun. Miles of forest roads crisscross the 35,000-hectare Orléans Forest—a legacy of the royals who hunted here over the centuries. You can hike, hunt, fish, eat, drink, and live like a royal here—without wearing a crown (or losing your head).

Royal gardens are a particular specialty of the region. Not only are they luxuriant, they're often centers for the gardening industry. Kitchen gardens, flower gardens, royal orchards, water gardens, and grassy parks permeate the land. Garden shops proliferate. The rich soil hosts bright buttercups, wild orchids, rare birds, and colorful butterflies. And of course the Loire is famous for dozens of varieties of mushrooms. Picnicking is *de rigueur*. And there is nothing finer than spreading out your *dejeuner* on a grassy knoll with a castle as a backdrop.

These are just some of the enticements of the Loire. Since it is one of my favorite places on earth, it's my pleasure to bring you the beauties of this captivating valley in *Intoxicating Greater Paris: Loire, Valley of the Kings*. In these pages, we'll explore the region's rich history and extraordinary estates. We'll examine the personalities, past and present, that influence the area. We'll sample the lifestyle, culture, art, cuisine, and wine that make this such a popular destination in France. We'll look at ethereal cathedrals such as Chartres and Tours, as well as the world famous 24-hour racecar extravaganza called Le Mans. And finally, we'll explore how to navigate the area, visiting the five major areas of the Loire that include:

- Anjou (Angers, Brissac, Plessis-Bourré, Serrant, Montgeoffroy, Saumur, Montreuil-Bellay, and Abbaye de Fontevraud)
- Touraine (Tours, Amboise, Clos-Lucé, Chenonceau, Villandry, Azay-le-Rideau, Ussé, Langeais, and Chinon)

- Orléanais and Blésois (Orléans, Blois, Vendôme, Chambord, Chaumont, Cheverny, and Sully-sur-Loire)
- Berry (Bourges, Sancerre, and Valençay)
- Northern Loire (Chartres, Le Mans, and Alpes Mancelles)

Last, I leave you with this tantalizing thought as we begin:

> A land of pleasure for the senses and the soul, the Loire Valley has hosted the lives and loves of the kings of France and inspired artists as diverse as Rabelais and Balzac. Still today, strolling the gardens of Chambord Castle, one can imagine François I greeting his cousin Emperor Charles V on these very paths with a bevy of young girls dressed as Greek divinities sprinkling the ground with petals. Or chance upon a masked 18th-century élégante in the French-style park of Villandry, where the topiary box trees and yews celebrate human emotion in four gardens dedicated to tender, passionate, flighty and tragic love…
> —Relais & Châteaux, *https://www.relaischâteaux.com*

Come now and join me in this magical place, the royal Loire Valley of France.

CHAPTER TWO

Navigating the Area

Originating in the rugged central Ardèche region of France and emptying into the Atlantic near the shipbuilding port of Saint Nazaire, the 1,000km-long Loire River is as French as the Mississippi is American. This is the river the French love best: for the soft green beauty of the regions it waters and because it has so profoundly shaped their culture and identity. The constellation of magnificent *châteaux* found in the Loire valley has stoked the world's romantic imagination, making the area between Orléans and Angers one of the most storied and visited destinations in France.

—Alexander Lobrano, "The Lure of the Loire: Where to Stay, Eat, Drink and More," *The Guardian*

Since 2000, the Val de Loire has been classified as a coveted UNESCO World Heritage site. This historical gem extends mostly along the Loire River from just beyond Angers to the west and Orléans to the east—a distance of about 174 miles covering 198,000 acres. The area includes:

- 2 regions (Centre and Pays de la Loire)
- 4 departments or counties
- 6 cities (Orléans, Blois, Tours, Chinon, Saumur, and Angers)
- 1 Regional Natural Park (Loire-Anjou-Touraine)
- 164 towns and villages
- A population of more than one million residents

The 300+ *châteaux*, mansions, and manor houses are the valley's great draw. These, coupled with the vineyards, orchards, windmills, caves, farms, ranches, greenhouses, and acres of abundant fruits and vegetables, make this a most charming Garden of Eden to meander through, whether you're atop a bike, on a hike, in a train, part of a tour, driving an auto, inhabiting a bus, or dangling in a basket under a hot-air balloon.

Logistics

Visiting the Loire is fast and easy from almost anywhere in the world. Options include:

- **Fly and drive.** Fly to Paris Charles de Gaulle, Paris Orly, or Nantes airport, rent a car, and drive to the Loire. A day trip from Paris is doable, as it's a fairly short distance of about 150 miles on super highways with tolls. But you'll probably have to leave Paris early that morning and return long after dark. You may only be able to see two or three castles.

- **Rail and drive.** From a hub like Paris or Bordeaux, take the TGV high-speed train from Paris into Tours' Saint-Pierre-des-Corps station. Then rent a car at Tours and drive around the Loire. Or you might hop on a bus or bike from any of the major towns and tour the area. The fast TGV train from Paris takes about 1.25 hours to Tours, 1.5 hours to Angers, and 2 hours all the way to Nantes on the western coast.
- **Packaged tours.** Rendezvous with your chosen travel company and travel around the Loire in a pre-planned format, often for one price. (I'll include recommendations later in this chapter.)
- **Private or group guide.** Many personal guides in the Loire act as experts for specific locales or activities. These can range from a few hours to a day, a few days, or a week or more. Pictured here, for example, is Nicholas Rodier from Balloon Revolution, who took me up for a spectacular hot-air balloon ride over Amboise and Blois. (I'll include other guide recommendations later in this chapter.)

Several books, articles, maps, and resources are available to help you plan your Loire visit. I highly recommend contacting the tourism office of each area (listed in this book at various points). They'll happily send you a packet of maps and local information to help you plan your trip, your activities, and your hotel and dining choices.

In *Intoxicating Greater Paris: Loire, Valley of the Kings*, I've laid out five distinct Loire areas detailing the main highlights with my recommended accommodation and dining venues. However, more than that, I've tried to put a face and a soul on these locations and people so you can sense the living, breathing history and culture that underpins these marvels as we see them today.

I've also attempted to streamline your selection process—and maximize your enjoyment—by prioritizing Loire locations according to these designations that follow each newly introduced location name:

   ***Must see
    **Could see
     *Might see

Note that some three-star *châteaux* are located in two- or one-star locales. You may want to drive to these special *châteaux* from your base of operation rather than visiting the area as a whole. Be aware that the Loire is a large area to navigate by car, due to busy traffic and narrow country roads.

The town of Tours has the most traffic as a municipality; so unless you're staying there, try to avoid the roads around it. But if you want to stay in a compelling town with a fresh vibe and plenty of history, old town Tours is your place.

The best overall location for seeing the most popular castles, however, is Amboise. Amboise is primed for tourism, yet it retains its medieval charms. When I was last there a few months ago, Amboise locals were proclaiming that there are at least seventy B&Bs, eight major hotels, four lesser but popular accommodations, and numerous other *gîte* and camping opportunities. You'll find accommodating eateries for any budget, and getting in and out of Amboise to head west to Saumur, or out to the castles in Touraine or Orleans, is easy and fast.

Logistically, avoid staying in the Touraine area if you want to see the sights in Anjou, since your drive back and forth will be at least 1.5 hours each way. Likewise, avoid staying in Anjou if you're seeing the Touraine or Berry areas.

Hence, stay near the castles you wish to see. Then change accommodations if you want to focus on new locations. Chinon and Angers make excellent accommodation bases for Anjou, for example (although I've stayed in Saumur at Hôtel Anne d'Anjou and loved Saumur as a base). I easily visited the castles at Saumur, Angers, and Chinon, as well as the vineyards, goat farms, mushroom caves, and other attractions in Anjou.

Amboise is a great starting point for the Touraine; from here you can easily access Villandry, Chenonceau, Azay, etc. Chambord and Blois are two handy central bases for the rest of the eastern Loire.

Christy Destremau, book contributor and head of France Off the Beaten Path Tours, also provides this gem:

> A little known pleasure for the more adventurous is to hire a bike and take a ride through the splendid Loire countryside. A scenic cycling path (also a wine route) lunges the entire 1000 km (621 miles) distance of the Loire River. Alternatively, riders can simply cycle through the countryside for a day or two. The wine route of the area, however, between Amboise and Onzain, is rich in quaint, unknown, privately owned *châteaux*, some open to visit. You can ride this entire wine route and see beautiful off-the-beaten-path France. It's like stepping back in time—and most visitors coming to the region miss

out because they don't know about the itinerary. This Amboise to Onzain route is similar to the course taken by the kings and their courts and families, particularly between their castles in Amboise and Blois. So if you want to travel like royalty, this is it!

The following is a comprehensive list of areas, towns, and top *châteaux* explored in this book, ranked by priority. The Index at the back will also help you locate specific names and destinations within the chapters. (Note: I use the term *châteaux* and castle interchangeably.)

**Anjou (stay in Angers or Saumur or at one of the overnight *châteaux* or *gîte* residences in the area)
      **Angers, the Plantagenet heart of Anjou
      **Brissac, the giant castle of the Loire
      **Plessis-Bourré, favored movie-set castle
      ***Serrant, symmetrical castle charmer
      *Montgeoffroy, time-capsule 18th century *château*

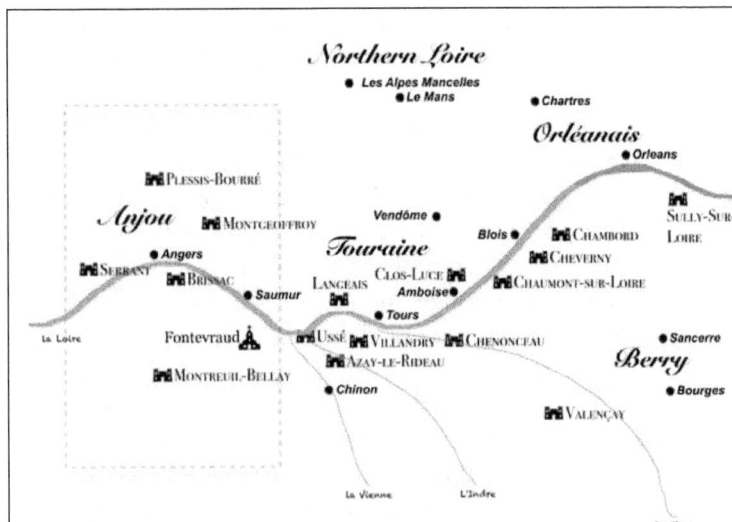

**Saumur, the white city of wine and horses
*Montreuil-Bellay, ramparted, unbleached castle and wine tasting venue
*Abbaye de Fontevraud, royal abbey extraordinaire

***Touraine (stay in or near Amboise)

**Tours, the smart and civilized capital of the valley
***Amboise, royal center and popular tourist haven still bustling today
*Clos-Lucé, Leonardo da Vinci's final home
***Chenonceau, the women's *château* and the prettiest in the valley
***Villandry, Renaissance-garden estate
***Azay-le-Rideau, jewel-like *château* floating on a lake
**Ussé, Sleeping Beauty's castle
* Langeais, moated fortification with a fine working drawbridge and ancient Keep
**Chinon, wine enclave and site of Joan of Arc's historical debut

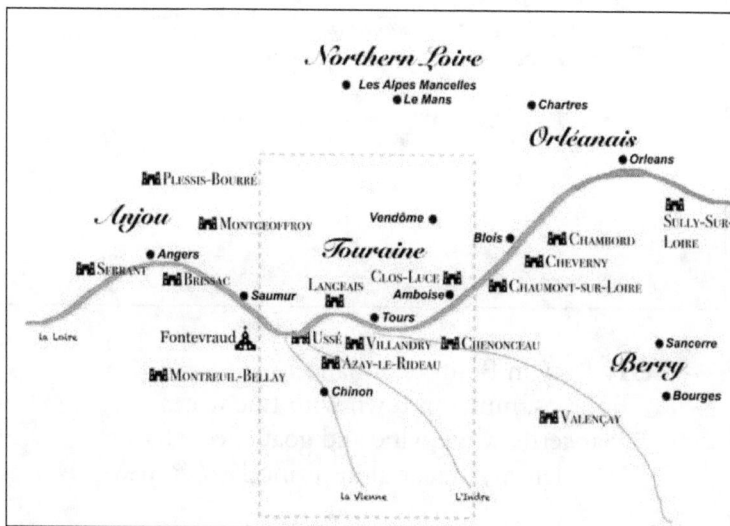

Northern Loire

● Les Alpes Mancelles
● Le Man

● Chartres

Orléanais

● Orleans

Plessis-Bourré

Anjou   Montgeoffroy   Vendôme ●   Blois ●   Chambord   Sully-Sur-Loire

● Angers   *Touraine*   Cheverny

Serrant   Brissac   Langeais   Clos-Lucé   Chaumont-sur-Loire
● Saumur   Amboise●

● Tours

la Loire   Fontevraud   Ussé   Villandry   Chenonceau   ● Sancerre

Montreuil-Bellay   Azay-le-Rideau   *Berry*

● Chinon   ● Bourges

Valençay

La Vienne   *L'Indre*

**Orléanais and Blésois (stay around Blois or Chambord)
   *Orléans, historical town of Joan of Arc's victory
   **Blois, lively Renaissance town with modern touches
   **Vendôme, serene enclave with troglodyte homes
   ***Chambord, the granddaddy and king of all Loire
châteaux with 425 rooms, 365 fireplaces, and 84 staircases
   **Chaumont, garden-rich Loire castle where Catherine
de' Médici consulted seer Nostradamus
   **Cheverny, gorgeous *château* that inspired Tintin's
creator and where the hound-feeding ceremony is
legendary fun
   *Sully-sur-Loire, 14th century castle frequented by
Voltaire, Enlightenment philosopher and writer

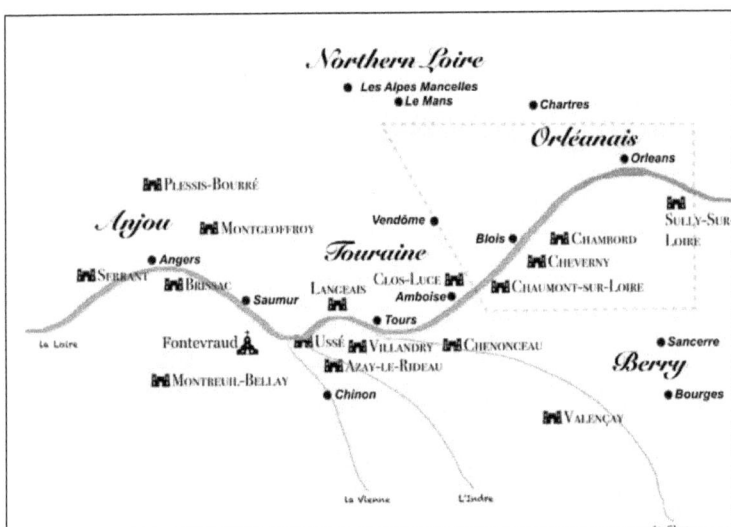

Northern Loire

Les Alpes Mancelles
Le Mans
Chartres

Orléanais
Orleans

Plessis-Bourré

Anjou
Montgeoffroy
Vendôme
Blois
Chambord
Sully-Sur-Loire

Angers
Touraine
Cheverny

Serrant
Brissac
Langeais
Clos-Luce
Chaumont-sur-Loire

Saumur
Amboise

Tours

La Loire
Fontevraud
Ussé
Villandry
Chenonceau
Sancerre

Azay-le-Rideau
Berry

Montreuil-Bellay
Chinon
Bourges

Valençay

La Vienne
L'Indre

   *Berry (stay in Bourges or Sancerre)
      Bourges, museum town with fine wines
      *Sancerre, white wine and goat cheese haven
      ***Valençay, the fabulous princely *châteaux*

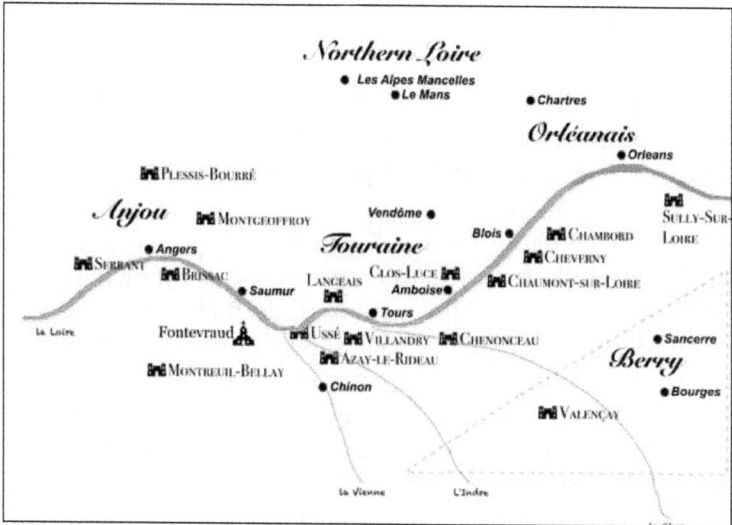

Map of the Northern Loire region, including Anjou, Touraine, Orléanais, and Berry, showing towns and châteaux: Plessis-Bourré, Montgeoffroy, Serrant, Angers, Brissac, Saumur, Fontevraud, Montreuil-Bellay, Chinon, Azay-le-Rideau, Ussé, Villandry, Langeais, Tours, Clos-Lucé, Amboise, Chenonceau, Vendôme, Blois, Chambord, Cheverny, Chaumont-sur-Loire, Valençay, Orleans, Sully-sur-Loire, Sancerre, Bourges, Les Alpes Mancelles, Le Mans, Chartres.

*Northern Loire (stay in Chartres or Le Mans)
   **Chartres, glorious cathedral town
   **Le Mans, Roman ruins and 24-hour motor races
   Alpes Mancelles, sport enthusiast northwest

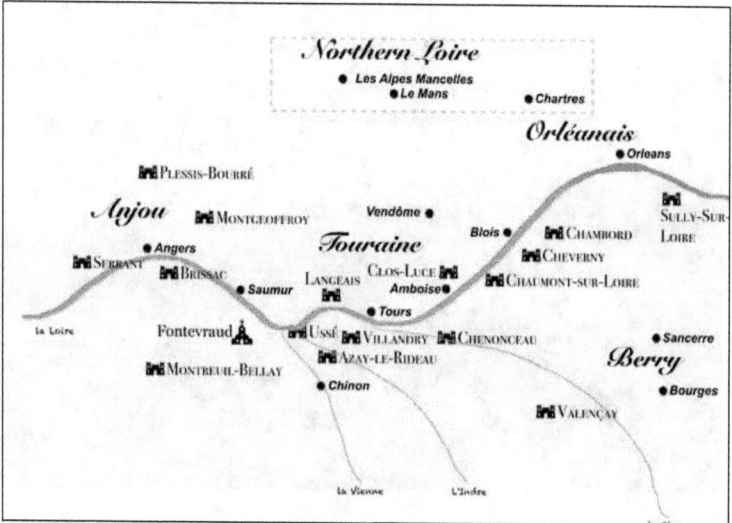

Map of the same region with the Northern Loire area (Les Alpes Mancelles, Le Mans, Chartres) highlighted in a dotted box.

What to Expect

Visitors have such an abundance of choices in the Loire it's sometimes difficult to decide where to focus your time and resources. Tour pro Christy Destremau offers this:

> The appeal of the Loire is its rich history not just of factual events, but also of quirky and intriguing anecdotes illustrating both royal life and commoner life from the Middle Ages through the Renaissance to modern day France. Additionally, the region offers some of the finest French cuisine, and is home to some of the country's best-loved bubbly, called a pétillant, from Vouvray and Montlouis.
>
> Hot-air ballooning, organized canoeing excursions on the Loire and Cher Rivers, or enjoying sundowners sailing on a wooden flat-bottom boat down the Loire are just a few of the more active options to complement any visit to the region.

My preference is to arrive in the Loire, and then take several days to explore the region, visiting the towns, villages, *châteaux*, and vineyards at leisure. There's plenty to keep you busy for days or even weeks. I tend to move at least once during my Loire visits, to cut down on my transit time between destinations.

You'll be pleased to hear the Loire is reasonably priced yet elegantly pastoral, despite the regal estates. Venues accommodate most any budget: Camping is common, while self-catered *gîtes*, B&Bs, and *châteaux* overnights run the gamut from thrifty to pricey.

Dining can be a picnic by the river. Or you can enjoy a street café, bistro, or high-end restaurant that you need to book in advance. Cost wise, the Valley of the Kings is now the "place of the people," so you can spend a little or a lot, as you see fit.

Whenever I visit the Loire in May–September, there's a summery vibe everywhere. Tennis shoes and shorts are preferable on many days; but in May and September there may be rain, so bring your umbrella or hooded coat. In October through April, there may be heavier rain and chill. As such, I take a heavier raincoat in the rainy months and a lighter-weight coat or jacket with a hood for summer. As always, pack for layering and wear good shoes for daily treks, depending on your activities. I tend to take dressier shoes for evening, although keep in mind that Paris elegance is missing here for the most part, and sometimes-treacherous cobblestones line most streets. Enjoying at least one riverside picnic is a must-do—and the experience will linger a lifetime in your memory.

The Loire and its tributaries, the rivers Cher, Indre, Vienne, and Loir (without the e) are burbling waterways that link the *châteaux*, vineyards, farmlands, forests, and ancient towns that rest on their banks. Several captivating river towns can serve as hubs for viewing the great castles. One is Tours, the busy industrial center and university town at the junction of the Loire and Cher Rivers. The Paris TGV train runs directly into Tours' Saint-Pierre-des-Corps station, although you'll have to take a local train, shuttle (navette), taxi, or bus into the Tours city center.

Proximity from Tours out to the nearby *châteaux* runs the gamut: Azay-le-Rideau (15 miles SW of Tours), Chenonceau (14 miles NE of Tours), or Villandry (12 miles SW of Tours). However, there is a lot of traffic around Tours, as I mentioned, which may somewhat hamper your mobility.

On the Loire's western end is the Anjou region where the towns of Angers and Saumur are found. As I said, I enjoy Saumur, the equestrian city, as a hub for visiting Anjou. But I like Angers too—it has an artsy youthful vibe while Saumur is more staid and horsey. (You'll see military personnel based here too, so it has a masculine aura about it.) When in doubt, try both!

At the other end of the Loire Valley in Touraine are the towns of Amboise and Blois. Amboise is my hands-down favorite for an efficient base for castle touring. But I like historical Blois too. Blois can be a charming hub, although it is less sophisticated than hip Tours or tourist-friendly Amboise. One of my Loire guides, Jeremy Kolbe, puts Tours versus Blois in perspective by calling Tours a "fashion-forward Paris girl" while Blois is a "French housewife." From Paris you can also take a fast train through Tours via the St. Pierre-des-Corps (TGV) station, and then get on a slower train to Blois. Once in Blois, which has its own castle, you can take a tour, join a bus ride, or rent your own car to drive out to the various *châteaux* like Chambord (10 miles E of Blois), Chaumont-sur Loire (12 miles SE), or Cheverny (10 miles SE of Blois).

Amboise is my favorite quirky "walking village becoming a town," with its own royal castle—but it's busy with tourists who like it for the same reason. As local expert

Christy Destremau adds, "Amboise is a village that's been rejuvenated by a growing influx of artisan workshops and boutiques, art galleries, and stellar dining options from gourmet sandwich shops and wine bars to gourmet bistros and Michelin rated restaurants. It's now considered the 'it' place to visit, eat, overnight, or use as base camp to explore the Touraine."

By the way, a *château* may be one or all of the following: a stately home, mansion, castle, fortress, or palace. I find that one of the enticements of visiting the Loire is the opportunity to stay overnight in a *château*. *Châteaux* owners often treat their guests to the *crème de la crème* of *château* living. *Châteaux* rates vary depending on amenities and grandiosity. Even if you cannot afford a *château* stay, however, hospitality is serious business in the Loire and guests are much welcomed.

Of the hundreds of *châteaux* estates in the Loire, about 100 are open to the public. If you take a packaged bus tour or group excursion, you'll be whisked through several of the public castles via fast group access. On large bus tours from Paris, you'll probably be limited to a one-hour visit per castle. Paris day-tour companies typically offer three castles in a day tour option. (Count on an early boarding time around 6 a.m. and a return to Paris late into the evening.)

If you plan your visits independently (my preference), you'll most likely run into crowds for the top five or ten castles unless you go early or later in the day. Chambord is by far the largest estate. And since outdoor fairs, *fêtes*, and other events occur here, the pay-to-stay parking area looks a lot like an American baseball stadium lot. (Wear your sneakers.)

The other estates are less vast, yet many have pretty parklands ripe for a stroll, a hike, or a picnic. Check their individual websites for details. Travel tip: If the *château* doesn't have a full-color website that looks fabulous, it's probably not worth a visit unless you are mining obscure history. On the other hand, the less-traveled castles hold some marvelous secrets—and you may encounter a friendly Count or two who will give you a personal tour with all the trimmings! (Yes, there are still "royals" in the valley, although many of them are vintners or farmers with "titles" who also have to scramble to pay for their castles' upkeep.)

Carriage rides by day are delightful. But nighttime can be marvelous in the Loire too. At dusk, the valley seems to come alive with a magical ambiance that must be some combination of wine aromas, ripe blossoms, gentle breezes, and "royal buzz." It's impossible to see this royalty-ripe area and not think you see knights on the horizon or courtly ladies disappearing behind a castle door. At night you'll actually see them show up on the *château* walls, since Loire is the heart of the Son et Lumière (sound and light show). These music-pumping Hollywood-type light-show extravaganzas projected onto the castle walls will zing you back 500 years in high resolution. These are fantastic experiences not to be missed. Many castles offer these shows at night, and Amboise, Chambord, and Azay have some of the most spectacular shows in the valley. Blois also has a marvelous light show—and those offered on Wednesdays are narrated in English.

Keep in mind that July in France is very crowded due to the festivals and pageants that occur during the month. August is busy, as it is the French holiday month—but some eateries will be closed since the owners are also on holiday (often in the South of France!). I quite enjoy visiting in May and June, as well as September and October. I've also gone to the Loire in November, despite the chill; although the flowers are not particularly in bloom, the crowds are thin.

Many Loire country hotels close for the winter at the end of October. Hotels in villages and towns will remain open year round, but they do generally close for a month's vacation sometime during the winter off-season. Many restaurants and shops close in November particularly.

If you are a meanderer (like me), you may use a combination of Loire venues and tour options—but also make time to follow your intuition along a country road or down a cobbled stone path. If you opt for a small group experience like France Off the Beaten Path Tours helmed by contributor Christy Destremau, you can access a comprehensive package that gives you a taste of the Loire with *château* visits, hot-air balloon rides (shown), cooking experiences, wine tasting, and access to Loire professionals in charming settings. Your accommodations and transportation are inclusive. Since I've been on a France Off the Beaten Path tour, I can vouch for its quality.

Christy (shown) reiterates, "Our tours offer guests opportunities to meet some of France's most talented chefs, artisan producers, and artists in a small group environment. My French friends are my guests' French friends."
https://www.traveloffthebeatenpath.com

If you plan your trip independently—which I've done for the last four or five years, I highly recommend you contact the various tourism offices in Angers, Tours, Saumur, and Blois to make choices about what you want to see and do. They can provide you with maps, day passes, and tour information, as well as offer local guide names, hot-air balloon and bike rental companies. They can also direct you to boating, horseback riding, and other delights. You'll find specific activity information listed in each section of this book by location.

Things to Do

There are several themed tours of the Loire for those who wish to travel independently rather than with a tour company. Local Loire tourist offices do a terrific job in providing visitor routes themed around wine, churches, *châteaux*, historic buildings, botanical gardens, and much more. Many of these are sign-posted routes that you can follow in your vehicle on your own. Some tour examples are the Plantagenet tour (tracing the lives of Henry II, his wife, Eleanor of Aquitaine, and their sons), the Wine Route, the Route de la Vallée des Rois (tracing the former royal residences), the Route François I, and the Route des Parcs et Jardins (tracing the famous Loire Gardens).

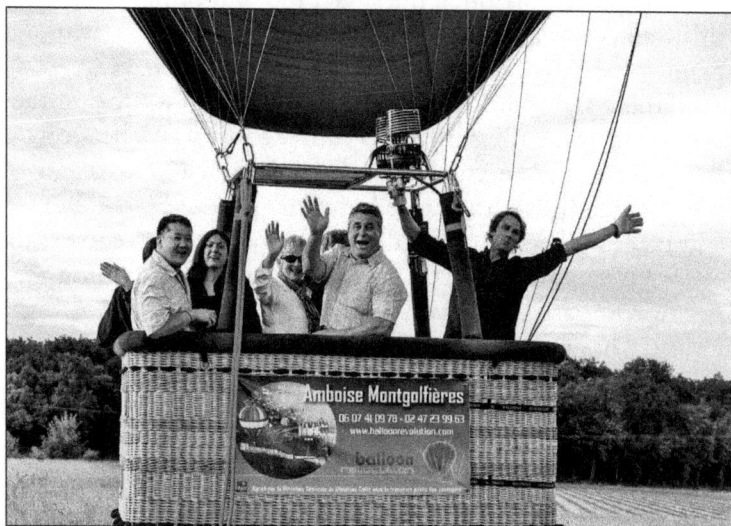

Shops in many of the towns rent bicycles by the day and can offer maps and suggest destinations. Pick up a La Loire à Velo brochure at any tourist office for details. Some trains allow bicycles, whereas others do not; be sure to check first if you expect to take your bike by train. And of course many of the major towns have Segway tours—one of my new favorites; I adore getting on a Segway and zooming down the medieval avenues like I'm on a magic carpet. Hot-air balloon rides are fantastic in the Loire too; you'll find many companies that provide rides. But if you want to really travel light and fast, motorbikes may be your very best mode of efficient, fun transportation.

One of the best ways to wander along "the most sensual river in France," as Flaubert called the River Loire, is to walk. The Grande Randonnée 3 is a long, marked walk that takes you along the Loire from its source at Gerbier de Jonc to its mouth at the Atlantic. This long-distance hiking trail (about 150 miles total) is clearly marked by signs that say GR with red and white horizontal lines. Get more information about this walk, as well as others in France and Europe, at http:// granderandonnee.com.

There are other short walks through specific areas of the Loire, including the Sancerrois (thirty short walks between 2.5 and 16 miles, each passing through the vineyards) and the Sologne (leaves the Loire between Gien and Chambord and takes walkers on a five-day journey through the forest).

Once a riverboat king for transporting goods from the Atlantic to Paris and beyond, the Loire commercial boating industry has now given over mostly to pleasure boating and barging. A delightful way to spend a morning or afternoon in the Loire is to hop on one of the long wooden boats called *toues* that will carry you on a lazy river cruise. Alain Bonnot, for example, who runs the wine showroom for Domaine de la Paleine (near Angers) takes passengers out for a wine tasting aboard Milady, his *toue*. With a glass of Saumur and some sausage or cheese in hand, this is one of the most delightful ways to treat yourself to the taste and feel of the languid Loire. It's all part of the *la vie est agreeable* (life is good) mindset that describes Loire river life.

As for parks, picnic spots, bird watching locales, fishing and hunting venues, golf, cycling, boating, and hiking, you could not ask for a more idyllic setting outside Paris. I particularly like the Loire-Anjou-Touraine regional park (Parc Naturel Regional Loire-Anjou-Touraine). This vast preserve, situated along the Loire River from Angers all the way east to Tours and down to beyond Chinon, is a fantastic outdoor area. The Park Discovery Book, offered by several local tourist offices in the vicinity, offers nature outings, nature and heritage tourist accommodations within the park, discovery trails, equestrian trails, mountain biking excursions, and canoe routes, among others.

One of my favorite things to do in the Loire is to take a hot-air balloon ride over the park and the Loire River, and then drive back through what I've just sailed over. Hot-air balloons are a terrific form of transportation by the way. They give an unparalleled view of the beauties of the Loire—and the castles spreading out across the valley. Not only is this a great picture taking opportunity, but you'll see the rolling Loire with its sandy islands that create a rich environment for river life. You'll spy tropical plants blooming along the banks. You may even glimpse boar and deer roaming in the distance beneath you.

Click on this link http://www.experienceloire.com for wonderful summary material on the Loire, including locale highpoints, street market days, festivals, etc. Great find! By the way, here's a comprehensive list of the main street markets as of this writing:

- Sunday: Angers, Montsoreau, Saumur, Blois, and Amboise (four-star rated), Montrichard, Chinon, Descartes, Langeais, and Tours
- Monday: Baugé, Candé, Doué-la-Fontaine, and Blois
- Tuesday: Angers, Cheverny, Bléré, Bourgueil, L'Île-Bouchard, Montbazon, and Tours
- Wednesday: Angers, Fontevraud l'Abbaye, Saumur, Blois, Romorantin-Lanthenay, Loches, and Tours
- Thursday: Angers, Saumur, Blois, Bracieux, Chinon, Cormery, Montlouis-sur-Loire, and Tours
- Friday: Angers, Saumur, Montrichard, Amboise, Bléré, Montbazon, Ste-Maure-de-Touraine, Tours, and Vouvray

- Saturday: Saumur, Blois, Bourgueil, Chinon, Loches, Luynes, Montréser, Saint-Aignan, and Tours

Tips for Maximizing Your Time in the Loire

Whether you have a limited or lengthy time to visit the Loire, here are some suggestions for itineraries:

One Day:
- Blois, Chambord, Chenonceau

Two Days:
- Blois Chambord, Chenonceau
- Amboise, Azay, Villandry

Three Days or more:
- Everything from the Two Day agenda above, plus
- Angers, Saumur, one wine tasting, one river boat cruise, one tufa cave tour or dining experience, one bike ride, and a visit to the International Garden Festival at Chaumont-sur-Loire (where you can also enjoy a superb, one-price menu luncheon in the pretty gardens)

I have two words of advice, however: Pace yourself. I'm also going to add a few words about "castle fatigue." Anthony Peregrine of the UK's *Telegraph* wrote:

> If you've been to the region, you will have noticed the Loire Valley Shuffle, the desperate slouch of visitors traipsing from one castle to another, one salon to another, driven to the very brink of despair by more Renaissance mouldings, more inlaid commodes, and endless 16th-century portraits of fellows with ruffs and bloomers.

I quite agree with Peregrine that castle fatigue is a very real phenomenon (and your feet will know it long before your brain does). So I'd suggest you see no more than two or three castles a day (two for maximum appreciation). As you'll experience in this book, I've attempted to write full-bodied descriptions of the places and castles since it's important to take the time to feel the life in these wonderful locales. History comes alive here—unless you're too exhausted to experience it.

As such, here are some suggestions for your Loire travel:

1. Read about the Loire and the individual castles before you visit. Be informed on what to expect and what you hope to see in a day, a few days, or a week.
2. Carry a book, map, guide, app, or audio guide with you. Better yet, take the guided tours by locals who can tell you not only the facts but the gossip as well. (There's a lot of it here, both past and present. Frankly, that's what puts the life in my coverage, since locals want to share what they know—or suspect!)
3. Select your castle visits strategically to maximize your time and energy. Start out with a good breakfast, take along some water, see the first *château,* and then stop for a wonderful lunch or picnic. Then, after some digestion time, pick up and head to the next *château.* Always give your brain and your feet a rest in between.
4. By sunset, most of the tour groups are gone; you'll have the *châteaux* practically to yourself. As the sun sets, you'll also get the most stunning photographs of these glorious abodes. You may also glean some insider tips from castle staff (especially about places to dine or have an *apéritif* nearby)—and sometimes your guide will even join you in the wine bar or café!

5. Talk to others along the way, whether they're in a parallel group, on a tour bus, on a honeymoon, or simply locals enjoying their history. I once spent twice the time I'd planned at Villandry because I met a delightful group of Australians who invited me to have tea with them in the garden tearoom. They even invited me to a wedding of one of their members! Another time, a French guide wandered alone into a bedchamber where I was studying the ancient bed linens and proceeded to share about 20 minutes of insider information about the castle we were standing in (Langeais), plus his own personal connection to the estate. Other times, I've had dinner or lunch with my guides and found out how the locals truly live amongst all this royal hoopla.

6. Be careful how many tours you plan for and pay for in advance. You may want to vary your pace depending on which castles you are seeing. Keep some free time for meanders.

7. Vary your activities to avoid castle coma. Do a wine tasting or a cave tour or a cheese tasting or a bike ride. And there's always shopping. You'll feel like you have had a more holistic holiday if you can pace yourself and vary your sensory enjoyment.

8. Avoid peak hours if you can. Avoid mid morning or right after lunch. Early or late is best. Sometimes I even go in the opposite direction from a big tour group—then I double back once they're gone or have passed me along the path.

9. Walk the gardens and grounds, stroll through the mazes, and wander by the rivers and creeks. These were as much a part of medieval life as living in the castles.

10. YouTube, Rick Steves, and other travel resources

provide short shows or programs that can give you an overview of the Loire. This will pique your interest as well as give you a frame of reference for your various destinations.

11. Make reservations for dinner, unless you seek a curbside café or brasserie. Nice dining options fill up fast. Unlike Parisian venues, Loire fine dining usually takes place in one seating from 7 p.m. to 9ish, so reservations are a must. Don't expect to eat around 6 p.m. unless you plan a picnic or a quick nosh. But one of my favorite dining venues is on the deck of my room or suite at my accommodation (if I have one). Most of the hotels and *châteaux*, as well as the B&Bs, also have wonderful gardens where you can enjoy a baguette, some cheese, and a bit of Loire bubbly at your own accommodation! However, take note of this next etiquette detail. Many owners do not allow onsite picnicking without permission. Owners feel it's a personal intrusion if you just show up with your food and expect to lay it all out in their garden without notice. Ask first.

12. Remember that when shopping, La Poste is your best friend. If I buy a tapestry or some crockery, I head to La Poste, buy one of their international shipping boxes, stuff my treasures inside, and then ship the box home. I avoid carrying things in my suitcase or on the plane (although I've been known to ship home no-longer needed clothing and pack my tapestries in my suitcase instead).

13. If you're a wine lover, sample the various Loire wines with different courses or at different eateries. The wines are wonderful and very affordable compared to other areas of France. Thus you can try several glasses to see what suits your palate.

Guides & Tour Operators

These are a few names I can recommend if you would like to try a private guide or tour service:

France Off the Beaten Path Tours helmed by American-French Christy Destremau and staff. Comprehensive group tours of the Loire with cooking classes, wine tasting, group and individual dining events, plus *châteaux* visits with local experts. Christy (on the right) is pictured here with well-known chefs Christophe and Angelique Quantin. Cooking classes with noted Loire chefs is part of Christy's fantastic group experience. https://traveloffthebeatenpath.com

Loire Valley Tours. Personable private guides and tour options. http://www.loire-valley-tours.com

Loire Guide Services. Prestige Loire excursions. High-end touring venues. http://www.loireguideservices.com

France Private Tours. Upscale tours with elegant components. http://www.france-private-tour.com/EN/paris-private-tours/Loire-valley-castles-private-tour.html

Brittany Ferries. Small or large touring venues and transportation. www.brittanyferries.com

Viator. Day trips to the Loire from various points in France. http://www.viator.com

Odyssée en Val de Loire. Guided visits and minibus tours. http://www.odyssee-valdeloire.com

Loire Valley Time Tours. *Châteaux*, wine, and food tours.

http://www.tourtheloire.com

River Loire. Local agency that specializes in Loire packages that can include accommodations as well as itineraries. http://www.riverloire.com

Nicholas Rodier of Balloon Revolution. Fantastic balloon rides with stellar views of the valley that are reasonably priced and exceptionally memorable. http://balloonrevolution.com

Jim Lockard (pictured). Adventurous wine and food tours in various parts of France for English speakers. http://deluxewinetours.com/ http://jimlockardonwine.com

Jeremy Kolbe, English- and French-speaking tour guide and driver (pictured with me in Chinon). Long-time Loire resident Jeremy provides full-service guide or driver services. He and his wife Julie also have *gîtes* (self-catering cottages) called *Les Bocages* for daily, weekly, or monthly rental. Les Bocages are restored from a former wine producer's property. They include pool and patio features. Contact: mobile +33 6 19 07 05 98, phone +33 2 54 70 20 52, http://loirevalleygite.com or office@france-tours.net.

Intoxicating Greater Paris: Loire, Valley of the Kings

CHAPTER THREE

History and Landscape

French monarchs and rich aristocrats selected this area for their *châteaux*—usually for their own use but often for their mistresses…Touraine seem(s) like a gigantic open-air museum with the world's largest collection of castles.

–Hubrecht Duijker, *Touring in Wine Country:*
The Loire

Extending over eight regional areas and spanning one-fifth of France, the Loire Valley is easily one of the country's most famous spots. It's dotted with pleasing villages, enterprising towns, and vital cities including Angers (population 147,000), Le Mans (population 144,000), Tours (population 134,000), Orléans (population 114,000), and Saumur (28,000). Pretty Loire is a magnet for enthusiastic travelers. In fact more than 15 million visitors come to the valley each year.

The Valley of the Kings is alluring to modern globetrotters with all kinds of tastes. The climate is favorable 80 percent of the year—hence it's a year-round destination. The cuisine is appetizing. The wine is superb, yet affordable. The people are friendly and forthright. And the one- to two-hour proximity makes it a perfect escape from the bustle of Paris, London, or Bordeaux. These are exactly the qualities that made the area alluring to early settlers as well as French rulers of centuries past.

Neolithic man left evidence of himself in the Loire from around 2500 B.C. The Celts arrived between 1200 and 400 B.C. They established important settlements that still bear a portion of the tribal names: Nantes (the Namnet tribe), Bourges (the Bituriges tribe), and Tours (the Turones). These settlements, plus others such at Angers, Chartres, and Orléans, became vibrant cultural enclaves that remain so even today.

When Caesar invaded and conquered the Loire (which the Romans called *Gaul*) around 58–51 B.C., he subdued the warlike Celts militarily. But by maintaining a light-handed Roman rule, the Celtic culture flourished. The two dynasties intermingled over time. By A.D. 250, Christianity had become recognized; the area's first archbishop, Martinus, came to Tours and founded a French monastery in 361. Celtic dominions such as Angers, Bourges, Chartres, Orléans, and Tours evolved into centers of learning during the spread of Christianity.

The Gallo-Roman culture remained intermingled until the fall of the Roman Empire from invasions by the Franks, Huns, and Visigoths. The Merovingians ruled from 500 to 751 A.D., and the Carolingians came to power in 752. Under their most powerful ruler, Charlemagne, western and central Europe was united and relative peace came to the widespread territory.

By 987, the Carolingian dynasty had died out. The power was then transferred to Hugh Capet, who became Duke of the Franks. Under his Capetian descendants, the kingdom of Anjou grew until it controlled nearly half of present-day France. But feudalism—the social system that established local warlords with enormous power and standing armies—continued to fuel conflict.

During the Middle Ages, fortified feudal residences built by the rich and powerful became warring focal points around which many Loire towns and villages grew. The area slowly began to coalesce around a handful of powerful dukes. In 1154 Henry Plantagenet ("Henry" in English, "Henri" in French), who could trace his lineage back to Charlemagne, became ruler of both Anjou and England. With Henry's marriage to land-rich Eleanor of Aquitaine (who ruled much of southwestern France), the pair controlled huge chunks of the territory. However, this did not include Paris or the lands to the south and east, which were still controlled by the French king. This created a chronic warring situation for Henry. He was frequently off fighting interlopers in France and England, giving Eleanor plenty of time to meddle in royal politics.

Henry and Eleanor's sons, Richard the Lionheart and John, each took the throne in turn as kings of England, as well as rivals to the French King, Phillip II. Eleanor even ruled England as regent when Richard went off to the crusades. She also had to travel to Germany to negotiate his release when he was captured.

After Richard's death, weak-willed John ruled England for seventeen years. Unwisely, he tried to strip his lords of power, but they forced his hand as a unified group: They were ready to chop his head off. As part of his negotiations with them, John forfeited the Angevin lands to French King Phillip. This is why Anjou is part of France today.

Still later, in 1215, John was forced by the British aristocracy to sign the Magna Carta, which severely curbed his powers. John, who later became known as "John Lackland" due to his loss of ancestral lands, is often referred to as the primary enemy of Robin Hood. He's also deemed one of the worst kings in English history.

After the Plantagenets' deaths, English descendants pursued continual claims to the throne of France as well as to the Loire and other areas of France. This, plus the continued incursion of Brits and other nations into much of Western and Southwestern France, resulted in the bloody conflict called the Hundred Years' War. The lethal conflict for control of France lasted from 1337 to roughly 1453.

Each side of the conflict drew many allies into the war. This accounts for the unusual alliance between England and French Burgundy; the Burgundians were angling for the French throne by defeating the weak Dauphin of the house of Valois (based in the Loire), who had the weightier claim to the throne.

This was one of the most notable conflicts of the Middle Ages. Five generations of kings from two rival dynasties fought for the throne of the largest kingdom in Western Europe. The war marked both the apex and the decline of chivalry, plus the development of strong national identities in both England and France. It also marked the beginning of the most significant practice of maintaining standing armies (many of them mercenaries) since the time of Rome. Between 1347 and 1352, the Bubonic Plague ("the Black Death") took its toll on millions across France and England.

In 1429 Joan of Arc, a militant Loire teenager with divine visions, met with the reluctant, some say terrified, Dauphin. The French royal family had disinherited him, since his parentage was in question. He was also staving off Burgundian claims to the throne. Joan came to him in Chinon. Here, she convinced the frightened Dauphin to crown himself Charles VII, King of France, while she rallied the local army and subdued the English.

After a grand demonstration of her divine mission, Joan left Chinon with an army and returned to Orléans with the Dauphin's blessing. There, she broke the siege of the feisty English in a matter of days. Using her army as a shield, Charles asserted his right to rule; he was crowned at Reims the same year. Unfortunately, the Burgundians captured Joan. Then they promptly turned her over to the English. The English and Burgundians took the opportunity to burn her at the stake in 1431 after a lengthy trial. She became a martyr who inspired the French to rally against the English and their powerful Burgundy allies. (Notably it is Joan's statue that dominates many towns in France. Charles is mostly a footnote.)

In 1435 Charles made peace with Burgundy, and the two French allies together ousted the British from northern France, save for a tip of territory at Calais. Keeping Calais was important to the British because it allowed them to keep control of the wool trade, which was vital for tapestry production. Charles finally moved the royal seat back to Paris. (The British continued to dominate in Southern France in the Bordeaux and Dordogne regions, however. They were instrumental in developing the French wine trade. I explore this dynamic at length in my *Intoxicating Southern France* and *Bordeaux Spotlight* books.)

The English were fully ousted by Louis XI, son of aforementioned Charles VII. Returning to Paris only on special occasions, Louis decided to hold court in the more attractive Loire vicinity at Tours around 1461. Tours subsequently became the capital of France.

Under Charles VIII (son of Louis XI), Brittany was added to the empire as a result of his marriage to 15-year-old Anne of Brittany in 1491. This wedded the rich area of Western France (including Nantes) with the area between

Mont-Saint-Michel and Rennes. Charles VIII's successor, his cousin Louis XII, also married Anne eight years later after Charles's death.

This may sound odd, but the binding marriage contract between Charles VIII and Anne of Brittany stated that she would marry Charles VIII's successor if there were no surviving male heirs. This explains how she ended up married to two French kings and was twice the Queen of France. Anne's daughter Claude went on to marry François of Angoulême, who, in 1515, ascended to the throne as François I.

During the years 1494–1525, all three kings were involved in wars with Italy. François I finally defeated Milan in 1515. Rather than rejecting the Italian culture, however, he adored Italian art and architecture and embraced it to spark a "new Renaissance" in France.

Vibrant François I ultimately became France's strongest Renaissance king. Reared there in his early years, François adored the Loire. With his retinue, François loved travelling out to the Loire to escape the stench and chaos of pre-revolution Paris. (The extended Louvre and Versailles were not yet built.) François and his retinue admired the Loire for its beauty, abundant sunshine, and incredible bounty. In fact, François spent half of his 32-year reign in the Loire Valley. Like his predecessors Charles VIII and Louis XII before him, François first modified the region's main royal *château* at Blois. But the king made it his main quest to mold the Loire into a Renaissance hub.

A "courtly French power" developed in the Loire under monarchial François I. His new worldview created an openness to new ideas, new beauties. America had just been "discovered" in 1492; it was deemed a "paradise on earth." The French laid down their weapons with the Italian victory at Milan in 1515. And the beautiful lifestyle of the Renaissance held sway for decades. I'd suggest the Renaissance propelled France, Italy, and England out of the Middle Ages and into the modern era. This is not to say that wars and skirmishes ended. But a deep-seated desire for a more serene way of living was bred during the decades of the beautiful Renaissance.

With a romantic zeal driving him, François was not content just to refurbish the old. As royal master of the French universe, François set out to build for himself the most opulent *château* in the Valley of the Kings at Chambord. Chambord, the magnificent estate that anchors the landscape like Buckingham Palace, was originally designed to be an expansive "hunting lodge." However, with its 425 rooms, it turned out to be the largest castle existing in the Loire today. During 28 years of construction over his lifetime, François invited the famous Italian artists and craftsmen of the day—including Leonardo da Vinci—to create fabulous structures, towers, staircases, and *décor* using Renaissance techniques. During François's reign, the magnificent art collection of the French kings, which can still be seen at the Louvre Palace today, was begun.

The French Renaissance grew out of the Italian Renaissance, which was fueled in part by the money of Florence's Médici family, as well as the powers in Rome. Michelangelo (1475–1564) and Leonardo da Vinci (1452–1519) were among those fueling the glorious rebirth of culture. Simultaneously, the Renaissance flowered in England through Henry VIII (1509–1547) and later his daughter Elizabeth I (1558–1603).

François I and Henry VIII were essentially rivals on the Renaissance world stage. They lived splendidly, outdoing each other in opulent living. Later, the Médicis even "infiltrated" France essentially by marrying Catherine de' Médici to François's son Henri II—uniting Italian and French dynasties.

Thus, when you visit the Loire, England, and Italy, you may see Renaissance themes repeating themselves over many venues. These show up in neck muffs and rich brocade costumes for the royals. They extend to the lush flower gardens with mazes and elaborate topiaries. They appear in fine art paintings, classical sculptures, and Renaissance estates with pretty embellishments. They infuse the era's romantic poetry. They create common melodies in Renaissance music. And above all, they fueled the stampede to more refined ways of living in the Valley of the Kings. There are moments, therefore, when you will walk through the *châteaux* in the Loire and almost forget whether you're in rural France, London, or Florence.

When François I embraced the Renaissance, the rest of his court followed suit. His minions hurried to construct their own handsome castles in the Loire—each with a king's chamber in case François happened by and needed lodgings for the night. Luckily, they found a sturdy Loire material that perfectly suited their construction needs: *tuffeau*. This soft, easily quarried limestone underpins much of the Loire. Built with great *tuffeau* blocks, hundreds of castles went up over several decades.

Huge estates like Chenonceau, Villandry, and Chambord became architectural masterpieces with fanciful towers, intricate stone staircases, carved friezes, huge walking galleries, expansive kitchens, and elegant private apartments. Sometimes the estates even had private chapels, armories, and stables. Many of the castles anchored palatial grounds framed by moats, lakes, mazes, and orchards. And most all had some form of magnificent Renaissance garden.

But the old abodes where not wasted. Ancient Loire fortresses were often remodeled as pleasure palaces. Middle Age defense elements like watchtowers became fairy-tale turrets. Moats became reflecting pools. When complete, the owners (and their wives, children, and mistresses) filled them sumptuously with gilded furniture, brocade fabrics, romantic wallpaper, expensive tapestries, Renaissance art, and rich china and crystal.

The resulting *châteaux* are the architectural crown jewels of France today: Chenonceau, gifted to royal concubine Diane de Poitiers by adoring King Henri II; Villandry, acquired by Jean Le Breton and known for its extraordinary gardens; Azay-le-Rideau, which appears to float on a lake; Ussé, Walt Disney's model for Cinderella's Gothic-Renaissance palace and Sleeping Beauty's castle; Chaumont, much loved by Catherine de' Médici and where she consulted seer Nostradamus on her family's future; Cheverny, with its famous hunting hounds; and dozens of others, which have exquisitely withstood the march of time.

Even Leonardo da Vinci, aged 64 when he left Italy and entered François's service in 1516, was given a royal estate. His manor house was called Clos-Lucé. Fortuitously, Clos-Lucé was within walking distance of the king's royal residence at Château d'Amboise. It was here that Leonardo da Vinci spent the last years of his life. Notably, he brought his masterpiece, the Mona Lisa, with him (see the Amboise Tourism light show depiction). Da Vinci painted very little during his French years, but he allegedly designed the double helix staircase in Chambord, as well as numerous inventions, including a mechanical lion that could walk.

By the time Northern France was finally united under the French crown, more than 300 *châteaux* spread out like gems across the valley. Over the full history of the Loire, Blois, Amboise, and Chinon all served as royal palaces. The rich land and waterways easily supported the luxuriant lifestyle with fine fruits, vegetables, flowers, grains, and wines. Fed by plentiful game, fish, seafood, and cheeses, the royal appetites grew sated with some of the finest products in the land.

François I was succeeded by young son Henri II, who not only inherited François's throne but also his mistress (and children's nanny), Diane de Poitiers. The incandescent Diane initiated Henri sexually at his father's request when the boy was a teen. Interestingly, she remained Henri's favorite paramour when he became king—despite his political marriage to the indomitable Italian Catherine de' Médici.

The two steely women fought for power over two decades; Château de Chenonceau became a pawn in their extraordinary diva fight. With Henri's death in 1559, Catherine de' Médici became absolute regent. She promptly kicked Diane out of her beloved Chenonceau. Then Catherine took possession of the beauteous estate for herself.

The very Catholic Catherine, whose royal sons were too young to rule, assumed power as regent. She ruled from

Amboise, Chenonceau, and elsewhere. Each of her young sons in turn became kings of France. There was much civil unrest and religious warfare over the ensuing decades, however, between the volatile Catholic and Protestant Huguenot factions.

These French Wars of Religion lasted from 1562 to 1598. The aristocratic houses of France were again at war—but this time over religion. Catherine and her royal sons worked desperately to maintain their royal dynasty. They allegedly tried to quell the religious conflict and continue their dominance in the face of increasing irrelevance.

At first, Catherine tried a diplomatic approach. Later, she resorted to hardline policies against the insurgents and perpetrated (or was blamed for) the bloody St. Bartholomew's Day Massacres of 1572. Five days after the wedding of her Catholic daughter Margaret to protestant Henri III of Navarre (the future King Henri IV), thousands of high-level Huguenot Protestants were massacred by Catholic mobs in Paris and elsewhere.

Catherine feared for the lives and political future of her offspring thereafter. Thus she turned to seer Nostradamus for help. Nostradamus provided medical consultation as well as regular astrological charts for the family. The bloody conflicts continued throughout Paris, Loire, and the rest of France until the demise of Catherine's fourth son, Henri III, in 1589.

Upon Henri III's death, newly crowned Henri IV became the first Bourbon king of France. Though raised a Protestant, Henri agreed to convert to Catholicism to take the throne and quell the unrest. He famously said, "Paris is well worth a mass." He firmly established Paris, instead of the Loire, as the seat of royal power. Most notably, he signed the Edict of Nantes, which gave the Huguenots freedom of religion. This act ended the conflicts that had dominated the Loire for decades.

"Good King Henry" was celebrated for his geniality and care for the welfare of his subjects. His court left the Loire once and for all in favor of Paris's Ile-de-France area. After his assassination in 1610, his young son Louis XIII reigned with his mother as regent.

Later, as an adult, King Louis XIII married Anne of Austria (daughter of Philip III of Spain), cementing military and political alliances between the Catholic powers in Europe. He famously installed Cardinal Richelieu as chief minister and instituted the practice in which men wore wigs. He also banished his "meddling" mother Marie de' Médici to Blois—now a royal backwater. He did this to keep his mother (and her Italian family) out of French affairs. Interestingly, Richelieu attempted to promote the Loire area by establishing a new town in southern Touraine; hence there is a town there called "Richelieu." His results were mixed.

Louis XIII mostly ignored the Loire. Instead, he began building his own suburban palace at Versailles just outside Paris in 1623. This was a shorter hop from Paris than the Loire—especially on horseback.

When Louis XIII's son Louis XIV ("the Sun King") ascended to the throne in 1643, he wanted no part of Loire life. In fact, he directly impacted the economics of Loire by revoking the Edict of Nantes and freedom of religion. This caused the majority of the Loire's Protestant middle class to flee, many to England and elsewhere. This left a huge gap in the infrastructure of the Loire; it took decades for the valley to recover.

Louis XIV finished the grand Versailles palace, and he and his progeny lived there until the French Revolution in 1789. Paris in those days was still a relatively filthy conflagration of nobility, businesses, beggars, prostitutes, and students. Garbage regularly rotted in the streets; the stench was palpable. The royals came into Paris only for state events—and escaped to the pleasures of Versailles.

This royal abandonment cemented the decline of the Loire as a regal power seat and playground. Nevertheless, river commerce accelerated to fill the gap in the 1600s and 1700s. Loire riverboat traffic increased. The bounty of the countryside and the vineyards still regularly supplied the royal entourage. But local businesses by and for the common man thrived. In 1789 the French Revolution and the execution of the royals brought new violence to the Loire, since locals took both sides of the conflict. Napoleon's rule some time later brought stability to the area, however. Work began on canals designed to connect Nantes at the Atlantic and the Loire Valley directly to Paris.

Industry grew in the Loire while agriculture predominated. Royal life returned to the Loire with the modest, short reign of Louis-Philippe. He revitalized some of the *château* elements at Amboise and Chambord between 1830 and 1848. But the monarchy again was banished, and Louis died in exile two years later in England.

In the mid 1800s, the Paris railway reached Tours. In 1873 Amédée Bollée began manufacturing steam-driven cars (the "Steam Omnibus") in Le Mans. Le Mans is where, a half century later, the great Le Mans auto race would begin. Nantes became one of France's busiest ports, though the Nantes shipbuilding industry peaked in the 1920s. Wilbur Wright, the pioneer US flying ace, upended European aviation with his new commercial biplane in Le Mans in 1908.

The Loire and its many tributaries were tamed from habitual flooding by the addition of embankments along the shores. The busy cargo trade fueled the valley until the arrival of fast railways and automobiles. Feverish bridge construction began to link the roads and span the waterways, as cargo trade lagged and casual river pursuits took over.

During World War I and II, the *châteaux* sometimes served as military headquarters and hospitals. Oddly, Chenonceau even served as a "wormhole" of sorts because it spanned the river between occupied and unoccupied World War II France. The French Resistance smuggled people right through Chenonceau under the noses of the Germans until they caught on.

During WWII, the Loire region was particularly devastated by the Nazi incursion and heavy fighting for dominance. Amboise, Angers, Nantes, Orléans, and Tours all suffered great loss. Many bridges at the key cities along the Loire were bombed, both at the beginning and at the end of the war.

Tours briefly became the seat of the French government in 1940 when the Nazis invaded Paris. Once the Germans were defeated, the area began renewal; and many of the bombed and damaged buildings and bridges have now been lovingly restored. Superhighways arrived to link the cities to Paris and elsewhere. But the country roads remained for local traffic and picturesque sightseeing. In 1989 the high-speed TGV train brought the Loire within comfortable commuting distance of Paris.

Today, the verdant Loire Valley is a busy enclave of commerce and tourism that bustles around the stunning network of restored castles. Luckily, many of the much-visited castles are located within minutes of each other. Most of the castles are splendidly tourist friendly. Several have guided tours and gift shops, and many have reception rooms, cafés, and full-service restaurants. Often, period furniture and *décor*, vases of fresh flowers, wine and food, and costumed characters fill the romantic rooms to provide visitors with a you-are-here feel to the history within.

Among the most popular *châteaux* and towns are:

- *Chambord*, the largest castle with 425 rooms, 282 fireplaces, and 84 staircases
- *Cheverny*, the most spectacularly furnished *château* still privately owned by the Marquis de Vibraye
- *Chenonceau*, the most romantic, built over the Cher river, sometimes referred to as the "castle of the six queens"
- *Sully-sur-Loire*, the castle constructed by the finance minister of King Henri IV and an authentic *château*-fort built at one of the few sites where the Loire can be forded
- *Villandry*, most famous for the extraordinary *jardins à la Française*
- *Azay-le-Rideau*, a charming *château* floating in the middle of a small lake
- *Langeais*, sight of the oldest dungeon in France, with an operating draw bridge, a magnificent tapestry collection, and the oldest Keep in France
- *Ussé*, "Sleeping Beauty's Castle," as it inspired Charles Perrault's tale of a slumbering princess awakened by her true love's kiss
- *Chaumont*, the handsome castle between Blois and Amboise that Catherine de' Médici exchanged for Chenonceau and which now hosts the International Garden Festival

- *Valençay*, the striking classical estate where llamas and peacocks roam the French gardens
- *Plessis-Bourré*, the movie-set castle still inhabited by original descendants
- *Blois*, the residence of several French kings in the middle of the town of Blois, where Joan of Arc also received her blessing before departing with her army for Orléans
- *Saumur*, the captivating horse enclave and *château* dubbed "the Pearl of Anjou"
- *Angers*, the residence of the cultured Duc René d'Anjou, which now houses the Tapestries of the Apocalypse

As you explore this marvelous landscape and the historical marvels in this book or on your own tour of the fabulous Loire, keep in mind these words:

> The Loire Valley is part of UNESCO's World Heritage's list as a living, cultural landscape... the largest listed site in France. It stretches for 280 km, between Sully-sur-Loire and Chalonnes-sur-Loire. Harmony is the keyword of this heritage site where men and women find their rightful place with nature. It brings together natural and historical heritage, *châteaux*, gardens, towns and villages, traditions and expertise of river culture and wine production, all in a rich symmetry [that you too can share].
> —Office de Tourisme du Saumurois

CHAPTER FOUR

Lifestyle, People, and Culture

My day starts with French sunshine. My days end with a bite of fresh fish or game paired with a glass of sparkling Vouvray or Chinon. In between, I've very busy moments in my tourism job. I love showing the Loire to excited people who want to enjoy our fragrant fields, our extraordinary lifestyle, and our splendid castles. I sleep well. I live well. What can I say? I'm happy here. Deeply happy. This may not be Eden, but my dreams think it is.

—Cynthia L., Expat Amboise resident

Indeed, most everyone I meet raves about the sweet *milieu* of the Garden of France. The lifestyle is intoxicating, yet grounded, steeped in the traditional values of *La France profonde*. This "Deep France" outlook favors the culture of village life over the hegemony of big cities like Paris and London. It translates to a pride of place—a pride that resists too much influence from global hustle.

Long lunches prevail. Strolling local festivals or enjoying bike rides on long weekends is typical. A sense of pleasure marks the little moments. The *chèvre* is sharp and goaty. The bread is as crisp and fresh as a wheat field gently browned. The apples smell of honey and roses. The wine-reduction sauces roll over the tongue like warm chocolate. The wines, sparkling in the sunshine, cast an ethereal light. Everywhere there is a dedication to life fully felt. And (in this Amboise Tourism photo) love among the vineyards is *de rigueur*.

No wonder the Loire has been described as prime territory for *la douceur de vivre*, "the sweetness of living." Its moderate climate, vine-rich countryside, fairytale *châteaux*, and easygoing habits make it a magnet for those seeking "the good life" in France. Life is genial, inclusive. Year round there's a continual series of *fêtes* and festivals devoted to local produce. Week to week, garlic may be king. Then apples run the show. Soon, tomatoes, melons, and even chitterling sausages become the festival celebrants. There are wonderful wine festivals to sip the divine Sancerres or palette-pleasing Chinons. And peasants, kings, lords, and ladies will happily transport you to yesteryear at costumed Renaissance and Medieval Days extravaganzas presented throughout the valley in various months.

Yet the Loire is complex. Although the area is rife with Renaissance trappings, modern life percolates here too. The influences of nuclear power, social media, and international tourism have forced the need to balance "Deep France" sensibilities with global connectivity.

Thus visitors will see nuclear power stations at Avoine-Chinon and Saint-Laurent-des-Eaux. With the advent of the hyper-fast TGV train, Paris is minutes away if you need something from department store Galeries Lafayette. And you may see a helicopter or passenger jet passing overhead as life in the sky rattles the ancient ramparts and disturbs the dozing cows.

Modern, yet medieval, the Loire is such a favorite that Parisians flock to the area, snapping up *residences secondaires* reachable in minutes from their busy offices in Orléans or Paris. Expats retire here in droves—or they acquire second homes to visit all year long. Thus you will meet many Brits, Americans, and Germans who spend joyous amounts of time in the Loire, buzzing around in local cars. And of course visitors arrive by the dozens in tour buses or vans to sample the joys of the Loire for a day, a week, or more. Many make it a habit to return again and again.

People

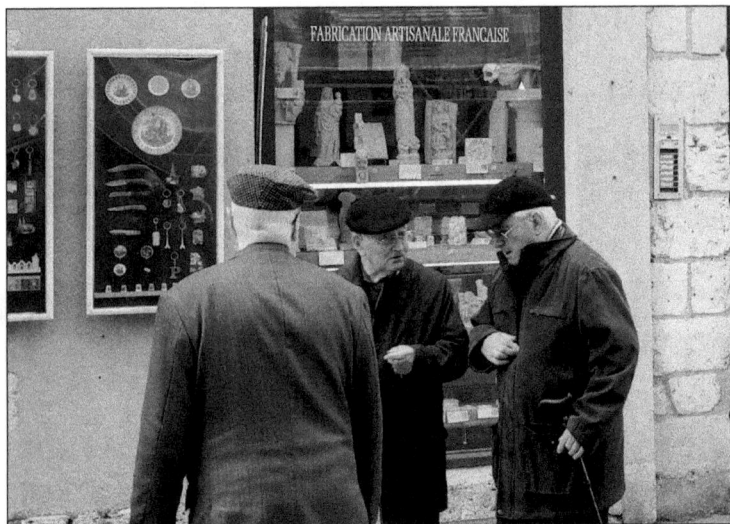

In this central region of France, the people have neither the brisk, sometimes brusque, demeanor of their northern counterparts nor the excitable nature of the southern provinces. They get on peacefully with their lives, benefitting from the prosperity generated not only by the region's centuries old popularity with French and foreign visitors alike, but also by a fertile soil and a favorable climate, which rarely succumbs to extremes of heat or cold.

—*Eyewitness Travel: Loire Valley,* Duncan Baird Publishers/DK Publishing

Loire life seems satisfying to these convivial locals working in the vineyards, biking along the rivers, breeding fine horses, creating locally based cuisine, running businesses, rearing families, and showcasing history through castle management and tourism. The food and wine industries play a major role in the local economies; up to 12 percent of the population is employed in the agriculture, food, or wine industries. There's also high tech commerce and entrepreneurship aplenty.

As for daily living, Loire people enjoy the *hypermarchés* and big-box home and garden stores, as well as the homey *boulangeries, pâtisseries,* and *charcuteries.* But there's always time for a bike ride and a casual picnic with a bit of cheese, a bite of baguette, and a goblet of wine enjoyed atop a flower-covered riverbank.

Still, the historical presence of ancient peoples is very evident. It's clearly not just the wind, sunshine, rivers, and land that characterize the Loire. It's also the strong personalities who shaped the very soul of the place. Thus we'll meet many individuals who drove the Loire's destiny in these pages. Among the key figures, in addition to the historic personalities already presented, are:

- François Rabelais, Chinon-born 16th century satirist
- Honoré de Balzac, Château de Saché–born novelist
- Charles Perrault, fairytale author of *Sleeping Beauty* set at Ussé castle
- George Sand, 19th century female novelist and Chopin lover reared in Berry
- Claude Monet, famed Creuse Valley painter
- Henri Rousseau, the famed French painter born in Laval
- Marcel Proust, novelist who uses Chartres settings
- René Descartes, mathematician and philosopher ("I think, therefore I am") born in Touraine
- Alexander Dumas, famed author who set his 1846 novel *La Dame de Montsoreau* in the *château* at Montsoreau
- Pierre de Ronsard, "prince of poets" reared in Vendôme
- Coco Chanel, much-revered designer born in Saumur

Modern Loire residents relish their history. It informs them. Yet modern Loire life becomes a balancing act between history-rich gravitas and modern commercial agility. Loire people are industrious yet relaxed, reserved yet chatty.

A wander through the local street market is a weekly must do for locals of all backgrounds. Not only does a market meander provide the freshest in products, it keeps locals grounded in the slow culture of provincial France.

Gossip is the jungle beat of modern Loire life, despite the proliferation of computers and Wi-Fi. Locals love to tell the stories of centuries old romances and clashes—then context them with modern-day shenanigans. The Loire is thus full of rumors and tales, both quirky and racy. (This is how I learned about the peephole in Diane de Poitiers' boudoir, as well as the genital oddity that impacted Henri II's sex life. Now that I've got your attention, you'll read more about these gossipy tidbits in later chapters.)

The Loire is, above all, cleverly practical. I see this often in France, but particularly in the Loire. The French are masters at capitalizing on a trend, maximizing a marketing opportunity, or turning their history into moneymaking extravaganzas. Yet art and culture remain supremely important to the French. You'll see many locals visiting art exhibits, festivals, concerts, and pageants. School groups often have field trips to museums, galleries, and historical sites because the French education system folds culture appreciation and history into its core education programs.

You'll run into many Loire groups of children—shepherded by patient teachers—in the major attractions. Paradoxically, you'll find them extraordinarily well-behaved.

This is something I wrote about in my *Intoxicating Paris* book. French children learn early on not to act like hooligans. They are taught to be respectful in all situations. You will see them quietly eating complicated dishes in French dining venues, using proper etiquette, and not leaving their table places littered with crumbs. The one place where I've seen them enjoying themselves with abandon, however, was in Villandry gardens. Here they ran deliriously around the acres of gardens, mazes, grapevines, and play equipment. (But the watchful teachers were close behind.) In this photo courtesy of Maureen Beals, you can see one of these joyful children in the maze at Villandry.

Finally, when pressed, Loire residents as a whole stand their ground—literally. When the TGV high-speed Paris-Loire train was proposed, locales coalesced behind an interesting stance. They lobbied for a very specific route for the bullet train.

But this was not to preserve the ancient *châteaux* or treasured waterways. They just didn't want the bullet trains rattling their underground wine caves! Naturally, the train system plans were deviated. Wine trumped efficiency. Loire locals have very clear priorities.

Culture

From the Middle Ages through the Renaissance, the Kings and Queens of the Loire Valley championed intellectual and artistic creation. The result is an endowment of accomplishments for all time in the arts and literature, as well as extraordinary examples of magnificent architecture and landscaping.

—Luxury Traveler.com

Beyond their exquisite majesty, the lands and castles of the Loire Valley stand as a monument to the French cultural evolution. The beautiful French Renaissance was born here at King François I's urging. François, a man of learning and letters, "invented" the French language, naming it after himself *naturellement.* This is the reason the Loire is known as "the Cradle of the French Language." By the way, the first pages of Francois's new language were written after his release from captivity by his cousin Charles V of Spain. This precious collection of language documents was originally stored at Blois castle; they're now the property of the archives at Château de Fontainebleau.

A deep appreciation for culture, art, architecture, and learning still threads through the Loire psyche. The Celtic and Roman ruins are shown with deep affection. Great Renaissance art, fine craftsmanship, handcrafted china and glassware, and cherished architecture are showcased in nearly every Loire enclave. Royal crests, fine paintings, sparkling stained glass, gorgeous handmade books, floor-to-ceiling tapestries, stunning statuary, and exquisite gardens add to the sumptuousness of this cultural powerhouse.

Many of the *châteaux* are not just regal estates. They're museum showplaces where all aspects of fine living are evident. And of course the Italian Renaissance—much copied by the French royals—is seen in the garden-centered lifestyle, the embellished edifices, and inlaid furniture. It shows up in the splendid silk clothing, the intricate recipes, the introduction of Italian foods like pasta and parsley, and the gilded decorations.

François I helped set the tone for this deep love of culture. He was a great fan of written documents and collected them at Blois. His collection, in fact, became the foundation for the entire French library system.

It's also well known that François (see his salamander crest) greatly admired Leonardo da Vinci and his extraordinary genius. Da Vinci's presence is evident in numerous architectural touches, inventions, and artwork seen in the Loire today. Note his statue near Amboise.

Regional artists were also nurtured over the centuries by an affectionate populace who showered them with money and accolades. Writers, poets, sculptors, musicians, painters, craftsmen, photographers, videographers, and filmmakers have all come to the Loire for inspiration—and they still do. Some of France's beloved sons, like François Rabelais and Honoré de Balzac, were born in the Loire. Many favorite sons and daughters seem attached by a metaphorical umbilical cord to their homeland—and their stories and films are set in the lyrical Loire.

On a techno note, Loire is the birthplace of the *Son et Lumière* light shows. This "sound and light show" concept was the original brainchild of Paul Robert-Houdin, who was the curator of the Château de Chambord in France. In 1952 Houdin came up with the idea of projecting light pictures onto the side of the castle. Then he matched them with sound and music. It worked beautifully, to the delight of the crowds. Historical figures appeared two stories high on Chambord's walls to heart-pounding music as they acted out their lives in glorious Technicolor.

Hereafter, these fantastical light shows spread to many of the other *châteaux*, as well as to other parts of France. Some of these spectacles are accompanied by pageants with live performers in Renaissance dress. During these shows you may see figures sail over your head, watch sculptures come alive, witness scenes from royal hunts, and cheer jousts set to music. The *coup de grâce* will be dramatic fireworks shooting into the sky.

Some of the best *Son et Lumière* shows in the area include Amboise (June–July), Azay-le-Rideau (July–August),

Léonard de Vinci

Chenonceau (June–August), Blois (May–September, Wednesday in English), Cléry-Saint-André (July), Valençay (July–August), and Le Puy-du-Fou (summer). (Check the tourist offices for specific dates and times.)

And throughout the Loire today, there are not only museums and art galleries to visit but a wealth of festivals to meet any interest. While this is by no means a comprehensive list, here are some of them:

- Cadre Noir de Saumur, celebrates horsemanship
- Festival de Chambord, summer-long extravaganza of tours, shows, and fairs
- Foire aux Vins, wine fair
- Foire aux Escargots, celebrates snails and wine
- Fête de Jeanne d'Arc, celebrates the life of Joan of Arc
- Le Printemps des Arts, theatre and music festival
- "Nights of a Thousand Lights" at Château de Villandry
- Château Royal de Blois, traditional fencing and early music show
- Domaine de Chaumont-Sur-Loire, annual international gardens extravaganza
- Jazz en Touraine, fantastic jazz festival
- Bastille Day, July 14th country-wide celebration of French independence
- Vegetable Garden Days at Château de Villandry
- Abbaye De Fontevraud, "La Cité Idéale" pageant

- Marché Médiéval, "medieval" market takes over the entire town of Chinon
- Festival du Film, Vendôme film festival
- Marché de Noel, Christmas markets held in various castles and towns

In summary, the Loire is a culturally rich, sensually enjoyable place to while away a day, a week, a month, or a lifetime with convivial people and places of endless charm. No matter your interest, palette, or budget, you'll find much to enjoy in the appealing Loire—and fascinating people to share it with you.

CHAPTER FIVE

Cuisine, Wine, and Shopping

Rillettes and Loire wines. *Crottin de Chavignol* goat's cheese and white butter sauce...The inventions of the cooks and farmers of the Loire have long delighted the palates of the whole country!

—*Cycling-loire.com*

In the Valley of the Kings, the garden awaits. Much of the year verdurous fields brim with bright yellow sunflowers, fire-red poppies, and fragrant wildflowers. Glorious gardens burst with sun-kissed blossoms and glistening edibles. *Potagers,* or kitchen gardens—some first sown centuries ago—overflow with bowling ball-sized eggplant, hefty asparagus, and spring onions the size of a fist.

Wine vines stretch over the Loire hills in graceful rows of succulent grapes that become some of the most luscious—and affordable—wines in France. Hot-air balloons hover like inverted teardrop earrings over the Loire River as freshwater salmon and lamprey swim in the waters beneath. Graceful white swans glide over *château* lakes as wild boar and deer scamper through the Orléans forests. And in the sandy western estuary where the river and the Atlantic meet, oysters, mussels, shrimp, prawn, anchovies, and sardines are harvested for some of the most delicious cuisine in France. The bounteous "Garden of France" once fed royal cravings. Now, this cornucopia of comestibles feeds the insatiable appetites of Paris and beyond.

Cuisine

> The Loire still specializes in the production of *primeurs*, the early vegetables that appear two to three weeks before those cultivated around Paris: *asperges* and *haricots* from the Touraine, *oignons* and *échalotes* from Anjou, and *artichauts* from Angers—all are whisked up to the capital's markets and restaurants every spring, as they have been since trade in foodstuffs began.
> —Hugh Palmer, *The Most Beautiful Villages of the Loire*

The Loire is a natural haven for growing things. The alluvial soil, temperate climate, and balmy river breezes create a uniquely fertile environment for growing food and grapevines. The produce is often *produit primeur*—first or early to the markets. Many of the grand *châteaux* naturally have charming flower gardens, serene waterways, and shrubbed mazes. But they also have unbelievably verdant kitchen gardens. Gardening here is not just a means of harvesting food; it's an art, as well as a science.

Loire food cultivation is an enormous industry.

The fruits and vegetables grown here account for about 20 percent of the entire domestic production in France. The cultivation of many of the Loire specialties dates back to Roman rule. And some specific varieties have a noble pedigree. The Reine-Claude greengage plum, for example, was named for François I's Queen Claude, Duchess of Brittany. Melons were introduced to the area by Charles VIII's Neapolitan gardener. Anjou pears were originally planted in the Anjou region. Later this delicious pear was exported to England and America, particularly to Oregon, which produces about 34 percent of the pears for the US (Family note: my uncle raises tracts and tracts of this very pear on his land in Southern Oregon; he supplies such food retailers as Harry & David Orchards.)

Ripe plums and prunes hail from Tours. Succulent strawberries grow abundantly in Saumur. Angers produces tasty apricots as well as its famous pears. Reinette apples from Le Mans make their way into desserts, main dishes, and cheese courses.

But vegetables are also much prized. There are actually two main areas of Loire vegetable production. The first is the vast stretch of valley between Angers and Saumur. The second is the Orléans region on the northern banks of the Loire. Many of the areas have delicate specialties that are much loved all over France. Plump tomatoes, beefy cucumbers, and delicate lettuces grow around Orléans. Colossal asparagus proliferates in Vineuil and Contres, while plump potatoes by the carload ship from Saumur.

French beans overflow baskets in Touraine; robust onions and shallots flavor the recipes of Anjou and Loiret. Tangy lamb's lettuce with its high mineral and vitamin content finds its way into many dishes. Vegetables are often cultivated under glass or plastic to ensure their pristine quality. And this is one of my favorite places on the planet to enjoy artichokes—slathered in butter and mayonnaise—since they proliferate in the fields near Angers. You can see by the photo of one of the weekly Blois markets how lush and large the produce grows. Luckily, preparing heavenly vegetables is one of the finest skills of French cuisine. No wonder French chefs love the Loire bounty!

But there's much more. Anjou grows blue-ribbon vegetables such as white radishes, savory herbs, and gray shallots for *beurre blanc* (the hot emulsified butter sauce made with a reduction of vinegar, white wine and savory shallots). Zesty French radishes with butter and sea salt, by the way, often begin a Loire meal.

Side vegetables are almost a meal in themselves. Thick sliced Saumur potatoes and tomatoes dressed with walnut oil vinaigrette can be a main course. *Noirmoutier* potatoes or white beans called *mogettes* cooked in buttered crocks make for a fine repast. Flavor-filled pumpkins show up in cold-season soups. (As I mentioned in my *Intoxicating Paris* book, the French famously love soup; their soups are not only fresh and tasty, but they help control the waistline as well!)

But where would the Loire be without truffles? *Diamants noirs* or "black diamonds" are particularly cherished; these prized truffles come from Marigny-Marmalade. This town deems itself the "capital of the truffle trade" (but don't tell Sarlat-la-Canéda in the Dordogne, which thinks *it* holds that distinction). More than seventy-four acres of truffle beds are found in the Loire. December 21 marks the start of the truffle market in France—and the Loire comes alive with truffle hunters, sellers, and ardent consumers.

Fungi proliferate here with good reason, since the Loire has some prime qualities for growing superb mushrooms. Chanterelles, morilles, buttons, shiitakes, and *cèpes* are cultivated in the *tuffeau* caves. These labyrinth quarries *(tufas)* were left after the great *châteaux* were built from the harvested limestone. Clever growers figured out how to repurpose the dank quarries and turn them into mushroom palaces where delicious fungi multiply by the thousands.

The button mushroom is king in the Loire, however. These diminutive *champignon* we call "button mushrooms" are actually *Champignons de Paris* in French. This is because they were first cultivated at Versailles by Louis XIV's famous gardener, Jean-Baptiste de La Quintinie. Prior to that, the only mushrooms available were those growing wild in the countryside during the spring and summer seasons.

In the early 19th century, clever growers began using the Paris catacombs and abandoned quarries to grow button mushrooms for general consumption. The dark, damp caves offered a consistent humidity and temperature for the varieties to flourish. However, the building of the underground Paris Metro around the 1890s pushed the mushroom growers farther beyond the city, although there are reportedly still a few mushroom farms growing under the streets of Paris.

The mushroom farmers of old, however, found a perfect relocation site in the old Loire limestone caves. But there's a little bit of science here. The *tufas* (limestone caves) originally produced the huge calcium carbonate blocks for the *châteaux*. Fortuitously, this moist stone underground typically becomes whiter and harder when it meets the air. This explains why the castles are in such good shape 500+ years after they were built.

In the abandoned underground stone quarries, however, the soft stone became the perfect host for mushroom cultivation. Cold and dank, the mushrooms loved the underground haven where they could grow in a controlled environment. *Voilà*! The Loire mushroom industry was born. Now, these "Troglodyte Gardens" account for one of France's finest comestibles. In fact, about 75 percent of all mushrooms found in France come from the Loire Valley.

Naturally wine growers also took note. Vintners began storing wine in the *tufas,* since they also made stellar wine caves. But the French have gone even further. Some people have created homes in these quarries or fashioned B&Bs for overnight stays. And there are some very fun restaurant venues where you can dine among the stones, eating some of the finest French "cave cuisine."

In Saumur, the old quarries do a particularly brisk mushrooming business. There's even a Saumur Musée du Champignon (Museum of Mushrooms) where you can have a grand time wandering among 200 species of fungi. More than 60 percent of all *Champignons de Paris* button mushrooms come from Saumur. On a recent visit here, my friend and colleague Peter Stewart of *France Magazine* related a couple of his experiences in this mushroom wonderland. "[In here] the temperature hovers around 8–10°C (50°F), the optimum conditions for cultivating all types of mushrooms…Round off your visit with a warming bowl of mushroom soup in the museum café." For more information, see Peter's entire article "Land of Troglodytes," *France Magazine*, March 2016. www.completefrance.com

One of the most popular dishes in France is a mushroom and goat cheese tart. This delightful appetizer or main dish is made with local *champignon* and Loire *fromage de chèvre* (goat cheese); these savory ingredients are combined with flavorings and then layered into a puff pastry and baked. A goblet of Chinon often accompanies this scrumptious dish.

Another fungi favorite is *galipettes farcies* (large mushrooms), which are filled with cheese or other concoctions and grilled over an open fire. But often they're simply served all by themselves, lightly fried in butter or garlic with a sprinkling of parsley. Alongside a glass of Vouvray or Sancerre, this makes for a fabulous meal.

By the way, a different mushroom farm across the valley called La Cave des Roches in Bourré (east of Chenonceaux) takes up about 75 miles of the valley's vast 2,000-kilometer cave network. Here, you can also tour a magical mushroom kingdom, as well as its mushroom museum.

Not a fungi lover? You'll be pleased to know that creature consumption is also popular in the Loire. Seafood and fresh fish form the foundation of many Loire dishes. *Poisson* are plentiful since the Loire River and its tributaries provide superb breeding grounds. Between the lakes, rivers, and trout streams, more than fifty species of fish are bred and caught. Migratory species such as mullet, shad, lamprey and eels, as well as other fish such as carp, pikeperch, and bream, keep fisherman busy (and diners happy).

Touraine specialties include *Matelote d'Anguilles*, a flavorful stew of eels and red wine; it's typically paired with a light red from Chinon, Bourgueil, or Saumur. You'll find tantalizing fish fare like pikeperch coated with gingerbread crumbs and served with creamed leeks and white butter sauce. Or you can enjoy sea bass marinated in lime juice and ginger or braised turbot with cream of Champagne sauce—

just to name a few.

Roast salmon, turbot, zander, bream, and shad are often served with a *beurre blanc* sauce or a rich wine reduction. These are usually paired with a ripe Chenin Blanc. Simple grilled fish, pan-seared halibut, and freshwater whitebait (young fish) dishes also taste delicious with a Muscadet.

Notably, *beurre blanc* sauce was invented by accident in the Loire. Chef Clémence Lefeuvre was preparing pike in her Loire restaurant La Buvette de la Marine in her village of Saint-Julien-de-Concelles (near Nantes). She was supposed to be whipping up a *béarnaise* sauce. But she got distracted and forgot to add the tarragon and egg yolks. She whipped up what was in the bowl, and surprisingly the most beautiful sauce appeared, and *beurre blanc* was born. Today, delicious *beurre blanc* sauce is made handily by skilled chefs with a hot emulsified butter, vinegar, and/or white wine (sometimes Muscadet), then reduced down until thick. Shallots are folded in with cold butter; the mix is blended off the heat to prevent separation. Then this divine concoction is poured over steak, fish, and even poultry—I've even been known to slather it on a baked potato.

At the Atlantic mouth of the Loire, however, seafood is king. The sandy estuary at the *Pays Nantais* provides a rich environment for fresh oysters, shrimp, mussels, prawn, and sardines. Oysters on the half shell are delicious; Vendée-Atlantic Oysters (found in the port at Bec) are highly prized. Muscadet wine pairs beautifully with shellfish to offset the briny taste. During the holiday season, oysters are a popular French favorite.

Mussels à la Marinère and mussel soup spiced with saffron are offered on many Loire menus. Prized mussels are specially cultivated on posts in the Bay of Aguillon. Saint-Gilles-Croix-de-Vie and La Turballe produce anchovies and sardines. Baby sardines show up in the valley markets from June to September; many of the French eat them raw or on bread with butter. Sauvignon wines are also great quaffing wines to accompany many of these seafood dishes.

White-wine stews of hare or fowl are popular. *Lapin farci* (stuffed rabbit) is served frequently in winter. Nantais ducks are prized for their meaty flavor; *Canard au Muscadet* is a roast duck simmered in pan juices deglazed with Muscadet. Challans or Loué free-range, grain-fed chickens make remarkable dishes like *Fricassee de Poulet*—which is especially yummy served with a light red or dry Chenin.

Fowl lovers may enjoy *Géline de Touraine*, also known as *La Dame Noire*; this is a *poulet* dish made from Loire black hens. Another bestseller is *Boudin Blanc,* or sausage stuffed with chicken meat. *Poulet George Sand*, named for the French novelist and memoirist, is young chicken (capons) served with a crayfish sauce. I enjoyed a similar *poulet* dinner (pictured here) at Château de Chenonceau's l'Orangerie restaurant (reservations required in advance of your visit).

Pork and meats are equally important components of Loire gastronomy. Stewing is a favorite preparation method; the 17th century dish *Noisettes de Porc aux Pruneux de Tours* is still prized, for example. This dish uses pork, hazelnuts,

prunes, cream, and Vouvray wine. *Charbonnée,* or pig stew with onions cooked in a red Chinon sauce, is often served. *Fressure* (hash), *Lard Nantais* (cutlets), and *Saucisses au Muscadet* (blood thickened sausage) are additional pork-based favorites.

The French classic *foie gras* is plentiful in the region. It's served as an appetizer or with main dishes such as Roast Fillet of Veal with pan-fried *foie gras* crowned with mushrooms and gravy. A Loire winter *pâté* favorite is *Terrine de Gibier (*game *pâté*), which I also enjoyed at Château de Chenonceau.

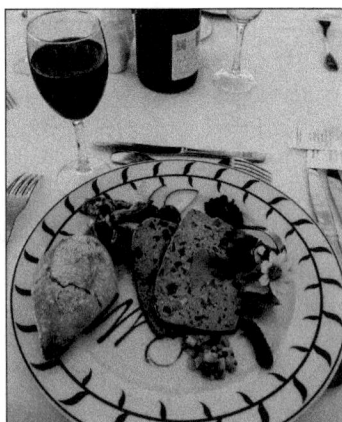

And while we're on the topic of *haute cuisine* meats and poultry, I have a story to share. At the risk of offending readers, I've included a photo of my Michelin-starred chef pal, Damien Garanger. Damien is the head chef of the well-known Le Médicis restaurant in Blois. He cheerfully gave a cheese lesson and cooking class in Blois one year.

At one point during our lesson, Damien suddenly left the room. He strode back in with a chilled pig slung over his shoulder! He slapped the piggy down on his carving table. Then he began selecting knives. As I realized he was about to debone this entire specimen, I hastily snapped a photo and left to sit in the lobby until he was done carving. (I didn't have the stomach to watch the "dissection," but I loved the mischievous look on Damien's face when he stood ready to give us a pork lesson from start to finish!)

By the way, I returned after all the carving was done, and completed my cooking course. We ate everything we cooked and it was delicious.

Processed meats, or *charcuterie*, figure prominently in the Valley of the Kings. Sausages of all types are plentiful, including *Saucisson sec* (dried sausage) and air-dried ham like *Jambon de Sancerre*. Many dishes are made with pork, goose, or duck. They go into *terrines, rillons* (morsels of grilled pork served cold), *rillettes* (slow-cooked pork or goose morsels stored in a pot), and *rillauds* (chunks of pork belly cooked in a vegetable stock with herbs). *Rillettes, rillauds*, and *rillons* are all variations on the 16th century word *rille,* meaning "small dice of pork."

In Touraine, pork belly is made into *rillettes* by taking sliced pieces of pork, pounding and salting them, and then simmering them in cast iron skillets for up to six hours. They're next packed in jars and then sealed with a thin layer of fat, usually goose fat. Later, these are served with toast as an appetizer, often accompanied by a chilled glass of dry Vouvray or Cabernet Franc.

Rillons are chunkier snips of meat fried briefly until crisp. *Anjou Rillauds* are not pounded like *rillettes,* and a little caramel is added to the dish to add that dash of sweet. *Boudin blanc* is a soft white pork sausage made with pork, veal, cream, and sometimes truffles. On the other hand, *Boudin noir* ("black pudding" or "blood sausage") is the traditional blood sausage. *Andouillette* is a chitterling sausage sometimes served grilled over vine twigs. Pork *pâtés* are typically made with prunes.

The Loire forests provide an abundance of quail, pheasant, partridge, deer, and wild boar, which serve as the key ingredients in many famous dishes. The succulent game dishes are usually prepared in rich wine sauces flavored with mushrooms and shallots. Much of the game meat is still prepared the royal way, as King François I loved—that is, roasted over spits or stewed slowly in great pots. The wines of Chinon, Bourgueil, St. Nicolas de Bourgueil, and Saumur Champigny beautifully accompany grilled or roasted meat dishes such as grilled steak with shallots and *Cul de Veau* (rump of veal).

Yet, the Loire is also a land of memorable *fromage.* One of my French friends says, "The Loire Valley is like one big open-air cheese platter…serving the right wine with the right cheese is no laughing matter here… it's to showcase the flavors of the cheese—some of the best in France!"

Some very fine award-winning cheeses hail from the Loire. These include St. Benoit, Crémet d'Anjou, Saint Paulin, Crottin de Chavignol, St. Maure de Touraine, Selles-sur-Cher, Pouligny St. Pierre, and Valençay. St. Maure de Touraine, Selles-sur-Cher, Pouligny St. Pierre, and Valençay are among the most prized.

Oddly, the Loire is a hotbed of goaty goodness. But how did goats get to France? The Saracens (Muslims) brought goats with them when they invaded France during the early Middle Ages. When Charles Martel, the grandfather of Charlemagne, defeated the Saracens in 732 at the Battle of Tours, they fled the Loire—but left behind their goats and cheese-making secrets! Having developed a taste for goat-milk–based *fromage*, Loire locals took up the practice and made it their own.

The Loire Valley today has six varieties of AOC

(*Appellation D'Origine Contrôlée*) status goat cheese of the total 48 in France. The most famous of these star-quality goat *fromages* is *Crottin de Chavignol*. This soft-ripened, crumbly mound of deliciousness come from the tiny village of Chavignol near Sancerre; it has only 200 inhabitants. A small disc of this creamy cheese becomes a *Crottin* only when it is older and drier. Younger *Crottins* may be soft enough to spread or to heat and serve on a bed of salad greens; older ones can even be grated. This cheese was originally conceived to accompany a crisp white wine. A classic dish is baked *Crottin de Chavignol* served on a green salad with a chilled glass of Sancerre.

Valençay is a world-class goat cheese served especially in prestigious restaurants. It's easily identifiable by its truncated pyramid shape. The cheese is dusted with ashes and therefore called *cendré*. Napoleon Bonaparte is said to have adored this nutty-flavored *fromage* but disliked its original shape since it reminded him of his defeat in Egypt. He therefore lopped the pointed top off and it has been produced in this shape ever after. This fantastic cheese goes beautifully with a red Sancerre or other Pinot Noire-type wine.

Chabicou du Poutou goat cheese has a delicate, sweetish flavor. It goes wonderfully with a Pouilly Fumé, which is made from Sauvignon Blanc grapes. The clean taste of Pouilly Fumé also goes well with Chabicou. *Pouligny St. Pierre* is a legendary goat cheese that has a full pyramid shape; it's golden brown with speckles of blue-gray mold. This pyramid of *fromage* is known as "Eiffel Tower" or "Pyramid" cheese. The center is bright white and has a smooth, crumbly texture; it has sour, sweet, and salty overtones when you bite into it. I can attest that it tastes wonderful on a French baguette with a glass of blush Rosé d'Anjou.

Selles-sur-Cher is an ash-coated goat cheese that nearly melts in your mouth. Well known for its blue, sometimes dark, color, this yummy *fromage* tastes of cheesy sweetness with undernotes of saltiness. Enjoy this with a crisp, fresh wine like a white Muscadet *sur lie*. It also accompanies west coast Atlantic Loire flavors like crab, shrimp and scallops.

Sainte-Maure de Touraine is a creamy, ivory-white cheese of cylindrical shape also coated with bluish ash. It brought fame—and AOC status—to the small town of the same name that produces it. It must be aged and goes beautifully with a red Chinon wine or other Cabernet Franc vintage. Other noted goat *fromages* are *Saint-Aignan* and *Pavé de Sologne,* a famous product from Vendôme.

You may not be aware that you can actually go "cheese tasting" in France. Along the country roads you'll see signs for *degustation* and *chevrerie* (goat farm). The smell of goats will assail your nose long before you see the signs. By the way, the paler the exterior of these cheeses, the younger and usually milder the product. Yellowing crusts indicate the cheese is drier and more pungent. When in doubt as to wine, a chilled Sancerre goes beautifully with any of these distinctive cheeses.

As I mentioned above, I had the opportunity for a lesson in French *fromage* from Chef Damien. Damien is a highly decorated chef with experience that has taken him on culinary adventures around the world.

After traveling extensively in places such as Cyprus and Moscow, he returned to his native Loire Valley to share his culinary experience and knowledge at his family restaurant. He's famed for adding tasteful twists to regional recipes. Cooking class with Damien (offered only through France Off the Beaten Path Tours) is both a hands-on experience and a demonstration of some of Damien's favorite recipes and cooking techniques.

Damien also gave us an extensive cheese course that I will remember for the rest of my life. He began by laying out a large map of France on his table (see the photo courtesy of Christy Destremau). Then he hefted out a huge tray of cheese from his chiller to begin the lesson. As he gave each of us nibbles of a particular variety, he'd ask us to guess where the cheese originated in France. Afterward, he'd slap the cheese hunk down on the map at its birthplace. Then he'd

tell us the story of its pedigree. After twenty or so cheeses, we were stuffed with insight *and fromage*! By the way, my understanding is that even those who are lactose intolerant can enjoy raw-milk French cheese with no discomfort. I'd highly recommend this *fromage* experience.

But we can't neglect Loire *pain* (bread). Some of it is even famous! *Fouace* or *fouée* is a Loire sweetheart with a romantic history. The beloved Renaissance writer François Rabelais made this airy, pita-like bread famous. Rabelais was born in Chinon; he brought *fouace* to the attention of the world when he published a recipe for it in his stories about the memorable giants Gargantua and Pantagruel. (I infer that the *Gargantua and Pantagruel* books were *The Hobbit* series of their day.)

Fouace is unfortunately no longer sold in the *boulangeries* (bakeries). But you may taste it in one of the regional restaurants. One version is plain and baked in a wood-fired oven, while the other looks and tastes more like *brioche* (cake-like bread). The puffy-pocket versions are often stuffed with rillettes, beans, or cheese (or all three) and eaten as an appetizer. *France Magazine*'s Peter Stewart described a delectable experience he enjoyed with these traditional breads in a troglodyte cave hotel, Hôtel Rocaminori, near Angers. "My companion and I [especially] enjoyed piping-hot *fouées*—bread rolls baked in a wood-fired oven—with accompaniments including salted butter, rillettes, butter beans, and goat's cheese." Sounds like heaven to me.

Other Loire specialties include *crêpes* (thin pancakes), *galettes* (thick brown pancakes), and *sables* (shortbread), which are served on many menus filled with cheese, meats, or poultry. Many *crêpes* are served for dessert, oozing with sweet strawberries, *framboise* (raspberries), white peaches, apricots, pears, or other fruit compotes that have been flambéed with rum or laced with orangey Cointreau. (Cointreau was invented in the 19th century in a small confectioner's shop in Angers. See more on Cointreau's history in the Wine and Angers sections.)

The aroma of savory breads, baguettes, candies, and cookies practically wafts down the Loire River. Adorable *macarons* come from Cormery. Tempting pastries sit fetchingly in *pâtisserie* windows all across Tours. Handsome dessert *galettes* (crusty pancakes flavored with fruit, honey, jams, jellies, or cream) are served throughout the day.

But my favorite cake-like-bread is lighter-than-air *brioche* (sweet bread). Many *pâtisseries* produce a creamy-custard-filled *brioche* in multiple flavors. But I confess I absolutely love plain old *brioche*— and I scoop up several wherever I find them. In fact, I almost prefer brioche over dessert (except for maybe a chocolate éclair or tarte Tatin…but I digress.)

Sweets are particularly popular in the Loire, including *forestines* from Bourges. These are the pastel, hard-candy shelled sweets that burst with soft praline, hazelnut, or chocolate centers when you bite down on them. Holidays and special moments aren't complete without *Quernons d'Ardoise* (little triangles of caramelized nougatine laced with almonds and hazelnuts coated in slate-colored, bluish-white chocolate).

Macarons, like elsewhere in France, are the extraordinary round sandwich cookies loved by the royals and made in quantity by Ladurée and others in Paris. In the Loire, they have their own twist on this famous cookie: *Macarons aux Fruits d'Orléans*. These little marvels are a relatively recent Loire invention since 2006. They come in four marvelous flavors: strawberry and Orléans vinegar, pear and spicy ginger, creamy hazelnut, and candied rose petals with lime and cinnamon.

I want to tell you the story of my first-ever *macaron* lesson with Chef Christophe Cosme of Au Rendez-vous des Pêcheurs restaurant in Blois. (These classes are offered only through France Off The Beaten Tours.) Michelin-starred Christophe is a skilled artisan who not only makes fabulous *macarons* but serves sensational fish dishes and other specialties at his sleek Blois restaurant.

You may recall that *macarons* were much loved by doomed queen Marie Antoinette. (I'd be tempted to make a very bad joke about her losing her head over them, but that would be *très gauche*.) At any rate, I picked up some royally impressive secrets on how to make the perfect *macaron* from Christophe.

First, these are essentially cloud-like meringue cookie sandwiches filled with creamy fondant. They're delicate little things; they must be baked properly or they'll fall apart like so much wet tissue paper. The artfulness comes not only in the baking but in varying the colors of the cookie and the fondant flavors to create extraordinary taste combinations (as well as pretty food photography).

As such, the egg whites used to make the batter must be glossy and fluffy and hold soft peaks (but not be over-whipped, so that the

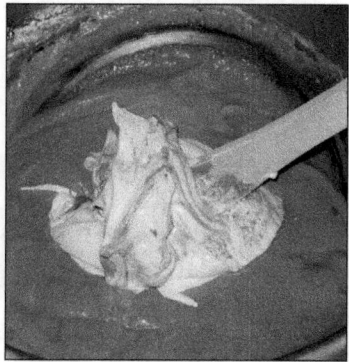

egg white has a chance to "grow" a little in the oven). First tip: After folding in the confectioner's sugar and almond flavoring, a sample of the batter piped onto a parchment-paper covered baking sheet should flatten immediately into a round disk. If it doesn't, you will have a hair-on-fire peaked cookie that looks like a tiny ice cream cone rather than a smooth topped *macaron*. (Try refolding the batter a few times before piping all of it onto the cookie sheet to make the cookies.)

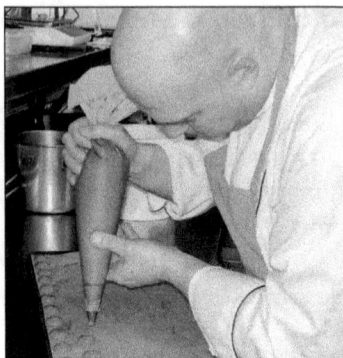

Second tip: The piped cookies on the cookie sheet have to sit out in the air in order to form a hard skin on top; some French chefs say 15 minutes, other designate up to an hour for this "rest period." Third tip: The cookies are baked at a relatively low heat until set, but not browned like a Ritz cracker. By the way, French bakers leave the oven door propped open slightly with a kitchen towel to allow a little air into the oven.

Final tip: Make your filling(s), but be sure they have thickened before piping them onto a cookie. Common flavors are buttercream, pistachio, ganache, chocolate, and coffee, but there's no limit to your imagination for creating your favorites. When filling the cookie with fondant, pipe a little of the mixture on the

flat side of a baked and cooled cookie. Then press another cookie on top, allowing the fondant to fill the space (but not ooze out).

Here's a basic *macaron* recipe if you'd like to make these divine treats in your own home:

Macaron Recipe

INGREDIENTS

- 1 1/4 cups plus 1 teaspoon confectioners' sugar
- 1 cup (4 ounces) finely ground sliced, blanched almonds
- 6 tablespoons fresh egg whites (from about 3 extra-large eggs)
- Pinch of salt
- 1/4 up granulated sugar

DIRECTIONS

- Preheat the oven to 350 degrees. In a medium bowl, whisk together confectioners' sugar and ground almonds. In a separate bowl, whip egg whites with salt on medium speed until foamy. Increase speed to high and gradually add granulated sugar. Continue to whip until stiff glossy peaks form. With a rubber spatula, gently fold in the confectioners' sugar mixture until completely incorporated.
- Line baking sheets with parchment paper; set aside. Fit a pastry bag with a 3/8-inch #4 round tip, and fill with batter. Pipe 1-inch disks onto prepared baking sheets, leaving 2 inches between cookies. Let stand at room temperature until dry, and a soft skin forms on the tops of the *macarons* and the shiny surface turns dull, about 15 minutes or more.
- Bake, with the door of the oven slightly ajar, until the surface of the *macarons* is completely dry, about 15 minutes. Remove baking sheet to a wire rack and

let the *macarons* cool completely on the baking sheet. Gently peel cookies off the parchment.

- To fill the *macarons*: Fill a pastry bag with the filling (see below). Turn *macarons* so their flat bottoms face up. On half of them, pipe about 1 teaspoon filling. Sandwich these with the remaining *macarons*, flat-side down, pressing slightly to spread the filling to the edges. Refrigerate until firm, about 1 hour.
- Variations: add flavorings or colorings to the egg whites after they are whipped.

Macaron Filling

INGREDIENTS

- 3 large egg whites
- 1 cup sugar
- 1 cup (2 sticks) unsalted butter, at room temperature, cut into pieces
- Flavorings as desired

DIRECTIONS

- In the bowl of an electric mixer, whisk egg whites and sugar. Set mixer bowl over a saucepan of simmering water and heat mixture, whisking often, until the mixture feels warm to the touch and sugar is dissolved, 3 to 5 minutes.
- Transfer bowl to the mixer, and fit with the whisk attachment. Whip on high speed until mixture is stiff and shiny, 3 to 5 minutes. Add butter, one piece at a time, and continue mixing until butter is thoroughly incorporated. The filling can be kept, covered and refrigerated, up to 1 week. Bring to room temperature before stirring.
- Variations: To make flavored fillings combine 1/2 cup of *macaron* filling with 1/3 cup finely ground hazelnuts, chocolate, espresso powder, or honey.

Beside *macarons*, biscuits and sweet nuts are also Loire favorites. Mazet pralines are particularly good. In 1903 Léon Mazet arrived in Montargis, where he set up Maison Mazet to sell his caramelized nuts, which are still being made today with traditional methods. Biscuit lovers will also find yummy *Vinaillou* biscuits, which are vanilla biscuits flavored with Cabernet d'Anjou. Other flavors include apple, honey, and rose.

But the Queen of Loire dessert is the famous *tarte Tatin*. *Tarte Tatin* is the caramelized upside-down apple pie invented by the Tatin sisters from the tiny Loire village of Lamotte-Beuvron. Here's their story. The pair ran the tiny HôtelTatin. Stéphanie Tatin apparently did most of the cooking. She was overworked one morning and started to make a traditional apple tart. However, she left the apples cooking in butter and sugar for too long. Smelling the burning, she tried to rescue the dish by putting the pastry base on top of the pan of apples. Then she quickly finished the dish by putting the whole pan in the oven as is. After turning out the upside down tart, she was surprised to find out how much her hotel guests appreciated the dessert. *Tarte Tatin* became a favorite all over France, particularly in Paris (which sometimes tries to take credit for inventing it, but most know it comes from the Loire).

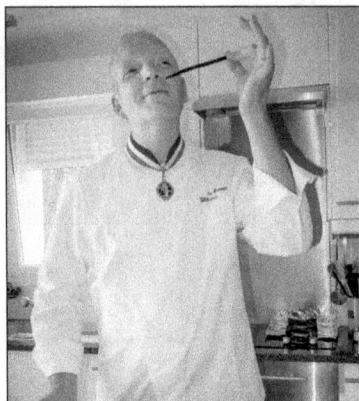

I had the unique experience of working with a modern-day master of this appley dessert; and he taught me how to make it in his very own kitchen at home! Christophe Quantin (shown), former Director of the Lycée d'Hôtellerie de Blois, and his charming chef wife, Angelique, invited me into their home one afternoon for a cooking lesson. I, and a few others from a France Off The Beaten Path Tours group, made a complete French dinner from scratch with Christophe and Angelique. It ended with the famous *tarte Tatin*.

I need to explain that Christophe is no ordinary French chef. In fact he's a highly decorated master chef. In 1993 Christophe won the prestigious Meilleur Ouvrier de France (MOF) culinary competition. This is why he gets to wear the blue, red, and white collar of the prestigious MOF. He's also a *Chevalier* in the Order of Academic Palms.

From 1998 to 2013, Christophe was the Technical Director at the Lycée Hotelier de Blois, working in partnership with the Pedagogical Committee of Ducasse Education in Paris. Since 2015, Christophe has been spending weekdays in Paris as right-hand man to legendary chef Alain Ducasse. Together they are training the French chefs of the future at Ducasse's professional cooking school in

Paris at Argentueil. For those of you who don't know, Alain Ducasse is one of the top ten chefs in the world.

One of the gratifying things about my friend and France expert Christy Destremau and her tours is that she not only helps groups tour specific France areas, but she also provides professional cooking classes and wine sampling with true French experts. Christy was born and raised in the US, by the way, but she's lived in France for over twenty-three years. Having met her French husband, Hugues, and reared two children in France, she's fluent in French and French culture. More importantly, she's exceptionally savvy about how to maximize the travel experiences of her groups in France.

Here is one of Christy's groups cooking with Christophe and Angelique (far right). You can see in this photo how Angelique is taking the group through various cooking processes in her own kitchen. (Note: a glass of wine helped make the experience even more relaxed.) The likable Chef Christophe then took the group expertly through the process of creating the renowned *tarte Tatin* dessert from start to finish, crust to filler to baking.

For do-it-yourselfers, here's a basic *tarte Tatin* recipe that you may enjoy making in your own home. It's easy to concoct and really delicious:

Tarte Tartin Recipe
INGREDIENTS

- Frozen puff pastry sheet (from a 17 1/4-ounce package)
- 1/2 stick (1/4 cup) unsalted butter, softened
- 1/2 cup sugar
- 1 t. calvados (optional)
- 7 to 9 Gala apples (3 to 4 pounds), peeled, quartered lengthwise, and cored
- Special equipment: a well-seasoned 10-inch iron skillet

PREPARATION

- Preheat oven to 425°F.
- Roll pastry sheet into a 10 1/2-inch square on a floured work surface with a floured rolling pin. Brush off excess flour and cut out a 10-inch round with a sharp knife, using a plate as a guide. Transfer round to a baking sheet and chill.
- Spread butter thickly on bottom and side of the skillet and pour sugar evenly over bottom. Arrange as many apples as will fit vertically on sugar, packing them tightly in concentric circles. Apples will stick up above rim of skillet.
- Cook apples over moderately high heat, undisturbed, until juices are deep golden and bubbling, 18 to 25 minutes. (Don't worry if juices color unevenly.)
- Put skillet in middle of oven over a piece of foil to catch any drips. Bake 20 minutes (apples will settle slightly), then remove from oven and lay pastry round over apples.
- Bake tart until pastry is browned, 20 to 25 minutes. Transfer skillet to a rack and cool at least 10 minutes.
- Just before serving, invert a platter with lip over skillet and, using potholders to hold skillet and plate tightly together, invert tart onto platter. Replace any apples that stick to skillet. (Don't worry if there are black spots; they won't affect the flavor of the tart.)

Brush any excess caramel from skillet over apples. Serve immediately. (Note: Tart can cool in skillet up to 30 minutes. It can also stand, uncovered, up to 5 hours, then be heated over moderately low heat 1 to 2 minutes to loosen caramel. Shake skillet gently to loosen tart before inverting.)

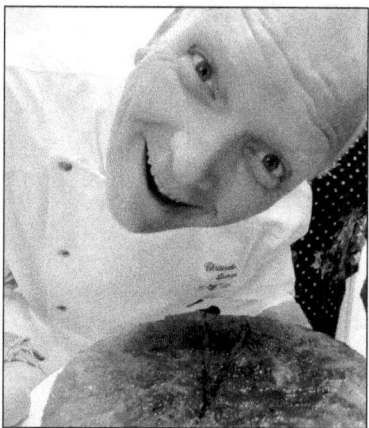

Here is Christophe with the finished *tarte Tartin* from his very own oven. He made it clear it is a very doable dessert for pros or amateurs alike.

Wine

The Loire is the garden of France, the land of castles, the place where the purest French is spoken. And it is the home of some of the most delicious, delectable, enjoyable French wines…The countryside is beautiful—wide expanses of vines, gentle slopes, grand castles and ancient cities, all dominated by the rivers and the milky blue light of the summer sky. If a vineyard [enclave] deserves to be called "pastoral," this is it.

—Roger Voss, "Decode the Wines of the Loire Valley," *Wine Enthusiast Magazine*

Loire is one of France's largest and most far-flung wine regions. It stretches about 186 miles from Nantes at the Atlantic to Pouilly-sur-Loire in the east. It has slightly more than 185,000 acres of vines—about two-thirds the size of southern wine giant Bordeaux. The geographical extent

of the region means that the *terroirs* and thus the grapes themselves produce wines of variable quality year to year. Climate conditions are much more unstable than those of southern France in Bordeaux or the Rhône Valley. Thus, the wines may vary with each vintage. Yet, over time, they yield affordable wines that go beautifully with most foods.

The Loire region has a wide range of wine styles. But freshness and finesse are their common qualities. The area is dominated by four major grape varieties—Sauvignon Blanc, Chenin Blanc (from which almost every conceivable variety of wine is made), Melon de Bourgogne, and Cabernet Franc. In fact, the Loire is France's third largest wine region. Plus it's the second largest region for sparkling wine after Champagne in eastern France.

Loire wine estates are generally small and often family owned. This opened the door for cooperatives several decades ago. Small growers often pool their resources to create some memorable wines. There's also a sizable network of *négociants,* or wine buyers, who bottle or sell the wines under their *négociant* name. (I often buy Loire wines through *négociants* in local wine stores, online in the US, or at Total Wine when I'm not in France.)

> There is scarcely a bistro, brasserie or restaurant in the capital [Paris] that does not have one of the agreeable, inexpensive Loire tipples on its wine list—a Muscadet or Sauvignon, Cabernet or Gamay.
> —André Dominé, *Wine*

The Loire lacks the highbrow reputation of Bordeaux or Burgundy. Still, the area produces some delightful wines, particularly Sancerre and Pouilly-Fumé made from Sauvignon Blanc grapes, as well as popular Muscadet whites and tasty Chinons. More than 100 of these high-quality wines with a regal history have been awarded the AOC (*Appellation d'origine Contrôlée*) designation.

French AOC laws specify and delimit the geography from which a particular wine (or other food product) may originate. And they dictate the methods by which the wines may be grown and made. To confuse matters further, the AOC designation is being changed to AOP over the next several years. The new AOP stands for *Appellation d'origine Protégée*. For several years to come, you may see both AOC and AOP designations on bottles.

There are many opportunities to sample and purchase Loire vintages when you visit the valley. The Maisons des Vins de Loire (local wine centers with expert information in Angers, Saumur, and Tours) are excellent places to start. Even more fun, individual producers will welcome you for tastings as you meander along. Look for *dégustation* (tasting) signs or inquire at tourist centers for wine tour and tasting information. Better still, you can book wine tours in advance with producers from their websites. Many will roll out the red carpet to greet you.

Wine pro and blogger Jim Lockard (http:// jimlockardonwine.com) describes the Loire Valley wine culture as "a host of smaller, really mom and pop producers, whose styles vary greatly. I like the soft whites with green fruit and spice highlights, as well as the mostly young reds that bring a taste of the soil into the glass. The Loire Valley has a wonderfully small-town feel." (Jim also conducts tours in France. http://deluxewinetours.com/)

Traveling through the Loire wine enclaves, you may come across this title: *Terra Vitis*. Terra Vitis is an organization that monitors participating vintners who practice organic methods. In 1990 some of the Beaujolais winemakers (in the Burgundy region north of Lyon) decided to adopt and formalize integrated eco-friendly vine-growing techniques. This spread to the Loire and beyond. The designation dictates the avoidance of herbicides, the application of fauna-safeguard measures (like grassing between the vine rows and limited pruning), and organic maintenance of the grounds and processing areas. Thus if you care about organic producers, this organization is your source. Terra Vitis provides a list of their members at http:// www.terravitis.com.

The chart below shows the principle Loire grape regions. These follow the course of the Loire River, west to east from Nantes at the Atlantic Ocean, then east to Pouilly-sur-Loire. As the crow flies, this is only about 350 kilometers (217 miles). But as the Loire River wends its way across the valley, the distance is much longer and the geography changes dramatically. The result? Diverse wine growing regions that produce sweet and dry white wines, as well as sparkling wines, rosés, Bordeaux-like Cabernets, and Burgundy-like Pinot Noirs. In between, there are the semi-sweet rosés of Anjou and the dry rosés of the rest of the Loire. We'll highlight these major wine growing regions as we travel west to east across the valley.

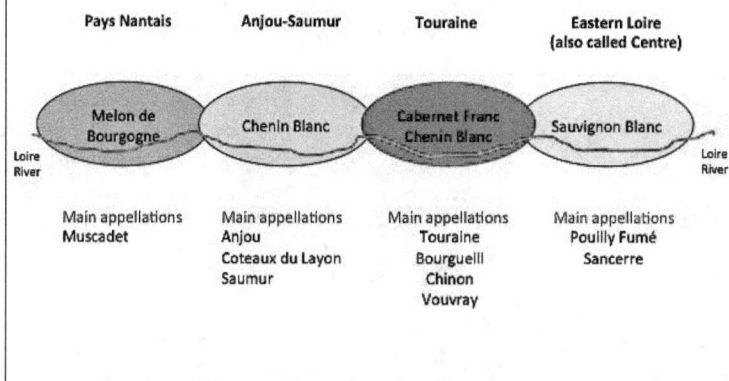

Loire Valley – Principle grape regions

Pays Nantais	Anjou-Saumur	Touraine	Eastern Loire (also called Centre)
Melon de Bourgogne	Chenin Blanc	Cabernet Franc / Chenin Blanc	Sauvignon Blanc
Main appellations Muscadet	Main appellations Anjou, Coteaux du Layon, Saumur	Main appellations Touraine, Bourgueill, Chinon, Vouvray	Main appellations Pouilly Fumé, Sancerre

Note: if you are a real wine fancier, you might enjoy following the Scenic Vineyards Route from Nantes to Sancerre (just under 500 miles). This is obviously an undertaking—particularly if you choose to "taste" along the way. But if you have a few weeks or a month, this could be a delightful way to meander through the Loire Valley as you wine taste and stop to view the breathtaking *châteaux* along the valley.

The following sections detail the specific regions to consider. As you meander, you may want to stop at the wine centers of each major town to get oriented to the area and buy/taste wine. They also have wine maps and details about specific producers.

Muscadet

The Loire is a land of moderation: It's cold in the winter, and never gets super hot in the summer. Vines can really only grow here because of the river and its tributaries, which raise the temperature just those few vital degrees and ensure long, leisurely autumn days for the harvest.

—Roger Voss, "Decode the Wines of the Loire Valley," *Wine Enthusiast Magazine*

Starting in the west near Nantes, we find Muscadet country. Muscadet extends from the mouth of the Loire estuary to the western fringes of Angers where the Anjou wine district begins (about 55 miles). The climate is maritime, with a higher rainfall and westerly winds that blow the sky clear but slightly salty. Dotted with magnolias, fig trees, laurels, cedars, and Mediterranean pines, the grapes produced here are clean and crisp.

In fact the colorful Nantes area was historically the bastion of the Duchy of Brittany until the 15th century. As such, it was more aligned with the coastal Brittany community that was Celtic in culture and sensibilities. (This is one of the reasons I will cover Nantes in my Brittany &

Normandy book next year, rather than explore it here in my Loire book other than the wine particulars.)

Later, the area was subsumed into the French Crown lands in the late 1400s. It became part of the Loire region with mixed reactions from the locals. The last time I visited Nantes, there was a movement afoot to spiritually re-establish Nantes as part of Brittany. They are culturally more Celtic/British than Loire/French, in my experience. The indomitable Celtic spirit shows up in Celtic music blaring in many of the Nantes bars. And of course you'll find hardy Brittany beers and Guinness on tap around the area. You can also get flavorful buckwheat *crêpes* called *galettes de sarrasin* that are designed to keep a fighting man (or woman) going. (These make the normally pale and delicate French *crêpes* look anemic.) Here's a photo of one that took up nearly my entire place setting.

Despite the beer fascination, Muscadet wine fanciers love the dry Muscadet wines made from Melon de Bourgogne grapes that thrive here. These perky vintages have low acidity and alcohol content. Muscadets often have a subtle apple and citrus aroma, coupled with pepper and a slight salinity evocative of the Nantes maritime locale. The wines are a favorite with fish lovers, as they pair beautifully with crustaceans and shellfish. You'll often find Muscadet on the menu as an *apéritif* too.

The four Muscadet appellations are Muscadet, Cotes de Gradlieu, Coteaux de la Loire, and Muscadet Sevre-et-Maine. Muscadet Sevre-et-Maine is by far the largest appellation. It spans about 55 miles (85 percent) of the total Muscadet wine growing area.

The Muscadet grape is rather subtle. Therefore the *must* (freshly pressed grape juice containing the skins, seeds, and stems of the berries) are often left *sur lie* ("on the lees"). That is, the must is left in the tank where fermentation takes place and affords the brew a much creamier taste. The wines are then bottled straight from the tank. Because they're not racked into another clean tank without fermentation, the *sur lie* wines retain oxygen. This gives the white wine a slight effervescence when opened. Other Muscadets are produced the usual way by tanking with fermentation, then tanking post-fermentation, and *then* bottled.

The area's second wine is Gros Plant du Pays Nantais, which is produced from the grapes of the same name (sometimes also called Folle Blanche). Gros Plant/Folle Blanche is also used in the production of Cognac and Armagnac. It's an exceptionally versatile grape

Since the Muscadet area is fairly small, it's enticing to simply drive around the area to visit some of the key producers. Some noted examples are:

- **Chéreau-Carré**: The most celebrated business of the Pays Nantais belongs to Véronique Günther-Chéreau, who produces an extraordinarily diverse range of excellent Muscadets. The *Sur Lie* versions are the best, with a green citrus flavor plus a pinch of minerality. http://chereau-carre.fr
- **Domaine de l'Ecu**: Ecu makes some of the region's best Muscadets, particularly the Expression de Orthogneiss with its citrusy, rich textured flavor. Expression de Granite is earthier and sweeter. Muscadet-Sèvre et Maine *Sur Lie* is a top-quality cuvée. http://domaine-ecu.com
- **Domaine Pierre de la Grange/Pierre Luneau-Papin**: All of these wines are made from the Sèvre et Maine

part of Muscadet. The Vieilles Vignes are powerful and full-bodied wines. L d'Or is intense with a spicy zest and a mineral core that ages well. Clos des Allées is the top wine, with intense floral aromas and fleshy, vibrant fruit notes. Their slogan is "A winemaker is like his terroir, always receptive." http://www.domaineluneaupapin.com/en/home/

- **Domaine la Haute Févrie:** The Sèvre et Maine *Sur Lie* styles are the best here, with bright but bitter pear fruit flavors throughout, as well as spicy, zesty herb notes close to the finish. Less intense, and closer to the $10 range, the non-*sur lie* style is more light and refreshing. http://www.lahautefevrie.com/en

For real Muscadet fun, attend the Muscadétours wine festival in October every year. http://lesmuscadetours.com. This high-energy event features local cuisine (especially lots of oysters, mussels, lobsters, fish, and *foie gras*) paired with the local Muscadet vintages. You will meet many friendly vintners as well--and perhaps meet some charming locals who will want to share sightseeing tips.

Anjou (Anjou, Coteaux du Layon, Saumur)

Anjou wines…a microcosm of the Loire Valley.
—Tom Stevenson, British wine expert

Anjou vineyards, near the storied towns of Angers and equestrian-oriented Saumur, are primarily south of the Loire River. This is the largest wine growing area of the Loire— more than 49,900 acres with 32 notable AOCs. The estates stretch from beyond Angers to the districts of Grand Saumur. Only the Savennières wines are located on the north bank. Anjou produces about one quarter of the Loire's total wines; it's France's third most important viticulture region.

The rich palette of wines includes sweet and medium-sweet whites, bright rosés, and memorable red wines, including one of the most famous reds in France, Saumur-Champigny. The Anjou AOCs are responsible for a broad spectrum of wines, including still red, white, and rosé produced with varying levels of sweetness. The "celebrities" of this area are the sweet Coteaux de Saumur, the sparkling Saumur Brut, and Crémant de Loire, plus the aforementioned Saumur-Champigny.

Among the wines of Anjou, Savennières is noted for its dry Chenin Blanc wines and the Coteaux du Layon for its sweet dessert wines that include the botrytized wines of Bonnezeaux and Quarts de Chaume. *Botrytis cinerea* is the "noble rot" grey fungus that raisinizes the grapes to produce a concentrated sweet wine when harvested and bottled. Quarts de Chaume is a notable pairing with appley *tarte Tartin*.

The general region is known particularly for its Rosé d'Anjou. This is a rosé that tends to be powerful, but many other styles of wines are made here as well. The Gamay grape of the Beaujolais wine region in Burgundy (which was transplanted in Anjou) has had a long history in the Loire; it has its own Anjou-Gamay AOC. Blended grapes from around the region can go into the mix for a basic Anjou Blanc and Anjou Rouge AOC wine.

Along with Touraine, the Angers area makes up what is known as the Middle Loire—the source of most of the Loire's best wines, especially Chenin Blancs. Chenin Blanc production dates back to the 9th century; this was also one of the first areas to utilize the practice of pressing grapes when Dutch traders in the 16th and 17th century introduced the sweet wine production concept to the region.

Anjou vineyards take up about 20,000 acres; 55 million bottles of wine a year are produced. Grapes include rosé and red: Cabernet Franc, Cabernet Sauvignon, and Grolleau. The white grapes include Chenin Blanc, Sauvignon, and Chardonnay. Chenin Blanc is sometimes termed the "white quick-change artist," since it is used for so many purposes.

"Anjou-Saumur's most extraordinary dry white wine, Savennières, is possibly the greatest dry Chenin Blanc in the world," says wine pro Karen MacNeil, author of *The Wine Bible*. "Savennières are densely flavored wines with such intensity, grip minerality, and taut acidity that they can be aged for decades." One of the most revered producers is Clos de la Coulée de Serrant. This seventeen-acre vineyard is farmed according to the principles of biodynamics. No pesticides are used. Planting and harvesting are done only in sync with the planetary alignment, as first espoused by Austrian Rudolf Steiner. This tiny-estate wine is so good it is its own appellation!

My French friend Jean-Pierre, who hails from Paris but worked in Saumur before emigrating to the US, says "Saumur is famous for its 'Methode Champenoise' that rivals many in Champagne. But it's also famed for its 'Saumur Champigny,' probably the only red wine that you can drink straight out of the fridge on a hot summer day. This 100 percent Cabernet Franc is light, fresh and dry... so much better than a rosé!" One of Jean-Pierre's favorite producers in the Loire is Château de Targé, which produces a well-regarded AOC Saumur-Champigny, as well as other wines. http://www.chateaudetarge.fr

Saumur is also famed for producing the Loire's top sparkling wines. Outside the very specific Champagne region to the east, the Loire is France's main source of sparkling wines. Champagne is the only area of France in which wine growers are allowed to label their sparklers as "Champagne," by the way. That is the reason "sparkling wine" appears on all other fizzy wine concoctions around the world—even in France outside the Champagne area.

The Loire wine makers produce tasty sparklers using the same *méthode traditionnelle* as the Champagne region. Despite the fact that they aren't permitted to use the name "Champagne" on any label, their Loire sparkling wines are delicious nevertheless. They can be found in either red or white varieties. Saumur Brut is a well-known sparkler, while Crémant de Loire is an even higher-quality product produced in much smaller quantities.

Interestingly, several of the main Champagne houses now own and produce sparkling wines in the Loire. (One can only presume that instead of fighting the competition, Loire and Champagne producers simply joined forces!) For example, Langlois-Chateau (http://langlois-chateau.fr/en/) is a noted sparkling wine producer that's owned by Bollinger, a grand-estate Champagne house.

Another producer is legendary Bouvet-Ladubay. Bouvet-Ladubay makes for a memorable visit in the Loire—and it has been one of my favorite tastings. Just a few miles from the center of Saumur, visitors get to access the nearly five miles of cellars (via vintage bikes if you like), as well as all the stages of sparkling wine making. My *France Magazine* colleague Peter Stewart visited recently and had this to say:

> Known for its Brut de Loire sparkling wines, the company was founded in 1851 by Étienne Bouvet and his wife Célestine Ladubay, who bought the caves to store the wine. These had first been quarried by 11th century monks, who had fled from their Abbey in Saint-Florent…On a vintage French bicycle, after attaching a miner's light, I was led deep underground by my guide Julie and saw hundred of barrels of wine fermenting around us…Wine tasting takes place above ground, where you can sample up to four wines and raise your glasses in your own toast to [the vintner's and monks'] work. (See Peter's entire article at www.completefrance.com in the March 2016 issue.)

My visit at Bouvet was similarly fun. We headed down to the miles of caves with our charming guide Lea, who took us through the ancient caves where the wonderful Bouvet's have been barreled, bottled, and produced for hundreds of years. Intricate carvings punctuate these much loved caves, so there was ethereal artwork nestled amongst the barrel chambers. Up top, we had a terrific tasting in Bouvet's elegant tasting room. I couldn't resist a few bottles of these bubbly beauties— and I admired Lea's official Bouvet jacket so much she let me buy one! By the way, this one-hour tour and tasting was a scant two euros per person. Yes, two euros. In Napa Valley, California this would have cost $85 on the low end!

An additional treat is Ladubay's ethereal La Cathédrale Engloutie, an underground "cathedral of sculptures" hewn out of the *tuffeau* stone caverns beyond the wine caves. The carriage house above serves as the tasting and reception area. It's a beautiful and romantic visit if you get the chance to go there. http://www.bouvetladubay.com

Here are some of the most well-known producers in the Anjou area:

- **Coulée de Serrant:** A leading biodynamic winery helmed by biodynamic viticulture spokesman Nicolas Joly. Cistercian monks first planted this seventeen-acre vineyard in a steep slope overlooking the Loire in the 12th century. During the past 800 years, it became so celebrated that it was visited by French kings and the Empress Josephine, who cherished the wines. It produces simply fabulous Chenin Blanc Savennières wines. Their slogan is, "I don't only want a good wine but also a true wine." http://coulee-de-serrant.com

- **Bouvet-Ladubay:** As detailed above, this is a top producer of sparkling wines, with a regal tasting experience. They also do some nice reds. Definitely stop in—and you can email for reservations online with no problems. http://www.bouvetladubay.com

- **Gratien-Meyer**: Large Saumur producer of still and sparkling wines. Reportedly, more than five million bottles are aging in splendid caverns beneath the Art Deco reception center. http://www.gratienmeyer.com

- **Château de Targé:** Run by charming Édouard Pisani-Ferry, who titles himself an "Independent Winemaker," the winery is also a *château* with stay-over accommodations. (The handsome *château* was originally a hunting lodge owned by Phelippeaux de Ponchartrain, secretary of King Louis XIV of France, in 1655.) Their AOC Saumur-Champigny and AOC Saumur-Blanc are vinified according to the traditional Saumur-Champigny method. Very good wines of several varieties are available. The winery is so highly recommended by my friend Jean-Pierre that I immediately ordered a bottle in Saumur—and instantly fell in love too! http://chateaudetarge.com.

- **Agnès & René Mosse**: Produces a marvelous Anjou Blanc from Chenin Blanc with zesty citrus and herb flavors. From its Mosse vineyard, a dark-berry layered Cabernet Franc is produced. http://domaine-mosse.com

- **Domaine des Baumard**: Varietal Cabernet Franc, particularly the Logis de la Giraudière produced by father and son, who are among the best wine makers in the area. Coteaux du Layons (sweet white wines) are also good. http://www.baumard.fr
- **Château Pierre-Bise**: Pierre-Bise is known for its offerings in Coteaux du Layon, but it makes excellent Anjou Blanc and Anjou-Villages wines as well. In good years, the sweet wines of Claude Papin are marvelous. http://www.chateaupierrebise.com
- **Château d'Epire**: Stellar Chenin Blanc Savennières. One of my favorite wine importers, Kermit Lynch, personally selects special lots of this wine to import into the US. The estate has rediscovered the fine aging abilities of their wines. http://www.chateau-epire.com
- **Domaine de la Soucherie**: Reasonably priced wines are made in both red and white styles. The red is generally more drinkable, with elegant red fruit flavors. http://domaine-de-la-soucherie.com
- **Château Du Breuil:** A 19th century *château* where you can stay and dine. It has been producing fine wines since 1822. It currently produces flavorful Cabernets and Coteaux de Layon-Beaulie from old, well loved vines. http://www.chateau-hotel-du-breuil.com

Other noted wine-tasting venues in Anjou are Les Caves de la Loire (www.cavesdelaloire.com), Domaine de Sainte Anne (www.domaine-sainteanne.com), and Domaine de Deux Moulins (www.domaine2moulins.com). For a delightful website that lists Saumur producers, check out http://www.ot-saumur.fr.

Touraine (Touraine, Bourgueil, Chinon, Vouvray)

> Touraine…it is a wine region befitting Cinderella [with] centuries-old storybook *château*, replete with turrets, moats, and drawbridges…
> —Karen MacNeil, *The Wine Bible*

Touraine, the prime area encompassing the "Garden of France," contains a far-reaching Loire wine tract. It extends from west of Chinon to the point where the River Vienne meets the Loire, past Blois, then miles further to the east. Busy Tours marks the region's center. Touraine is where the climate shifts from coastal maritime to Loire central with its hot summers and extremely cold winters.

This vibrant area is not only filled with vast forests, fragrant fields, and extensive vineyards but dotted with some of the most majestic *châteaux* in France. A jewel box of Renaissance castles like Chenonceau, Villandry, and Azay-le-Rideau, its gardens and vineyards—some of them planted centuries ago—are also quite regal in the quality of the grapes produced. Everywhere the scent of honey, flowers, and grapes permeate the air.

In keeping with its regal pedigree, Touraine's lush terroir produces quite a few wine stars. The specific wine growing locations include Chinon, well known for fine red wines from the Cabernet Franc grape, and Vouvray, famous for its legendary whites. More than two million cases of wine are produced here a year— although only a few are associated with the *château* estates scattered over the region. Unlike Bordeaux in southwest France, where the great *châteaux* estates like Mouton Rothschild, Latour, and Margaux produce their namesake wines, Loire wines are produced more by hardworking families and cooperatives without a title—or a castle—to their names. The occasional royal baron making wine does crop up, however.

More red wine is produced in Touraine than in all other parts of the Loire combined. Historical references to Vouvray go back to the Middle Ages. A pioneering role in Loire wine making occurred when Martinus of Tours came to the area as the first Archbishop of Tours in 371 A.D. The papacy was always interested in growing wine for sacraments and for pleasure. Martinus was similarly invested in winemaking. Wandering through one of his vineyards one day, he stumbled upon something that impacted the wine business ever after. His donkey clumsily broke some twigs off a grapevine. Later, the remaining branches bore much more fruit than the other vines in the vineyard. Result? Pruning was invented!

Martinus was later canonized—and the exceptional Touraine AOC was awarded to this heavenly wine domain in 1939. Vouvray and Sancerre are some of the most famous appellations. Lovely wines abound in Touraine: light-bodied Gamays (made to be drunk young), reds of Cabernet Franc, Cabernet Sauvignon, and supple whites bottled from Sauvignon Blanc, Chenin Blanc, or Chardonnay grapes. The bubbly vintages and some of the fine Touraine sweet wines pair beautifully with rich sauce dishes and memorable cheeses.

The most famous red wine appellations of the entire Loire originate here. These include Chinon, Bourgueil, and St.-Nicholas-de-Bourgueil. All are made from Cabernet Franc grapes. Among the noteworthy reds are the Chinons from Charles Joguet. Joguet says, "Wine is always the fruit of a love story between vines and strong personalities." And colorful vintners producing sublime wines are a powerful combination here. Paris *bistros* are famous for serving these supple, affordable reds, especially in summer. Flavorful Bourgueils from Pierre-Jacques Druet are also quite good.

By the way, I had a wonderful luncheon at L'Etape Gourmande in Villandry geared around Bourgueils. This fantastic off-the-beaten-path restaurant just up the road from Villandry castle is a rustic charmer; the dining room has a fireplace right in the middle of it, providing the utmost in charm—and warmth. The delightful owner, Madame Béatrice de Montferrier, gave me a much-appreciated lesson in how to say "Bourgueil" (Bor-gay) as well as exactly which delicious Bourgueil to have with lunch, since one of us had ordered fish while my companion was having veal. Madame came to the table personally to check on every aspect of our dining experience—and sat down for a few moments to talk to us in perfect English. (Her grandmother had been English, it turned out!)

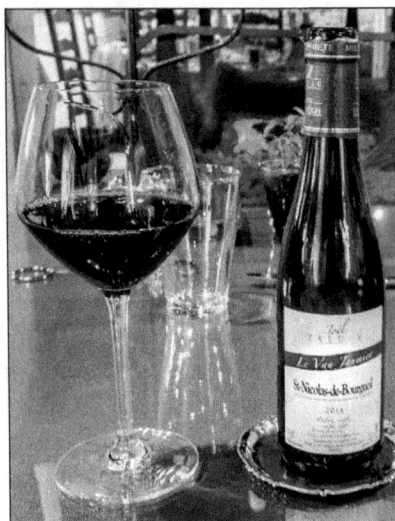

We lingered in Madame's "farmhouse" eatery, sipping our Bourgueil for a couple of hours. Outside, we snapped a few pictures of the couture rabbits she kept nearby. That Bourgueil, by the way, cost under $20—and the entire three course meal, stretched over 2.5 hours, cost under $80! I promised Madame we would come back for Christmas someday—and she said she'd have a table ready for us. http://www.letapegourmande.com.

There are additional Touraine Rouge quaffing wines that are made from a blend of Loire grapes: Gamay, Cabernet Franc, Cabernet Sauvignon, Côt, Pineau d'Aunis (a favorite of Henry Plantagenet), and Grolleau. Azay-le-Rideau, the locale of the famous *château*, produces a few good wines, as do several other communes immediately adjacent. Château de Chenonceau produces some nice wines from its own vineyards (and there are wine consortiums near the grounds of the estate where you can also buy them)

Vouvray, however, is in a class by itself. A famous white wine known all over the world, Vouvray by law is made from 100 percent Chenin Blanc. Vouvrays are divided into four sweetness categories, depending on the level of residual sugar and the degree of acidity: *sec* (dry), *demi-sec* (medium dry), *moelleux* (medium sweet and very mellow), and *doux* (very sweet with more than 4.5 percent sugar per liter).

Unlike many other whites, Vouvrays are sometimes held in a wine collection for half a century—such is the level of some of the best vintages. However, some Vouvrays are not in the top tier as the rarified few; these grapes are purchased and bottled by local *négociants*, which is why you see many of them in your local wine stores. The price will tell you which is which. Often Vouvray is used to make fine sparking wines—although this varies with the season and the quality of the grapes. I am completely smitten by sparkling Vouvray at the moment; it is like a rich, bubbly champagne, but at a much better price point!

Aforementioned travel guide Jim Lockard (http:// jimlockardonwine.com) recalls visiting a small producer, Domaine Jérôme Godefroy, just outside Amboise.

> The winery was in three small caves off a back road. The caves were lined with black mold. A little old man and woman who spoke no English were the only people there—the winemaker and his wife. After a lot of flailing around with language and some wine tasting, we bought a few bottles of their

wonderful Vouvray for 5 euros each. That is the Loire Valley.

Jim and his wife Dorianne (pictured) say this is one of their most enjoyable memories of wine tasting in the Loire.

Vouvray, Montlouis, and Saumur have a reputation for producing excellent sparkling wines. One of the oldest wineries in the Loire Valley is Château Moncontour, which overlooks the village of Vouvray. The estate surrounds the castle, which dates from the 15th century.

These sweet/acid Vouvrays work particularly well with cuisine that has complex sauces or local charcuterie (meats and sausages). It's a treat to see some of the Vouvray vineyards that cling to the top of cliffs where cellars are cut into the soft *tuffeau* rock. Nearby Montlouis also produces some similar wines of quality, especially Domaine Delétang.

Touraine AOC is another basic appellation. It has four satellite appellations of its own, however: Touraine-Mesland, Touraine-Azay le Rideau, Touraine Noble-Joué, and Touraine-Amboise. Touraine Sauvignon and other Touraine whites are lesser wines that blend Chenin Blanc, Sauvignon Blanc, and Chardonnay juice together in varying quantities. These wines taste similar to a Sancerre; you'll see them in carafes at the table as "house wines."

If you are really interested in Tours winemaking through history, stop by the Musée des Vins de Touraine. It contains a rich collection of artifacts and wine details. The Comité Interprofessionnelle des Vins de Touraine is located nearby; this is the organization that promotes the region's wines.

Some of the top producers of the Touraine include the following:

- **Domaine Bourillon Dorléans**. Produces some very fine Vouvrays. http://www.bourillon.com
- **Domaine Delétang et Fils:** Red and white sweet wines. http://www.domaine-flamand-deletang.com
- **Clos Baudoin (François Chidaine):** A large producer with several noted Vouvrays and Montlouis-sur-Loire. http://www.francois-chidaine.com/accueil/les-vins/aoc-vouvray/clos-baudoin/
- **Domain des Aubuisières**: Bernard Fouquet produces creamy Vouvrays using biodynamic methods. His sweet (*moelleux*) wine called Le Marigny is a rabid favorite in Europe. In the international press, Aubuisières is considered one of the top three Vouvray producers in France. http://vouvrayfouquet.com
- **Clos Roche Blanche**: This is the Touraine's most ambitious producer of multiple wines like a basic Cabernet Sauvignon, an ultra-complex Pineau d'Aunis rosé, a tasty Cuvée Cot, a pungent Malbec, some refreshing Beaujolais-like Gamays, and a zesty, herbal Sauvignon. (These wines are carried by online merchants.)
- **Domaine Marc Bredif**. These are very nice Vouvrays produced in the heart of the Touraine valley, where you can tour the caves and sample their wares. (The winery is owned by de La Doucette of Pouilly-Fumé fame.) http://www.deladoucette.fr
- **Charles Joguet**: Cabernet franc Chinons, often found in Paris *bistros*. Readily available in many US and UK wine stores. http://en.charlesjoguet.com

- **Domaine-PJ Druet**: Quaffing Bourgueils and rosés. http://www.domaine-pjdruet.fr/fr/index.php
- **Baudry-Dutour (Domaine de la Perrière, Chateau de Saint Louans, Chat de la Grille, and others)**: Well-loved Chinons and Vieilles Vignes. I popped into their tasting room while meandering down a back road on the way to Chinon. The grounds were fantastic—with quirky shrub sculptures, vines aplenty, and a fabulous mini-*château* being restored for public visitors. My tasting was fantastic—and I again came away with a few bottles of Chinon—some of

the most delicious red wine in the world—but under $25 a bottle! http://www.baudry-dutour.fr
- **Domaine de la Chevalerie**. A lovely family-run vineyard in Restigné in Chinon with terrific Bourgueils. http://www.domainedelachevalerie.fr

Upper Loire Wines (Pouilly-Fumé, Sancerre)

The eastern Loire is about 300 miles from Muscadet wine country and the Atlantic coast. Here, the famous dry white wines Sancerre and Pouilly-Fumé dominate. And, while Chenin Blanc dominates the white wines of the Middle and Lower Loire regions, here Sauvignon Blanc is king. The wines are greener in flavor. They have a sharp tang. And they're known for being bitter and austere, albeit in a fresh and intriguing way. As Karen MacNeil puts it in *The Wine Bible*, "With their racy gunflint, herbal, and smoky flavors, the best of these wines are true to the word *sauvignon*'s root, *sauvage*, meaning wild."

A popular food/wine pairing is to serve a tangy disk of Crottin de Chavignol goat cheese with a chilled glass of Sancerre. Sublime. Spring vegetables like artichokes and asparagus can be tricky to pair with wine because they can make the wine taste sweet or metallic. But citrusy Sauvignon Blanc goes beautifully with these vegetables.

Sancerre is undoubtedly the best-known wine area of the Upper Loire. (It's my go-to white wine in France.) This charming old wine growing area is named after the village of Sancerre that's situated on a hill overlooking the river. The fourteen communes of this appellation are stretched out over several rolling hills and valleys.

Almost all the Sancerre appellations lie on the left bank (south slope) of the Loire, opposite Pouilly-Fumé. It's well regarded for and primarily associated with Sauvignon Blanc. Some Pinot Noir is also grown, accounting for around 20 percent of the region's production. This is made into mostly inexpensive quaffing red wine under the designation Sancerre Rouge. A rosé style from Pinot Noir is also produced in a style similar to Beaujolais.

White Sancerre is the star of the party, however. White Sancerre was one of the original AOCs awarded in 1936. It has an aroma of ripe gooseberries, along with vegetal hints, which is why it goes particularly well with asparagus, *fruits de mer* (seafood), and zesty goat's cheese. It also shows up on many *bistro* menus.

Across the river is Pouilly-Fumé, the original appellation for Sauvignon Blanc. Unlike Sancerre it has a crisp, green flavor and the definitive Sauvignon Blanc "tang." But it also has something more: the distinct nuance of smoke. (The word "fume" means smoke.) This wine is the inspiration behind California Fumé Blancs as well as New Zealand Sauvignon Blancs. It's not to be confused with the similarly sounding Pouilly-Fuissé, a Chardonnay appellation in Burgundy. Interesting tasting note: few people can tell a Sancerre and a Pouilly-Fumé apart in a blind tasting—unless they are local experts!

Orléans is the newest AOC in the region since 2006. The two red Pinot grapes, Pinot Noir and Pinot Meunier, are used to make intriguing red wines. But the Chardonnay grape makes the best wines of the area. Quincy and Reuilly also produce some nice wines, but they are small in comparison to the big producers of Sancerre and Pouilly-Fumé. Look for the wines from Domaine Mardon in this area.

Key producers include the following:

- **Domain Henri Bourgeois** (Sancerre): A family-run estate producing clean, clearly defined Sancerres and Pouillys with the latest winery technology. http://henribourgeois.com/en/
- **Domaine La Porte** (Sancerre): Tasty Sancerres with a spicy edge. http://www.laporte-sancerre.com/#/en
- **Domaine Henry Pellé** (Sancerre): A high-end estate that produces wonderful Sancerres, especially their delicious Menetou-Salon. http://www.henry-pelle.com
- **De Ladoucette** (Pouilly-Fumé): One of the most famous Pouilly-Fumé producers. These largest and most famous Pouilly-Fumé vineyards have been in the hands of the Comte Lafond and Ladoucette families since 1787, when the Comte Lafond purchased the estate from the illegitimate daughter of the French king, Louis XV. The estate is now owned by Baron Patrick de Ladoucette, a descendant of the Comte Lafond. Pouilly-Fumé has earned a reputation as one of the world's great white wines. After taking over Ladoucette in 1972, the Baron extended his activities to Sancerre, Chablis, Vouvray, and Chinon. The entire consortium produces a huge variety of wines. http://www.deladoucette.fr
- **Didier Dagueneau** (Pouilly-Fumé): Dagueneau, the man himself, was considered a rebel, but a genius, in the Loire. He died tragically in a plane crash in 2008 near Cognac. His family carries on his bold vision. They make big-style, oak-fermented Pouilly-Fumés that appeal to an international market. (Sold by various wine importers like Kermit Lynch.)

Overall, the Loire is a delightful area for wine tasting and learning about winemaking. As you drive through the Loire, you'll see signs offering *dégustations* or wine tastings that welcome passersby without reservations. As mentioned, the major estates also have full-blown websites where you can make reservations for tastings.

If you would rather visit the Maisons des Vins in major towns for centralized wine tasting, you can get a comprehensive list at http://vinsvaldeloire.fr. I often use both the tourism locations and the individual websites to book wine, dining, and accommodations near each other for individual days or weeks. I find especially if I am touring without a guide that contacting the wineries for a reservation offers a visitor many additional perks.

It's also delightful to pick a town like Tours or Sancerre on which to base your wine tasting operations. You can then hire a local wine expert to take you out to specific vineyards for sampling. I love doing this. It alleviates the need for driving yourself and provides you with insider information from a local who knows both the wine details and the producers.

Liqueurs & Beer

Liqueur lovers will be familiar with some of the most famous products of this region: Cointreau, Triple Sec, Royal Combier, and Chambord. Cointreau hails from Angers, while Triple Sec and Royal Combier were developed in Saumur. Chambord was developed fairly recently as an adjunct to marketing Chambord castle. It's become quite popular worldwide.

You can tour the distilleries of many of these flavored liqueurs. Of particular note is the Combier distillery, the oldest in the Loire Valley at Saumur. In Angers, you can learn the secrets of Cointreau, the famous orange liqueur distilled since 1849. Also in the Anjou area, you can enjoy Guignolet, a supple cherry liqueur.

Chambord hails from François I's most regal Château de Chambord. It's the yummy infusion of red and black raspberries, Madagascar vanilla, and XO Cognac. The drink was first made in 1982 and was inspired by a raspberry liqueur produced for King Louis XIV during his visit to Château de Chambord in the 17th century. It makes a wonderful after-dinner drink, and it's yummy over ice cream as well.

Traveling along the orchards, you may also see this amazing sight: pears growing inside bottles on trees. This is pear brandy in the making right on the tree. *Eau de vie de poire* is a favorite distilled brandy made from the delicious fruit of the region. In the orchards of Orléans, the bottles are placed directly on the trees. The fruit that grows inside each bottle gives the *eau-de-vie* all the more flavor. (To the north a bit, you will also find you are in Calvados country, home of the famous apple brandy that packs a real punch.)

Noted beers in the Loire include Mélusine and Dumnac (from Brasserie Melusine in Angers), and 1664 (from Kronenbourg in Strasbourg, although the Loire has adopted it as "their own"). There are many others to choose from when your meal calls for a "brewski" rather than a "vino."

I will discuss some of these high-octane liqueurs and beers at length in their various places of origination. But if you'd rather just enjoy the delightful brews, bubblies, wines, and liqueurs over a meal or during an afternoon, you'll find many Loire wine and beer bars worth a visit. These are some of the most well known:

- **Le Caravage, Loches**. Le Caravage is a fun and friendly place where you find lots of "ready friends" also enjoying the liquid delights of the Loire. It's famed for quirky cocktails, themed party nights featuring Cuban salsa, African-Caribbean, karaoke, and live jazz. http://barlecaravage.com
- **Le Cercle Rouge, Angers.** This is Angers' popular wine bar, where you can sample limited-production vintages from the area's new generation of natural (no sulfur) and organic winemakers, as well as old standards. Winemakers and importers will be in the crowd, too. Since the French almost never drink without food, you'll find yummy plates of charcuterie, cheese, and rich homemade *terrines* and *rillettes*. http://petitfute.com
- **Les Becs à Vin, Orléans.** In the old quarter of Orléans you'll find this darling *bistro* by day and wine bar by night. One of the owners is funky Thierry Puzelat, one of the Loire's best-known natural winemakers. The food is also fun, and much of it is organic, including the *rillons*. http://www.becsavin.com

Shopping

Loire shopping is fantastic. You can shop on the street, in the boutiques, at the *châteaux*, at the street markets, and sometimes right out along the lanes and parking lots! Tapestries, French lace, French wire earrings, pretty clothing, artful scarves, fine porcelain, delicate crystal, charming

dishware, tea towels, and other home goods are some of my favorite items to bring back from the Loire. Especially in France, items are temptingly packaged—so even the wrappers are part of the fun.

Be aware that shops in France open in the morning for a few hours. Then they often close for a long lunch, not opening again until late afternoon but staying open late into the evening. The French take their lunch hours (or two or three) very seriously, so don't expect them to be available around midday.

I've learned to shop between 4 and 7 p.m., basically, after I've done my touring and activities for the day. Then I drop my treasures at my abode or ship them from La Poste, and have a walk until dinner anytime from 8:30 p.m. on—the later the better. Of course you'll still find big box stores like Printemps open all day long—but you'll find few of these since you are in the countryside, after all, where local shopping is *de rigueur*. Here are some of my shopping favorites in the Loire.

- **Tapestries.** Tapestries, that sign of medieval luxury favored by the royals and their wealthy courtiers, is very popular. Paris and Flanders were the centers of tapestry weaving in the 14th century, where skilled weavers followed an artist's "cartoon" to weave a beautiful picture. Threads were stretched vertically (called the *warp*) on a loom to the length of the finished piece. Then, colored threads called the *weft* were woven horizontally across the warp to create beautiful pictures of French life, royal or domestic. In recent decades, tapestry creation has seen resurgence in France, as well as elsewhere. Pablo Picasso and Henry Matisse both experimented with the medium during their most productive years. Whenever I go the Loire, I typically bring home a tapestry of some kind. You can buy them in small or large versions, and many are made as pillowcases or ready to be framed. There are fantastic tapestry stores all throughout the Loire. Many of the *châteaux* have them in their boutiques as well.

- **Lace.** Northern France has some of the finest lace makers in Europe. The Loire is thus a wonderful place to find lace dresses, bonnets, parasols, and handkerchiefs, as well as tablecloths, napkins, and other lace products.
- **Wicker.** During the 19th century, residents from Villaines-Les-Rochers (near Château Azay-le-Rideau),

grew willow wicker and made a living from it. Today, the area still produces such high-quality wicker products as baskets, picnic baskets, lampshades, sun shields, outdoor structures, and high-end luxury items such as Hermés handbags and Jean-Paul Gaultier wickerwork dresses.

- **Confectionery.** Delectable cookies and biscuits, yummy candies and marzipan, and sweet fruits make wonderful gifts to take home (or enjoy while you're here). Vinaillou Biscuits or wine-flavored vanilla biscuits come in such wine flavors as Cabernet d'Anjou. Other flavors include apple, honey, and rose. *Macarons* and marzipan appear in many shapes, colors, and styles. Artisan chocolate making, as in Paris, is very big. Chocolates are a French favorite, and you will see bonbons after almost every meal—and especially in the irresistible boutiques.

- **Foodstuffs.** There is a staggering amount of beautiful food products in the Loire. Much comes perfectly packaged for traveling or shipping home. Near the game-heavy forests of Berry you can buy jars and tins of *pâtés* and *terrines*. Firm goat cheeses are packaged for travel. Heather and lilac honey, nut oils (walnut, hazelnut, almonds, truffle, and more), and *foie gras* in many containers abound. Mushrooms, Pomme *tapées* (baked apples flattened by mallet pounding, then placed in jars for use in baking or in tapenades), and *confiture* (jellies) come in many flavors.

- **Flower products.** Flower products like rose water, floral perfumes, and aromatic soaps access the abundant floral industry. Pretty boxes and bags of flower products are everywhere—you'll find much to choose from.

- **Home goods.** Weather vanes, flags, garden paraphernalia like seeds, plaques, stakes, and gardening tools are plentiful, since this is a garden haven. Stained glass elements show up in lanterns, signs, windows, hanging pictures, and much more. You'll find lots of portable home goods like platters, coasters, cups, dishware, tablecloths, aprons, spoons, and much more. Loire *faience* (pottery) is quite pretty in a variety of shapes and colors.

- **Artisan products and souvenirs.** Most of the *châteaux* have well-stocked shops that offer souvenirs of your visit, such as glassware, pillows, small tapestries, posters, jewelry, notecards, and more. In small shops around the towns, you can find unique artisan products such as gilded books and bookmarks, fine boots and French shoes, replica playing cards, *château*-themed soaps and jewelry, medieval art stenciling, and lyrical paintings and home artwork.

- **Clothing.** I particularly enjoy the artfulness of the clothing in France. At fairly reasonable prices (unless you are buying *haute couture*), you can pick up hand-loomed

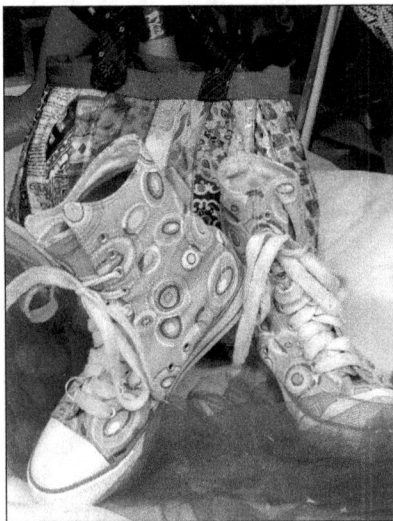

scarves, stylish hats and berets, unique jewelry pieces, pretty sweaters like my cream-colored fitted sweater with gold butterflies from Blois, quirky tennies like these shot by Maureen Beals, men's fine-cotton shirts (my husband has picked up a few of these), and more.

- **Fine wines and Liqueurs.** Shipping home a case of high-end Loire wine or champagne is easily done here. If you like the potent liqueurs, you can buy Cointreau,

Chambord, Triple Sec, and Royal Combier, for example, almost anywhere. However, I find it fun to purchase these on site at their place of origin.

- **Mistletoe**. This may seem like an odd item to include in a Loire shopping list. However, the story behind mistletoe is worth telling as it depicts the entrepreneurial spirit of the Loire as well as a particular aspect of the French psyche. My Loire pals noticed my puzzling over the gobs of mistletoe (actually an evergreen parasitic plant) hanging off the poplar trees that grow like weeds across the valley. I learned that local gypsies pull the mistletoe off the trees and sell it wrapped up with bows at the local markets and Christmas fairs. They know foreigners like it for the Christmas "kissing ritual." When I asked why the French ignore this "kissing plant," I was told, "Because the French know they don't need it!"

In sum, the Loire is a wonderful place to enjoy delightful cuisine, great wines and beers, delectable desserts, fun shopping, and enchanting company—whether you are enjoying alfresco dining, fine cuisine venues, pubs, wine bars, street cafés, open marchés, boutiques, castle shops, or everything in between.

As I explore each section of the Loire in the pages to follow, I'll detail some exceptional dining, food, and shopping experiences I've enjoyed. And together we'll walk where kings have walked and lords and ladies have danced in this most beautiful and historic land called the Valley of the Kings.

CHAPTER SIX

Anjou
(Angers, Brissac, Plessis-Bourré, Serrant, Montgeoffroy, Saumur, Montreuil Bellay, and Abbaye de Fontevraud)

> The [Anjou] landscape can be very beautiful: vineyards, fields and meadows alternating with orchards, woods and nurseries. The undulating terrain provides beguiling, constantly changing panoramic views.
>
> —Hubert Duijker, *Touring in Wine Country Loire*

One sunny afternoon in June, I was cruising along the country roads heading east from Nantes to Angers. The windows were down and the sunroof wide open, My crimson scarf whipped out behind me in the breeze. Aromas of magnolia and roses filled *ma voiture*. Green fields fanned out before me like huge nature carpets. Cows dozed under canopies of trees nestled along fertile riverbanks.

As I sped along, the grassy parklands and crisscrossing rivulets wooed me to linger for a picnic—though I'd yet to stop for a fresh baguette, a mound of cheese, and a bottle of dry white Savennières for toasting. That would come later.

I motored on through the unspoiled Anjou villages. I passed inviting manor homes surrounded by grasses and gardens. River marshes fluttered with life, especially if I honked, since they were migratory homes for all kinds of birds. At last the verdant carpet gave way to tracts of wine vines zipping over the hillsides.

The sight of grapes and more grapes reminded me that Anjou is known as much for its royal history as its distinctive wines. When suddenly windmills came into view, I recollected that the Dutch traded heavily in the sweet wines of Anjou in the 16th and 17th centuries. And they've left their mark in these few remaining windmills, some of which still grind grain today.

As I sped around a hill, at last I glimpsed the cream and slate limestone walls of the stately *château* of Angers—only one of many grand estates in Anjou. Many of these castles have pretty Angevin towns at their feet. The handsome dwellings too are made of the white *tufa* stone, but they're capped by prominent grey-slate roofs, not turrets. And around each estate and hamlet are patches of splendid flower gardens edged by swaying trees and palms that make nearly every view Instagram ready.

The history is as complex as the myriad wines here. Anjou, serenely pastoral now, was nevertheless the seat of a monumental royal power struggle in centuries past; this struggle shaped not only France, but England as well. When at last I pulled up in front of the great fortress-castle at Angers, I was reminded of the royal conflicts that went on before my modern 21st century visit.

Since around 880, Anjou had served as a territorial duchy. Its fortunes rose and fell with those of its rulers over the next several hundred years. Not yet a part of France, Anjou became a seat of bi-country power when Henri Plantagenet, then reigning Count of Anjou, inherited the kingdom of England in 1154. As newly anointed Henry II of England (note the new English spelling), he became the formidable ruler of England and major parts of France. This "Angevin Empire" at its peak spread all the way from Ulster (Ireland) in the British Isles past Bordeaux to the Pyrénées at the furthest southern point of France. It was one of the most powerful kingdoms of its age. From the feudal Plantagenet capital of Angers, Henry ruled from a castle situated where Anger's barrel-chested fortress now sat before me.

At the tender age of 18, Henry married powerful southern France heiress Eleanor of Aquitaine. She had inherited her father's lands at age 15 and became the most desirable bride in Europe. She controlled a huge swath of territory that spread across southern France. At age 30, Eleanor was newly divorced from stuffy Louis VII, King of the Franks. Eleanor's cultured and worldly ways allegedly conflicted with Louis's pious and quiet life.

Post divorce, Eleanor is said to have run gleefully into the arms of dashing young Henry, her third cousin 12 years her junior. They were a medieval match made in heaven: he had the titles and she had the land—more even than the King of the Franks. When Henry and Eleanor became king and queen of England in 1154, the pair ruled for 40 years over a turbulent period in French and English history that lasted several hundred years beyond their deaths.

The couple appears to have both loved and loathed each other. The pair nevertheless sired eight children; two of them—Richard and John—also became kings of England. Henry ended up imprisoning Eleanor in a drafty castle in England to stop her from encouraging rebellion among their sons. Ultimately, as described in an earlier chapter, inept King John lost most of the Angevin kingdom. He also tried to bully the enraged English nobles but finally capitulated to them by signing the Magna Carta in 1215 at Runnymede.

This "Great Charter of Liberties" gave power back to the mid-level lords (while they basically held a sword to King John's neck). Later, this seminal document served as a basis of common man rights. The basic tenets still underpin much of today's constitutional law, not only in England, but in the US and beyond. Thus, worldwide, we moderns are the inheritors of this democratic canon of law that began with the Plantagenets.

The Angevin Empire disappeared in 1204–1205 when it was seized by Phillip II of France. There were no more counts of Anjou once the French king downgraded the area to a dukedom. Over the next few centuries, Anjou was absorbed fully into the French crown's lands. In the wake of the French Revolution, Anjou rule was finally returned to the people. Royal watchers, however, can pay their respects to this powerful Plantagenet regime. More than 15 family members, including Henry, Eleanor, son Richard the Lionheart, and son John Lackland were buried at Fontevraud Abbey near Chinon (although only a few effigies remain). As both a couples therapist and Francophile, I can appreciate the legacy of this indomitable couple. They repose now for eternity side by side, conflicted in life, but bound forever in the great eternal legacy we call history.

Though the royals are long gone, there is still an indomitable royal quality about many of the famed Anjou highlights. Following are my favorite sites to visit: 1–Angers, the old kingdom's center; 2–Château de Brissac, the tallest *château* in the Loire; 3–Château Le Plessis-Bourré, a memorable pre-Renaissance *château*; 4–Château de Serrant; 5–Château de Montgeoffroy; 6–Saumur with its famous *château* and riding school; 7–Château Montreuil-Bellay; 8–the Abbaye de Fontevraud, and other attractions like the Zoo de Doué and a network of windmills still operating in the Loire area.

To get oriented, the Angers Tourism Office (http://www.angersloiretourisme.com/fr), as well as the Saumur Tourism Office http://www.ot-saumur.fr), can provide maps and literature so you can plan your itinerary. I particularly like their City Passes. For one low price you can get access to dozens of the local sites, *châteaux*, wine tastings, museums, and more. You can buy these at the two tourism offices, and they'll give you quick access to the key Angers and Saumur locales, as well as save you loads of time and hassle.

The tourism office maps are particularly useful, since they not only provide activity-specific routes but also give specific business details to aid in planning your days. Included are museums and places of interest, *château*

opening and closing times, cruise and boating companies, canoe and kayak consortiums, golf courses, Loire-by-Bike tours, picnic spots, family-friendly venues, wine tasting opportunities, and more. You can even attend fishing school, if you like, or take a bird-watching cruise. But my favorite Loire fun is a hot-air balloon ride. You'll cherish your experience aboard a Loire hot-air balloon—I guarantee it. Many companies offer sky-borne experiences; check local websites or the tourism office for the specifics.

Angers**
(See the Navigating chapter for a key to the "" rating system)*

Today's Angers, the capital of the province of Anjou, is a friendly city a mere 190 miles from Paris. It's situated on the short River Maine, about five miles from where it unites with the River Loire. By the way, the inhabitants of both the city and the province are called *Angevins*. Unlike the rest of the area's "*châteaux* country," where most castles were forged out of the creamy white *tufa* stone, the old city of Angers

was built from dark slate. (Angers, by the way, is pronounced "On-jay" not like "Angers away.")

"Black Angers," as it was dubbed, was the cradle of the proud Plantagenet dynasty. Once the Plantagenets lost their lands and power, Angers became the center of a modest Anjou dukedom. Angers' last great champion was Good King René of Naples and Duke of Anjou (1409–1480).

As previously mentioned in the history section, René was a great lover of culture and domestic harmony. He was fond of his subjects—and he lived and worked among them more as an equal than a royal. He transformed the once-somber Angers fortress into a lyrical castle known for its cultural enlightenment that was the envy of all Europe. He turned the old castle moat into a menagerie for example. King René also engineered the installation of several surrounding gardens with sculpted shrubs, bright flowerbeds, and inviting kitchen gardens, which are still well-tended today. (René personally introduced the carnation and the *Provins* rose to the region.)

Despite René's civilizing efforts, Angers continued to be a magnet for political intrigues. The 1500s brought great strife to Angers with the Catholic vs. Protestant conflicts known as the Wars of Religion. Massacres were frequent. In 1619 Louis XIII of France gave the governance of Anjou over to his mother, Marie de' Médici. She settled there with her chaplain, Cardinal Richelieu. The pair were part of many intrigues as the crown sought to maintain control of various French lands.

After the French Revolution, Angers and the entire Anjou area was markedly influenced by the transformation in Paris over the next two hundred years. Universities expanded. Streets were widened. Art deco buildings were constructed, along with charming parks and green belts threading through the town.

During World War II, the Germans made Angers the seat of its regional Kommandantur. Allied bombing destroyed the train station and surroundings, but these were reconstructed in the 1950s. After liberating the northern France Arromanches (Normandy Beaches) and Rennes in 1944, General George Patton and his 5th infantry division swept into Anjou as the people cheered. Along with French Forces of the Interior, they liberated Angers from the Germans, who retreated until their ultimate defeat.

Today's Angers has been rebuilt, and most vestiges of war are long gone. It's now a gentle enclave of beauty and education. Called the "Green Capital" of France due to its splendid array of flora, fauna, fruits, and vegetables, it's a bustling garden community with a high-tech edge. Angers' diversified economy mixes horticulture, electronics, and tourism as its main pursuits; and the city percolates with youthful energy since it's also a college town forever incubating the French geniuses of tomorrow. Angers touts itself as "first among all French cities for quality of Living and Life." And judging from the happy people I've seen bustling about on any given day, I'd suggest this may be closer to fact than fiction.

Angers benefits particularly from its massive urban development projects. These include highways, shopping malls, two universities, and the recent redevelopment of the chic Saint-Serge quarter just north of the historical center. One quirky note is that the population of modern Angers is fairly young; 48% of the population is under 30! This makes it a family-friendly locale, as well as a hotspot for the latest engineering and technological trends. (Packard Bell and NEC have plants here.)

The town is a magnet for conventions, and notably it's one of the top employers in all of northern France. Since Angers is also Europe's largest horticultural center, there's a delightful emphasis on clean air, bounteous vegetation, and serene living. The town practically bursts with blooms, particularly hydrangeas. Hydrangeas, by the way, are France's most important flowering plant, with more than six million plants being grown in the Loire alone.

Whether or not you're a gardener, you'll find much to see and do in this delightful municipality. Angers is a charming place to visit for a morning, a day, or more. Some even make Angers their base for visiting this part of the Loire—and they won't be disappointed if they do.

As a thriving university town, Angers has wide boulevards brimming with boutiques and lovely squares. At the same time, history whispers from many corners of the narrow streets at the foot of the royal *château*. And if you like street markets, Angers is your place. There's a market here almost every day of the week. (To find them just note the direction from which shoppers are emerging with their carts and shopping bags brimming with fresh baguettes, ripe vegetables, and huge sausages.)

Logistically, the Maine River divides Angers in two. The town's southeast side is guarded by the imposing Château d'Angers. This 13th century fortress was the main residence of the dukes of Anjou in the 14th and 15th centuries. The heavyset structure, complete with foreboding drawbridge and seventeen towers, seems more feudal fortress than Renaissance estate. But inside, you'll find a delightful enclave of comely buildings, pepper-pot-roofed *chatelet* (gatehouse), aromatic gardens, and aviaries added by King René.

Today, the castle has also been transformed into a modern day "Guardian of the Apocalypse" museum and historical art center. It beautifully houses the sublime *Apocalypse Tapestries*. The Royal Apartments, handsomely decorated, also house a beautiful collection of 16th and 17th century tapestries.

The famed *Apocalypse Tapestries* are the largest and oldest of

France's tapestry assemblage, dating from the 14th century. (Many will be familiar with the Bayeux Tapestry now in exhibition a few hundred miles to the north in Bayeux near the Normandy beaches; though that tapestry was woven in the 1070s, it was in fact made in England and is therefore not considered a "French" tapestry.) The *Apocalypse*, however, is the most luxurious of all medieval tapestries. The collection was originally created for Duke Louis I of Anjou to illustrate the visions of St. John from the Bible's Book of Revelations. Not only were the tapestries symbols of extreme wealth, but they decorated the thick, stone walls of the vast rooms and helped cut the chill.

In the wake of the French Revolution, the majestic tapestries were unfortunately cut up and used as horse blankets, bed canopies, and worse. Eventually the bits and pieces were reclaimed, and restoration began in the 19th century. Today, visitors can view 338 feet of these refurbished tapestries in a specially designed gallery. Like France itself, these tapestries still stir with their vibrant beauty 600 years after they were created. (The last time I visited, there were two very well behaved classes of first-graders going through the exhibit; they were quiet and enthralled. I found the children as fascinating as the tapestries. I noticed that since the tapestry hall is exceptionally dim to preserve the inks and ancient fabrics, the teacher was using an iPad with photos of the tapestries that were actually right behind her. The low light level also accounts for my rather indistinct photo.)

Though tapestry making declined in the 16th century, it has enjoyed a renewal in the 20th century. Angers naturally has become a center for these fabric master weavers—and many sell their creations for quite reasonable prices in and around the town. (I confess this is my shopping Achilles heel. My home is festooned with French tapestries—and they make me smile each time I walk through my house and remember where I've bought them. I've even purchased a few tapestry pillowcases, and then had them framed and mounted on my walls instead of displaying pictures. I have a tapestry pillow from Amboise behind my head as I write these words.)

Bringing tapestry art full circle, the Apocalypse collection inspired a modern artist to create a modern response to the end-times theme. His name is Jean Lurçat. His creation is called *Le Chant du Monde*, (The Song of the World). It's an equally impressive tapestry that stretches 260 feet. Woven between 1957 and 1963, this massive tapestry can also be seen in Angers at the Musée Jean Lurçat in the old town across from the château. Lurçat is largely credited with reviving the art of tapestry, by the way. A short distance from the museum is one of my favorite sights: the Centre Regional d'Art Textile. This collection of workshops for around 20 warp-weavers offers tours and classes in the art of tapestry weaving. (And you can buy tapestries in many sizes here as well, naturally.)

A few steps from Château d'Angers stands the majestically furnished Cathédrale Saint-Maurice. Inside this grand 12th–13th century church is a massive 18th century organ and a monumental 19th century pulpit. An intricate statue of St. Cecilia by famed sculptor David d'Angers stands before the carved stalls. The church itself is also a major landmark, since

its two 246-foot spires can be seen for miles. (Good King René is buried here.) Around the church are narrow streets lined with dozens of timbered houses. Maison d'Adam (shown), a 15th century merchant's house (now a craft shop) on place Ste. Croix is one of the most visited. The structure is embellished with wooden carvings of sirens, animals, musicians, and lovers.

The opposite side of Angers, called La Doutre, is well worth a visit for its well-preserved timbered houses, apothecary's house, restored church, pretty squares, and pavement cafés. Also worth a visit is the Musée des Beaux-Arts, which features Angers archaeological history through enamels, carved wood, and statuary, as well as canvases from various eras. This is a fine museum, and my afternoon here was a wonderful dip into visual history. Afterward, I had a scrumptious, low-priced lunch at Café Des Orfevres, the museum eatery. I ordered the lasagna and salad. It came piping hot from the oven, made fresh that day, no additives, no microwaving. My lasagna was so delicious, my companion and I oohed and ahhed over it, as well as her fluffy quiche with all the trimmings.

Afterward, I had a most unique experience. At the table next to me sat a pair of Angers *grands-mères* (elderly grandmothers). This is the cohort I find it most difficult to have meaningful interactions with in France; I suspect they are put off by "loud" English speakers who come to France and throw money around and hog the pleasures in their beloved pastoral enclaves. (Who can blame them?) I noticed out of the corner of my eye that the little grandmother opposite and across from me had on the "ensemble" of my own little grandmother when she was alive: a fading, nondescript housedress, a baggy white sweater, ill-fitting undergarments that made her body resemble a sack of potatoes, knee high stockings rolled up to the calves that were clearly visible for the entire room to see, and black "grandma" shoes equally good for vacuuming, mucking out the garage, or having lunch in town.

Lest I sound too "snarky," I loved my unfashionable grandmother (who used to do most of her shopping out of the JC Penney catalog with its yellowing pages). But I have endeavored not to assume this particular "look" personally, although I do see myself sliding slowly toward this "I don't care" presentation (despite my Victoria's Secret underwear, *haute couture* scarves, and Guess earrings).

As the *grand-mère* opposite me stood to leave, I prepared myself to be ignored or clucked at, since I wasn't a locale and I was inhabiting prime luncheon real estate. To my shock and chagrin, this little *grand-mère* stopped beside me and put her hand on my shoulder! She told me in "Franglish" how pleased she was that I had eaten the same dish that she had eaten and found it "Très, très bien."

I agreed and then told her how much I was enjoying her beautiful Angers. She replied that I was very welcome—and that she was glad to have me in her city. She then squeezed my shoulder and made her way to the exit. Watching her go, I had tears in my eyes. I had judged her harshly, but she had sweetly connected with me. I blushed at my error. And then I smiled in thanks for her acceptance and waved *Au Revoir.* Such are the beautiful moments I often encounter in France—very real, very memorable.

Not far from the art museum, art lovers can enjoy the stunning Galerie David d'Angers, featuring the work of favorite-son sculptor Pierre-Jean David. Inside are massive sculptures from this modern-day master who seems to have inherited the genius of Michelangelo.

Along the other byways, you'll see shops selling Angers' most famous product, Cointreau. More than 15 million liters of this famous liqueur are produced every year. The local distillery was founded in 1849 by the Cointreau brothers. These clever liquidologists were confectioners famous for their exotic tonics. Their first success was in making the cherry liqueur Guignolet. But it was one of their sons, Édouard, who created the original recipe that is used today, which is based on sweet and bitter orange peels.

Édouard had noticed consumers' interest in the taste of oranges, which were a very precious commodity at the time. He realized that this universal flavor appealed to both men and women. He experimented zealously until he created the perfect blend of bitter and sweet orange peels. His passion finally gave birth to the original Triple-Sec that is known today as Cointreau.

An estimated 13 million bottles of this orangey nectar are sold annually; 90% is exported. Besides being enjoyed neat or over ice, Cointreau is used in many popular drinks, including margaritas and cosmopolitans. The Cointreau Rickey is a refreshing drink that some may want to try. (But remember that Cointreau is 80 proof!)

Cointreau Rickey Recipe
INGREDIENTS
- Cointreau, 2 oz.
- Lime juice, 1 oz
- Club Soda, 3–4 oz.

DIRECTIONS
Add ice, stir well, garnish with an orange lime twist, and enjoy!

Though now merged with Rémy Martin, a visit to the Cointreau Museum in Angers's St. Barthélémy district makes for a tasty tour. Inside, you'll find some fascinating depictions of the distilling process from the late 1800s and early 1900s. Ladies in Gibson-girl hair, long dresses, and starched aprons are shown carefully pouring the rich liqueur into what look like gallon bottles. (My biggest question: Were these prim ladies allowed to tipple?)

In 1889 Édouard and his famous drink captured the Unconventional French Spirit award. Soon, recognition—and fans—came from all over the world. Like Toulouse Lautrec during his years in Paris, Édouard had an eye for advertising. He invented the character of Pierrot de Cointreau, the Cointreau-sipping clown. He became the much-loved ambassador for the heady drink. To this day, Cointreau is one of the most consistently honored products of France.

If you travel to Angers in July, you'll be pleased to find yourself in the middle of the fantastic Anjou Festival. It draws huge crowds that have a riotous time sampling Anjou fruits and vegetables, sipping Anjou wines, and carting off seeds, flowers, and medicinal plants, as well as home goods. Almost like Mardi Gras in New Orleans, revelers have a grand time enjoying the parades, bands, jazz ensembles, theatricals, pavement stalls (booths) and the fine *Son et Lumières* (light shows).

If you pop in to Angers, you can get a friendly orientation to the sites at the Office du Tourisme on Place Kennedy near the entrance to the *château* (http:// angersloiretourisme.com/fr). You'll come away with a town and area map, as well as tips for maximizing your time. You can purchase the famous City Pass that affords low-priced access to many Angers museums and exhibits. As of this writing, the passes are for 24 hours, 48 hours, and 72 hours; all sell for just a few euros each.

Wine lovers eager to sample Anjou wines can visit the Maison du Vin de l'Anjou on the same square. Here you can hop on one of the little white trains (which remind me of Disneyland) and get a quirky ride around town in about 45 minutes. (This is one of my favorite travel trips for visiting new places in France; these petite trains in most places provide a wonderful overview of the towns *and* save you having to explore them all on foot. That way, you can select a few favorites to return to at your leisure.)

The Tourism Office's very readable map in French and English offers two trails, or walking routes, for discovering Angers. The first is the one-hour *Parcours Facile.* This route is marked by bronze nails on the pavement; it's perfect for families with strollers or wheelchairs, as well as those who want an easy stroll through the town. The second is the 2.5-hour historic trail called the *Circuit Angers Historique.* It explores many of the sites I've mentioned above.

Here's a basic plan for visiting Angers: Allow a half-day for seeing the old town, including two hours to explore the *château.* Have a pleasant lunch at a pavement café on one of the old streets (recommendations follow). Then, wander through the lovely gardens off Boulevard du Mal. Foch, which includes the Jardin des Plantes. The Jardin des Plantes is a serene botanical garden filled with rare species of trees like the Davidia or handkerchief tree. There's also an aviary filled with birds and lively parrots.

Take a second day to view the tapestry museums and the other art galleries and sights. A fantastic family experience is the Terra Botanica plant theme park (especially good for children). The Terra Botanica, by the way, is Europe's first themed park dedicated to plants and nature. With more than 275,000 plants from six continents, it's truly a garden paradise. There are rides, activities and enjoyable eateries at this unique park.

Angers Accommodations

Traditional hotels proliferate in business-minded downtown Angers, including The Best Western Hotel D'Anjou (with La Salamandre restaurant); Hotel de France, one of Angers grandest hotels; the Mercure Angers Centre; and the Ibis Angers Centre Château. These are standard hotel accommodations, most with restaurants.

Le Mouton, a B&B situated in the hamlet of Port Valée near Angers, is an oblong house and tower that functioned as an inn and tollhouse in centuries past. Now a homey five-room riverside B&B with Jacuzzi, swimming pool, and *pétanque* court, it also has six independent summer-only *gîtes* for rent. http://le-mouton.fr

Château de Noirieux is a fabulous Relais & Châteaux property just outside Angers run by Anja and Gérard Côme. This magnificent *château* turned hotel, with romantic grounds along the river, has wonderful patio and terrace dining, poolside service, and fabulous rooms. (Maids put rose petals in your bath.) *Warning:* If you stay here, you will never want to leave. http://www.chateaudenoirieux.com/uk/index.php

Château de Brissac, situated about 24 miles from Angers, is the tallest castle in France. Day tours are a treat, but this venerable castle is also available for overnight stays May–September only. http://www.chateau-brissac.fr

Angers Dining & Wine Bars

Auberge Belle Rive is a popular veranda and patio restaurant with excellent food and romantic views.
http://restaurant-bellerive.com
Auberge de la Lieue offers a traditional French menu serving local dishes with seasonal ingredients.
http://www.restaurant-angers-49.com

L'Entracte has fine dining in one of the oldest restaurants in Angers. It contains lovely stained glass windows and an exceptional interior; the menu offers popular dishes and a great wine list. http://www.lentracte-angers.fr/

Le Dix Septieme is a cute and modern French bistro, more reasonably priced and more charming than others nearby . http://restaurant-ledixseptieme-angers.fr

La Chabada, on Blvd. du Doyenné in the north area of the town, is your local headquarters for live rock and pop. Other late-night bars, some with music, can be found around Rue Saint-Laud in the old quarter. http://www.lechabada.com

Château de Brissac**

At seven stories high, this 204-room castle is the tallest in the valley. Known as the "Giant of the Loire," Brissac has a long dramatic history. Situated about 24 miles south of Angers near the River Aubance, this grand castle was

originally built by the Counts of Anjou in the 11th century. In the 15th century, Pierre de Brézé, Minister to Charles VII and then to Louis XI, took ownership of the castle.

In 1502 Brissac was acquired by René de Cossé. During the French Revolution, the *château* was ransacked. It lay in ruins until 1844 when the remaining dukes of Brissac began restorations that continue to this day. The private estate is now the residence of direct descendants, the 13th Duke of Brissac and his family.

On my visits, I've always been overwhelmed with the serene beauty of the *château* and its gracious environs. By day, the castle and public rooms are startling examples of royal life with sumptuously ornate furniture, intricate tapestries, beautiful art, and rich décor. The cultivated parklands are wonderful to wander through. By twilight, the air around the estate is magical—as if it comes alive each night in some sorcerer's spell. You can almost believe a royal cavalcade will come riding across the lawn, horns blaring, at any moment.

The meticulously refurbished estate is a magnificent example of luxury restored. At the entrance, a domed 17th century pavilion soars to 120 feet between two 15th century towers. Inside, there are stunning ceilings, precious furniture, and a gorgeous Belle Époque theatre that seats 200 for Opera or theatrical performances. The Golden Drawing Room houses family souvenirs from the ages; the dining room reveals a royal table laid, awaiting royal guests.

A public tour allows visitors to follow in King Louis XIII's footsteps in 1620 when he visited the estate. It includes several royal bedrooms, portrait galleries, the chapel, and the private theater. The tour leads at last to the wine cellars, where various Château de Brissac wines are available for taste and purchase. The *château* has 28 hectares of splendid vineyards producing three well-loved AOC wines. Of particular note are the ruby red Anjou Villages Brissac wine and the salmon pink Rosé d'Anjou.

The tour finishes at the gift shop. Afterward, you may shop, wander the inviting park grounds, or enjoy a repast at Le Pavillon des Cédres. Le Pavillon des Cédres offers light lunch in July and August and tea and cakes the rest of the year. Brissac is also famous for hosting several yearly events like the Spring Fashion Flower show, the May Antiqua antiques fair, Brissac Paint & Picnic Days for picnickers and artists, and the annual Christmas Fair usually attended by more than 7,000 visitors. (The estate is available for weddings and receptions if you'd like to go all out for a wedding, anniversary, or corporate party.)

One ghostly note: A double murder allegedly occurred sometime in the 15th century within the walls of the castle. The persistent result is sightings of "La Dame Verte" or "the Green Lady," who sometimes reportedly wanders the halls in a luminescent green dress. She was supposedly murdered here—and her moans can sometimes be heard in the early hours of the morning. The current residents, the Duke of Brissac and his family, have become accustomed to her roaming the rooms, they say, but she *has* startled a guest or two. (I've not seen her.) This adds even more charm to this unique location as one of the most memorable castles of the Loire. Be sure to make reservations for a visit, since this is still a private castle and you may be turned away if you do not reserve in advance. http://www.chateau-brissac.fr

Château Le Plessis-Bourré**

The tidy Château Le Plessis-Bourré is a creamy-stoned *château* topped by gray slate, set stoically in a wide moat bordered by greenery. In the 1400s, Jean Bourré originally built this aristocratic estate. Bourré served Louis XI faithfully as Financial Secretary and Treasurer of France from 1461 onward until his death. He was the king's favorite confidante and wrote all of the king's private correspondence.

In 1469 Louis XI established an order of chivalry in the name of Saint Michael. Thirty-six knights took the Saint Michael oath to the king; Jean Bourré was one of the first. Bourré also functioned as the captain of several castles in the area, including Langeais and Angers, cleverly morphing them from fortresses into pleasure palaces. He later served as the tutor of Dauphin Charles VIII (who succeeded Louis XI at age 13 after a twenty-year reign). Bourré thus exercised much power in France during his lifetime, which spanned three kings' reigns.

Statesman, counselor, and alchemist, Bourré was a meticulous, efficient man. He thus completed Plessis-Bourré in just five years. Today it perfectly maintains its original structure with only modern upgrades like electricity and plumbing. Classically built in what is known as "Transition Style," the estate has both fortress elements (a double drawbridge, gatehouse, parapet walk, dungeon, and expansive moat) and stately living components (a large courtyard, arcaded gallery, and well-lit rooms with mullioned windows, rich decorations, and intricate ceilings). As Bourré was also very interested in Alchemy (very popular at the time), there are numerous esoteric symbols (sun, moon, stars, pentagrams) represented in the ceiling decorations and *façades.* These create a mystical atmosphere worth studying in detail as you visit.

After a succession of owners, Plessis-Bourré was purchased in 1911 by Henry Vaïsse, the great uncle of the present owner. As a lover of fine art, Vaïsse enriched the castle with fabulous paintings and statuary. In 1931 the castle was deemed a historical monument; in 1955 it opened to the public. Today, the castle functions more like a country-manor house. It's open for public and private tours, corporate seminars, and weddings.

As you enter the castle you'll find a complex of state apartments, a Parliament hall, a dining room with a vast fireplace at one end, a spectacular spiral staircase, a guardroom, a warm library, and a strolling arcade. The library fireplace bears some interesting graffiti: three coats of arms were defaced by some angry rebels during the French Revolution. The current owners have kept it exactly as is—a reminder perhaps of the now egalitarian nature of France.

Despite wear and tear on the six-centuries-old exterior stonework, I was impressed by how well maintained Plessis-Bourré is in general. Its handsome coffered ceilings, polished floors, and period furniture very accurately depict what wealthy medieval life must have been like centuries ago. The chapel reflects the abiding faith in a higher power; Jean Bourré's heart is buried here.

Around the castle is 20 acres of parklands, meadows, and gardens. This is my favorite part of Plessis-Bourré. Century-old ash and oak trees, plus Oriental plane trees, cedar, cypress, honey locust, and greenery, make the moat surroundings a delight. The medieval Alchemy garden is particularly charming. Plants with healing powers and the labels of the secret language of science pop up as you meander through this verdant enclave.

During pageant days, swan-helmed knights ride regally alongside elegant ladies in period dress on great steeds. Since it is such a photographable castle situated on what amounts to a sparkling lake, Plessis-Bourré has been a shoot location for numerous French films, including *Louis XI*, *Jeanne d'Arc* (1989 telefilm), and *The Princess of Montpensier*.

Easy to access and only 10 miles from Angers, Plessis-Bourré can be toured in a morning (pack a picnic lunch for enjoying the grounds after your visit) or afternoon. Public tours are offered in both self- and guided-tour formats. http://plessis-bourre.com

Château de Serrant***

Château de Serrant is the privately owned, most westerly of the great castles. It's located an easy drive 10 miles west of Angers. Construction of this unspoiled *château* with its pleasing symmetrical corners was begun in 1546 by Charles de Brie on the foundations of a medieval fortress. He modeled the structure after Renaissance-style Château de Fontainebleau (where French sovereigns lived on and off for eight centuries). Multiple owners completed Serrant over the next three centuries. Its pale *tufa* stone alternates pleasantly with the dark schist *façades*. Stately, rounded cupolas cap the corner towers. The result is a classical, dignified structure surrounded by massive trees—all reflected in calming waters—a beautiful sight indeed.

De Brie and subsequent owners in the early centuries failed to complete the original grand plan for the estate. But in 1636, Guillaume de Bautru, wealthy wit and counselor to

Louis XIII and Louis XIV, continued with construction as de Brie had originally outlined. Both towers were completed, as well as two wings and two lodges. Later a stately grand staircase was added.

De Bautru's granddaughter married the Marquis of Vaubrun, Lieutenant General of the king's army. Upon his death during the Spanish War, she commissioned a magnificent chapel to be built on the estate in his memory. Childless and nearing death, she sold the estate in the 18th century to Antoine Walsh, a member of the Irish nobility. Walsh had followed James II into exile in France. A clever and industrious man, Walsh became a wealthy ship-owner in nearby Nantes.

Over the decades, the Walsh family redecorated the interior and created an English-style park and pavilions around the castle. The family also added an imposing entrance gate crested by their Walsh coat of arms. In 1830 Valentine Walsh de Serrant married the Duke of la Trémoïlle, one of France's oldest families. Trémoïlle restored Serrant once again, added parapets and cornices, and additionally installed the coat of arms of the La Trémoïlle family.

In the 20th century, the *château* was finally modernized and cellars and electricity were added. The current owners, the Prince and Princess de Merode-Waterloo, are descendants of the Trémoïlles. Since 2004 they have offered splendid tours of the medieval rooms, Grand Salon, library, Napoleon bedroom, and restored kitchen.

As you enter the grounds, you are greeted by pretty fields, chestnut trees, and a gently flowing moat spilling into a wooded lake. Despite its enchanting ambiance, however, Serrant today is a working estate, both within and without. The exterior needs a bit of refurbishment, but this belies the busy activity within.

Inside is a sumptuous mansion that often rings with the drama of "medieval life." Visitors enjoy regular "performances" by costumed actors in various rooms, conducting the medieval business of the day. For example, in the wide kitchen lined with copper pots and ancient cooking instruments, you'll happen upon the head cook relating the latest news to her maids as they prepare luncheon.

In the elegant dining room, fine ladies are enjoying a feast of elegant *chocolate chaud*, *macarons*, and tiny sandwiches—and of course fine wine and gossip.

In the great *château* center is one of the most memorable Renaissance staircases in the region. A fine collection of 18th century furniture, wooden carvings, and Flemish tapestries decorate the handsome private rooms, many of which are open to the public on a regular basis. The majestic library is the real draw, however; it houses more than 12,000 books—many embossed with the Trémoïlle seal.

The apartments are classically furnished and capture royal grandeur at its peak. Of particular note are the bathrooms hidden in cupboards. *Quirky note:* Napoleon Bonaparte and Josephine famously visited this château; special furniture had been built and upholstered with fine Beauvais tapestry fabric in their honor. Alas, Napoleon did not sleep overnight in this handsome estate; he stayed for only two hours.

The Orangerie (conservatory) is being restored in 2016 to begin offering a venue for seminars and weddings. Guided tours are available June through October. Check the website for details. http://www.chateau-serrant.net

Château de Montgeoffroy*

What sets Montgeoffroy apart from other Loire *châteaux* is simple—it has remained the same as it was when it was built. A time capsule of sorts... Nothing of Château Montgeoffroy has changed through the centuries...Every piece of furniture, painting and accessory remains in the house as it did when the *château* was first designed. Even the kitchen retains its original 260 copper pots, which look remarkably in vogue today. Even more amazing, the same family still owns the *château*. Thus, a visit to Montgeoffroy is witness to the most beautiful

period in design—the 18th century. Time truly stands
still at Montgeoffroy.

—Joni Webb, *Cote de Texas* Blogspot

Sitting resplendent amid green fields stretching out
for miles is the splendid 18th-century-style Château de
Montgeoffroy (photo courtesy of Château de Montgeoffroy).
Montgeoffroy is a masterpiece of perfectly preserved
château living. Different from many of the Loire castles,
Montgeoffroy has a much more recent history.

Montgeoffroy was built between 1773 and 1775 by
Parisian architect Sir Benoît Vincent Barré for Field Marshal
Louis Georges Erasme de Contades (1704–1795). Contades
was the 6th Marquis de Contades, as well as Seigneur de
Montgeoffroi. (A Marquis title ranks below a duke but above
an earl/count. A duke is typically part of the royal family.)

Contades was born in Anjou; he rose to be one of
France's most extraordinary military commanders of the day.
He became Marshall of France for King Louis XV and served

as a major battlefield commander during the Seven Years War (1755–1764). (This was actually the first "world war" since it involved belligerents from Great Britain, Prussia, Hanover, and Portugal against France, the Holy Roman Empire, Russia, Spain, Sweden, and Saxony.) Contades later became governor of Alsace near Germany in northeastern France.

Contades is famous for several amusing lifestyle choices. The great man's chef invented *pâté de foie gras* for him—and it was originally known as "*pâté à la Contades.*" Most notable for the time, the Marquis was not extravagant as a rule; in fact, he lived exceptionally well within his means. This was exceedingly rare among the free-spending 18th century nobility; their profligate squandering of money led to the uprising of the starving classes and ultimately the bloody French Revolution.

Eyeing retirement, Contades had planned to return to his Loire Valley birthplace for a much-earned rest in a serene locale. He'd married Marie-Françoise Magon in 1724; she was the daughter of a wealthy merchant. They had three children. But, like many of the Frenchmen of the day, he'd taken a mistress. His was the formidable Marie-Hélène Moreau de Séchelles. The couple had a male child. This child was Jean-Baptiste Martin Herault de Séchelles; Jean-Baptiste became the father of Marie-Jean Herault de Séchelles, who eventually was guillotined during the French Revolution, despite the fact that he was a noted member of the Revolutionary Council.

When it came time for Contades to build his retirement castle in the land of his birth, however—using mostly his wife's money—he decided frugally to construct a new *château* on the remains of a 16th century estate. However, he put his mistress, her relatives, and his legitimate son in charge.

The mistress, rather than the wife, ultimately lived at Montgeoffroy. What's more, the Marquis apparently had a few additional mistresses, which he ensconced in secret rooms he had built into the *château*. (I always find it amusing to run across these French families with multiple paramours and out-of-wedlock children who get along so amicably. The French are superb, at least historically, at operationalizing the concept of "blended families.")

When Contades' architect Barré set to work on reshaping the estate, he began by burning the old *château* to the ground. But since he liked the horseshoe configuration, he decided to build a brand new *château* in its footprint while keeping the two original towers, the surrounding moat, and the chapel that dates from 1543. The entire estate and its furnishings miraculously survived, almost completely intact, the mayhem of the French Revolution (1789–1799), as well as the Revolt in the Vendée. One of the reasons is that the family remained at the *château* during the conflict and was thus able to protect it. (I suspect lots of money changed hands as well.)

Today, Montgeoffroy remains miraculously in the hands of direct descendants. The current Marquis and Marquise de Contades have only recently opened the castle, more than 300 years after it was built, to welcome public visitors. Though the family reportedly lives in Paris most of the time, they come out to the *château* regularly. It's very much a country home now, rather than a regal estate. Many of the current family's photos still sit just below the 18th century portraitures, lending a modern/old vibe to the cozy environs.

The inventory records reveal that almost every object a visitor sees today throughout the *château* was designed for Montgeoffroy in the 1770s. Each item is still found in the same room for which it was originally destined. The family's second-floor living quarters (which visitors do not see) apparently have the only modern changes: several small servant bedrooms have been made into modern bathrooms.

Inside the main structure is a superb collection of Louis the XV, Transition style, and Louis XVI furnishings. Much of the sinuous furniture is stamped with renowned artisans of the area, including Gourdin, Rousseau, Blanchard, and Durand. There are also famous portraits painted by Van Loo, Rigaud, and Drouais.

As you tour the Grand salon, which is flooded with light from huge windows overlooking the courtyard, you may be awestruck by the elegant surroundings that have no fewer than 34 chairs. Many of these are in the charming rounded cabriole style. Warm parquet floors underpin the follow-on square salon, apartments, and handsome dining room. As a whole, it's wonderfully inviting.

The 18th century *décor*, with modern upgrades, prettily highlights the ancient pieces. Much of the furniture has been newly reupholstered by fabric genius Pierre Frey. Colorfully paneled walls meld handsomely with ancient tapestries, jacquard weaves, and draperies of patterned Braquenie fabric. Louis XV chairs and divans sit delicately alongside intricate fireplaces and consoles. Chandelier-lit china and glassware give a romantic glow to sumptuous dining rooms. And everywhere flower-filled cut-crystal vases add a fresh aroma to each of the suites.

Another interesting note is that you'll see fine examples of the typical 18ᵗʰ century bed styles here. The gigantic four-poster is known to most of us, and these are handsomely represented in Montgeoffroy. One of the more unusual versions is the angel bed *(lit d'ange* or, later, *lit à la duchesse)*. It was dubbed the "angel bed" because it has a very high tester (or drapery) that was said to "fly," since it was attached to the wall rather than the corner posts.

Most interesting to me, however, is the *niche* bed, which tucks sideways into an alcove for added warmth. During his time as American Ambassador to France, Thomas Jefferson fell in love with the French *niche* bed. He later installed some of these beds in his home at Monticello in Virginia. In fact, one of his personal niche bed designs allowed him to roll out of bed into one room, but if he rolled out in the opposite direction, he was in a different room! (Jefferson was a noted inventor and tinkerer.)

Montgeoffroy's vast kitchen is gleaming with dozens of brass pots mounted below the heads of hunted prey now holding court over kitchen workers. (You may even smell the aromas of roasted game and truffles.) The tack room and stables are enjoyable for their authentic detail. A quaint shop housed in the stables offers French kitsch to buy or ship home. Surrounding the *château* are some extraordinary parklands and gardens filled with fountains, topiaries, and live deer. These make for a serene stroll to contemplate what you've seen in the castle.

I would highly recommend a visit to this sumptuous *château,* particularly due to its beautiful furnishings and comprehensive *décor.* Unfortunately, many of the Loire *châteaux* (particularly Chambord) are so large they do not have furnishings in all rooms. This castle, however, provides a rare glimpse into exactly what 18ᵗʰ century regal life must have been for the lucky few who had the opportunity to enjoy it. http://chateaudemontgeoffroy.com

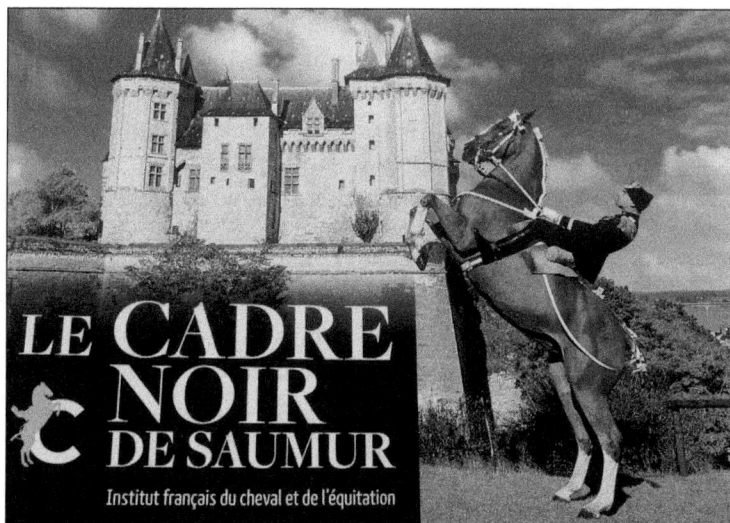

Saumur**

> Dream with your eyes wide open! Saumur has a soft *tuffeau* heart, a myriad of *châteaux*, manors, sixty listed churches, the largest monastery in Europe, but also dozens of megaliths. Nature, landscapes, and a gentle climate have inspired humans here for many millenniums!
>
> —Office de Tourisme du Saumorois

As I meandered along the Loire River road from Angers to Saumur, I came around a bend to behold an otherworldly castle high up at the edge of a dreamy stretch of the river. Standing guard as the Loire rolled past, Saumur's stately *château* was my first glimpse of this legendary part of Anjou. The limestone *château* topped by fetching slate blue towers reminded me more of the castles along the Danube than the *châteaux* of France. I soon discovered that this gem of medieval architecture is the crowning centerpiece of Saumur, the "Pearl of the Anjou."

Saumur, as well as the banks of the Loire nearby, are all part of the Loire UNESCO World Heritage site. Saumur and its *château* were built with the same gleaming *tuffeau* of the limestone plain that spreads south of the Loire. Hence its visual charm makes it a favorite for photographers.

But Saumur also has character as a stately equestrian city with a fantastic history of elegant showmanship that lives on today. "Grand Saumur" is the name given to Saumur and its surrounding areas. It's one of the most intriguing areas in the valley—though it sometimes takes a backseat to castle-heavy Touraine further to the east. Nevertheless, Saumur and its *château* anchor a dramatic region that showcases troglodyte caves, the Royal Abbey of Fontevraud, some of the finest vineyards in the region, and France's most famous equestrian school. If Touraine to the east is the feminine heart of the Loire with princess-like castles at Chenonceau, Uzès, and Azay-le-Rideau, then Grand Saumur is the masculine Loire core. It's filled with strapping horse riders and military zeal. The power and testosterone punctuate the air and seep into the troglodyte caves and underground, fertilizing the robust Saumur grapevines.

I find valiant Saumur a fantastic center point from which to see the rest of Anjou. (When I move to the more feminine Touraine area, I typically stay near Tours or Blois or in Amboise to enjoy the daintier vibe.) No matter where you lay your head in gallant Saumur, however, you can nearly always see the majestic castle, standing guard like some ancient defender in stone. At its feet is the inviting old town, which runs haphazardly down to the banks of the river.

On the outskirts of Saumur is France's most famous Cavalry School. Here, the finest French Cavalry officers trained in years past. This is also where valiant teenage cadets defended Saumur from the Germans in 1940. Later, the townspeople of Saumur worked brilliantly with the Allied forces to block German Panzer Divisions from reaching Normandy in 1944. (For these heroic efforts, the entire town was awarded the famous *Croix de Guerre*.)

Saumur is now home to the Armoured Branch and Cavalry Training School, the officer school for armored forces. This is one of the reasons you'll see military men and women around the town in uniforms or fatigues.

Historically, Saumur was situated precariously between the powerful counts of Anjou to the west and the irascible counts of Blois to the east. Theobald I, Count of Blois, originally built the foundation of the Château de Saumur in the 10th century as a fortified stronghold against the Normans. Fulk Nerra, Count of Anjou, captured the castle in 1026 and passed it on to his Plantagenet heirs. As previously mentioned, the most famous of these later Plantagenets was King Henry II who ruled England. Henry rebuilt the remains of the fortress into a castle in the late 12th century.

Phillip Augustus (Phillip II), the first French King from the Capetian dynasty, initially captured Saumur in 1203 as he extended the French monarchy into the Loire. Later, beloved René d'Anjou redecorated the interior of the castle in the 15th century. Under Louis XIV and Louis XV, the castle became the residence of the governor of Saumur.

The castle subsequently changed hands over the next several centuries; in time it served as an army barracks and then later Napoleon Bonaparte's state prison. The town itself finally acquired the castle in the 20th century. The Château de Saumur is now a Monument Historique of France.

If you decide to stay in Saumur, you will find it a well-built walking town—with plenty to see, do, eat, and imbibe. (The office of tourism provides an excellent walking tour map.) The winding streets follow the same course as in centuries past (although it's a bit of a hike up to the castle from the river). Between the great *château* and the bridge, you'll find half-timbered medieval houses side by side with newer construction. Of particular note is Eglise Saint-Pierre, a beautiful 12th century church that has been refurbished over the centuries and now contains a fine tapestry collection.

Rue St. Jean, the main shopping street, is a natty place to find Saumur treasures like sparkling wines and mushroom paraphernalia. Place St. Pierre is the center of things, and there's usually much to see, taste, and do here. Along the way, there are many churches to admire, as well cafés, restaurants, and wine bars to visit for a glass of Saumur Champigny plus some savory goat's cheese on a baguette with a side of arugula salad (my favorite *dejeuner* when I am here).

Wine and liqueur lovers will find accessible spirits. The Loire Valley Wine Centre (La Maison des Vins de Loire de Saumur) near the Saumur tourism office provides tour information, maps, and wines to taste and buy. http://vinsvaldeloire.fr/SiteGP/EN

The Combier Distillery (makers of Triple Sec and Royal Combier liquors) can be a fun visit too. Gustave Eiffel designed the stillroom for his friend and confectioner Jean-Baptiste Combier. http://www.combierusa.com

However, an initial tour inside the storybook Château de Saumur is a wonderful introduction to this intrepid town. Though it began as a fortress, the castle with its "pencil" turrets is today quite decorative and comfortable. Since it served most recently as a genial country home, it has spacious rooms, pretty balustrades at the windows, fine furniture, highly buffed wood floors, charming spiral staircases, and gorgeous artwork depicting the images of the time. Within and without, visitors may come across live re-enactments, with actors in regal costumes acting out daily Saumur life from medieval times. Other times, you may hear horses' hooves or glimpse carriages filled with happy tourists rolling along nearby. From the grassy ramparts, there's a panoramic view of the river and lively town below. At night, mostly in summer months, there are spectacular light shows projected onto the walls of the castle.

Across town are the Musée des Arts Décoratifs, the Musée de la Cavalerie, and the Musée des Blindés. The first offers a collection of paintings tapestries, furniture, statuettes, and ceramics dating from the 13th to the 19th century. The second is the Cavalry Museum, founded originally by a veterinarian at Saumur's cavalry school. The third is the Armored Vehicle Museum that displays weaponry and tanks from wars past; it has one of the most extensive collections on the planet.

The Cavalry Museum tells the story of the Saumur School of Cavalry nearby; it's now called the École National d'Équitation. This French military academy was founded in 1828. Designed to provide training for commissioned and non-commissioned officers for the French cavalry, the elite graduates participated in many wars and skirmishes in the 18th and 19th centuries. The museum has a rich display of their souvenirs, uniforms, and armor that trace the heroic deeds of the French Cavalry since the 18th century. In my most recent visit there, I even saw an elaborately carved Russian sleigh that reminded me of the movie *Dr. Zhivago*.

No wonder I picked up the Russian connection. My guide pal, Jeremy Kolbe, pointed out that if you look in the Saumur phonebook, you will see many Russian names. Apparently, many White Russians left Russia and came to live out their days in Saumur after the Russian Revolution. They contributed greatly to the Saumur equestrian culture— which still characterizes Saumur today. Outside the museum, some of

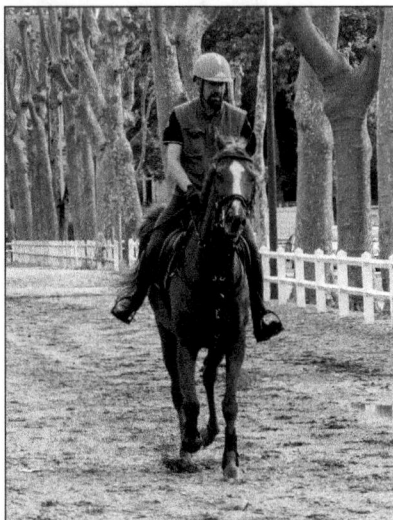

the riders were rounding the training path, so I had the opportunity to snap some extraordinary photos.

After World War II, the elite riders of the Cadre Noir began performing as the Republican Guard, mostly in a ceremonial capacity. However, France's pride in its long history of horsemanship helped morph the academy into a national riding school under France's Ministry of Sports. In 1972 the National Riding School was constituted around the Cadre Noir as the core teaching staff. They are named the *Cadre Noir* (black frame) due to their posh black and gold ceremonial uniforms. The horses themselves are also handsomely bedecked in tassels, braids, and ribbons. Horse and rider pairs appear in most Saumur marketing materials—and they are the "face" of this equine locale.

But these horses are no ordinary steeds. They're trained in a very distinctive style of ancient *dressage*. The horses are taught perfect balance; they learn to demonstrate intricate choreography and extraordinary jumps that highlight their natural equine grace. Many are statuesque Lusitano horses that demonstrate 16th and 17th century baroque riding styles. Thoroughbreds and Anglo Arabians are also in the mix. (Later, I will detail how I got to meet and pet some of these imposing animals that were as friendly as puppies despite their extraordinary size and elite status.)

Horses with riders appear in spectacular exhibitions called the Grand Prix dressage (formal horse riding events). One of the most photographed events features horses completely suspended in air! Other stunts have riders on bucking horses that rear up in perfect formation with one another. Many of these horses and riders have participated in Olympic events over the years, by the way. In 2008, the organization began accepting women into the Cadre Noir—and there are some very fine female riders.

Today's Cadre Noir puts on spectacular shows in its Olympic-sized indoor riding rink and training complex. A few miles from Saumur central, on a grassy expanse of land, sits this extensive Cadre Noir Training facility. I was wild with glee as I wandered around this fantastic compound one morning. (Entrance fee is only eight euros per person.)

With my English-speaking guide, Oriel, I surmised we would be shepherded around the outskirts of the complex at a circumspect distance. Wrong! We got unprecedented access to these fabulous riders and horses. We walked the stables, petted these million-dollar animals, and even watched an Olympian training to represent France in 2016.

Visitors are allowed to sit in the grand ring and watch the training. We were not allowed to film the Cadre Noir Masters as they rode; however, we were allowed to photograph and film their students—while the Cadre Noir Masters coached them from the benches.

In the stables, we were allowed remarkable access to the inner workings of the facility. We watched the riders coming and going in the stables. We visited the horse stalls and chatted with some of the trainers, who cheerfully helped move the horses to the front of their stalls for our photographs!

We peeked in at the *cheval douche* (horse shower) and the horse "heat lamp spa" where the horses stand under lamps to dry (much to their delight). To my surprise, these fantastic animals, with rippling muscles across their backs since they have to jump in the air on command and execute all kinds

of fantastic steps to music, were as docile as pets. As we wandered along, many of them begged for scratches.

To top off our visit, some of the Master riders themselves happened by. I admit as I wandered around the complex, smelling mown hay and watching these graceful animals being put through their paces by individuals in thigh-high boots, I've had a few fantasies. Most harken back to bodice-ripper novels I've clandestinely read. Inhaling the aroma of horse sweat and watching perspiration trickle down the neck of a chiseled Frenchmen is titillating indeed. But don't take my word for it. This is something you definitely need to experience for yourself.

My French pal Jean-Pierre spent a year in the military in Saumur as a young man. He recalls the inspirational time he had there. The military tradition of proud France is much on display in Saumur, he explained. "The dedication to the beauties of equine activities, a fondness for the culture of *haute* militarism, the traditions of "white glove" allegiance to France, are all part of my boyhood memories of Saumur." One of the things he told me he particularly enjoys there is the collection of military uniforms since 1445, as well as the samples of formal riding wear.

Tickets for visiting the training facility are so inexpensive I encourage you to bring the whole family. The formal Cadre Noir shows are also very reasonably priced.

Tickets can be purchased at various outlets as well as at the Office de Tourisme du Saumurois. Visitors to the facilities will see the main arena, master stables, and tack room, as well as memorabilia. (This is an exceptional family venue—your kids will love it!)

On another note, Saumur and the Cadre Noir have also dramatically influenced French fashion. Gabrielle Bonheur "Coco" Chanel was born into poverty in Saumur. Later she was reared in convent orphanages elsewhere after her mother died and her father disappeared. As a grown woman, Coco grew fond of horseback riding and the wealthy horsey set. Most fans know her *haute couture* history with military lovers, as well as wealthy patrons who supported her budding fashion empire.

What I suspect is that as a child she became acutely aware of the dashing élan of Saumur's famous cavalry and their uniforms. It may in fact be these dramatic childhood images that fueled her psyche for life—and added fire to her considerable design flair. The panache, the streamlined style, and the penchant for accessorizing are all there in the Cadre Noir, as well as in the Chanel "look." (The famous cropped Chanel jacket looks a lot like a feminized Cadre Noir jacket to me.)

Quirky note: By the outbreak of World War II, Coco had established herself in Paris. She lived and worked across from the Ritz Hotel, which she frequented. When the Nazis took over Paris and ensconced themselves at the Ritz, Coco fell in love with a German officer named Baron Hans Gunther von Dincklage. Together they took up residence at the Ritz, where they lived out the war until they escaped to Switzerland. (I suspect Coco had difficulty resisting a handsome man in uniform.)

But returning to the travails of Saumur, modern warfare has made its mark. The barn-sized Armored Vehicle Museum (Musée des Blindés) harkens back to more recent conflicts that tested the town's mettle. During World War II, the Nazis marched in and occupied Northern France, while the capitulated Vichy Government of France "loosely" governed the rest of the country (save for the Italian zone in the southeast portion of France). The Loire River was roughly the dividing line for a major part of the Nazi-occupied area (save for the entire coast of western France all the way to Spain through Bordeaux).

I find this German occupation of Northern France particularly fascinating, since two of my uncles landed on the Normandy Beaches as part of the Allied Invasion in 1944. Normandy is just a scant 192 miles directly north from Saumur as the crow flies. I've easily visited both the Normandy Beaches and the Loire Valley in a week, since they're so close together. It's a sobering reminder that the beauty of the Loire *châteaux* is only part of the history of this fabled, often conflict-ridden, area.

In the commemoration of all these mighty wars, the Musée des Blindés has an exceptional collection of more than 880 armored tanks and vehicles—many of them in perfect working order. These include several Panzer and Tiger tanks (German), Sherman and Lee tanks (US), Saint-Chamond and Schneider tanks (French), and Matilda and Churchill tanks (UK). There are also some Post War Pluton missiles and various other types of weaponry. Needless to say, this military collection is much in demand for films. (*Note to military fanciers:* Many tourists miss Les Invalides, the military museum, in Paris. This complex contains not only a fascinating historical exhibition but also Napoleon's tomb. Even though I am not typically a military aficionado, I can attest that Saumur, Normandy, and Paris's Les Invalides have held me in thrall each time I've visited. There is something about the proud show of service to one's country that is both inspiring and sobering. (I plan to write an additional *Intoxicating Greater Paris* book about Northern France, with special focus on the Normandy Beaches, as well Mont St. Michel, Honfleur, and Brittany.)

When you're ready for some genial carriage rides or exciting horseback riding adventures for yourself, however, Saumur is also your place. The Saumur tourism office has several equestrian venues for horseback riders of all levels. Check out www.equitation-saumur.fr for riding opportunities—you can also rent a donkey if you prefer a gentler pace!

Depending on when you visit Saumur, you'll likely find one of the many yearly Saumur events taking place. These include the Yearly Carrousel de Saumur, a spectacular event that celebrates the end of Officer Training in the Cavalry School (third week in July). It's been held each year for more than a hundred years! The annual Saumur Grandes Tablées du Saumur-Champigny is an all out wine–food–street-theater, two-night extravaganza that rivals New Orleans. (Check the Saumur tourism office for dates.)

Festivini is another epic event, this one stretching over eight days. During the event, revelers learn about wine and specific vintners and, of course, taste the exceptional wines. Throughout July and August, Place Saint-Pierre and Place de la République are alive with music for curbside diners and revelers. Nearby, in the suburb of Saint-Hillaire–Saint-Florent, several bars in *tuffeau* caves have music and dancing. In Saumur proper, don't miss my favorite shops: La Duchesse Anne (gourmet cakes and sweets), Festina Lente (art stencils near Fontevraud-L-Abbaye), and Barre de chocolat, a chocolate factory and shop in the heart of Saumur with bonbons galore and much more.

The Grand Saumur countryside is alive with unusual pleasures. Located at the cross point of the Loire and Thouet Rivers, Grand Saumur is a realm famed for its medal makers, mushrooms, and, above all, its exceptional wines, especially sparkling vintages. Chinon, Bourgueil, Coteaux du Layon, and Vouvray produce some of the Loire's favorite wines in this area, as I detailed in the food and wine chapter. Visitors can street-market shop and taste wine throughout the entire Grand Saumur.

Other popular events in the area include the Anjou Vintage Bike Festival, the Cadre Noir Galas, Book and Wine Fair, and the Great Banquet of Saumur-Champigny, to name just a few. (In spring, summer, and fall, Loire is alive with festivals from one end of the valley to another. The French, above all, know how to celebrate!)

The Loire Valley as a whole has an extensive network of honeycombed *tuffeau* quarries. Grand Saumur itself has more than 932 miles of these underground quarries and caves. Many of them have been repurposed into unconventional restaurants, B&Bs, mushroom farms, homes, wine caves, and beer distilleries.

Mushroom caves are especially popular in Saumur. As mentioned in the cuisine chapter, clever farmers transferred mushroom cultivation from the underground caves of Paris to the Loire. The result is the most extraordinary collection of mushrooms and snails on the continent. In addition to the famous *champignons de Paris* (button mushrooms), mushroom lovers will find oyster, shiitake, and blue-stem mushrooms, just to name a few. Though you may not be an *escargot* fan, seeing the Saumur snail farms (also underground in caves) is also a wonder.

Cave Aux Moines is one of the most famous venues for exploring mushroom and snail farming—and you can dine afterward in their very elegant eatery. Other noted cave venues include Cave Vivante du Champignon (Living Mushroom Cellars) and Champignonnière des Saut-aux-Loups (Saut-aux Loups Mushroom Cellars).

In Saint-Hilaire–Saint-Florent (about 12 minutes by car from downtown Saumur) is the noted Musée du Champignon (Mushroom Museum). This organization is much more than a history center for mushroom growing. Twelve tons of mushrooms are harvested within its caves annually. During their tour, you can see the many steps in growing and harvesting mushrooms, as well as see the striking *pied blue* mushroom (blue footed mushroom), plus more than 500 species of morels (some of them poisonous—but none of these are for sale!) Children will be fascinated by the collection of tools for mushroom farming. The shop sells all kinds of mushroom-related goodies, including books, comics, food, and more.

Near the Mushroom Museum sits a truly unique attraction: Pierre et Lumière—a miniature park of stone and light. A clever entrepreneurial team decided to carve a miniature version of Touraine and Anjou into the soft limestone of the caves. Beautiful churches, villages, and the grand *châteaux* of the area all appear in this wonderland of sculpture. All the pieces are lighted with planetarium-type lights of luminescent blues, reds, greens, yellows, and shimmering whites. The effect is a natural wonderland of backlit cave art. Do-it-yourselfers will find the attraction especially intriguing; it allows anyone, especially children, to use blocks of *tuffeau* to craft their own take-away artwork. http://pierre-et-lumiere.com

Since it's at the heart of the regional Park of Loire-Anjou-Touraine, Saumur is a prime spot to enjoy the beauties of nature. A glide down the river on a barge, boat, or canoe gives extraordinary views of the darling villages and castles, as well as the vineyard vistas. Interesting too are the sand barges, with their teeming life of fish and fowl.

Cycling or hiking excursions can take you up and down the rivers, offering fresh air and vibrant views. Cycling holidays for families, couples, or singles are particularly popular. One of the best vendors is Abicyclette, which puts together turnkey stays and weekends (www.abicyclette.net).

Saumur is such a lush, blue-skied area that flying

just over the treetops in a hot-air balloon gives stellar opportunities for a wide-angle view of the Loire. From up top, the grand *châteaux* are uniquely accessible to the naked eye (http://www.ballooning.fr/book-a-flight/). And if you are *really* adventurous, you can also do a parachute jump or two from the Loire skies.

The best news is that Saumur has one of the most helpful tourism offices in the area, Office de Tourisme du Saumurois. It provides a wonderful packet of material if you contact them via their website. They can also arrange walking tours, general tours, and local accommodations to suit your needs. http://ot-saumur.fr.

Saumur Accommodations

Hôtel Anne d'Anjou (pictured). This is a beautiful 18th century mansion with fabulous Trompe l'Oeil ceilings and castle or river view rooms. It's situated on the banks of the Loire within walking distance of the historic city center and castle with a very romantic garden, a bar, and a fine restaurant, Les Ménestrels, on the premises that is both picturesque and delicious. I can't say enough about this wonderful venue. Jean-René and Mary-Lyn Camus, plus their attentive staff, bend over backwards to be sure your stay is fantastic. They also can direct you to specific castles and make dinner and tour

reservations for you. They offer superb service at every turn. http://hotel-anneanjou.com/en/

Hôtel Kyriad is a city-center business hotel handy to downtown. http://kyriad-saumur-centre.fr/en

Château de Verrières is my other personal favorite in Saumur. This charming B&B is a gorgeous place to stay in the area. A *château* turned *chambre d'hôtes*, Verrières is set beautifully in a four-acre park and offers *château* living at an affordable price. Inside are sumptuous rooms with sculpted wood paneling, painted ceilings, Belle Époque furnishings, and a lovely fireplace where you'll find a cup of steaming tea or glass of Saumur wine awaiting you. Owners Yolaine and Thierry are personable hosts who will make your stay very comfortable. http://chateau-verrieres.com

Hôtel Les Terrasses. This is a peaceful accommodation on the Saumur outskirts. It has a spa and the Restaurant Bistronomique. http://www.lesterrassesdesaumur.fr

Château de Targé. This location also produces some excellent wines, mentioned in the wine section. It is now a *gîte* plus winery. http://www.chateaudetarge.fr

Camping L'Île d'Offard. Five star camping is available here. http://en.flowercampings.com

Saumur Dining & Wine Bars

L'Escargot offers fantastic five-star Parisian-style fine dining. http://www.ot-saumur.fr

Le Gambetta Presents its guests with elegant, Michelin starred fine dining. http://www.restaurantlegambetta.fr

Les Ménestrels has vaulted ceilings and a memorable interior, delicious food, and even a very favorable vegetarian menu. I had a marvelous dinner here in five courses, just steps from my castle-view room at the Hôtel Anne d'Anjou. http://www.restaurant-les-menestrels.com

Le Tire-Bouchon. Here you'll find bistro-style dining.

(There is no website as of this writing.)

Mercure Bords de Loire. This hotel and restaurant offer great views from the island. http://www.mercure.com (*Note:* Whenever I want an American or British-style hotel experience, I look for a Mercure. This is my favorite accommodation chain in France for clean, efficient stays; they always meet my expectations. They offer standard accommodations and dining options you can count on.)

Auberge Saint Pierre (shown). Wear your jeans and hunker down for some down-home French food in a funky atmosphere. When I want to chill out in my sneakers, I go here. Be sure to try the quirky desserts. This funky eatery has a cartoon-type menu and a fantasy *décor* of chainmail and armor. Located on the busy square, it has a superb luncheon menu and a truly wonderful wine list, plus an adorable bar. I could have stayed for hours. The staff became such great pals they gifted me with one of their newspaper-sized menus. http://www.aubergesaintpierre-saumur.fr There are a number of pavement brasseries ringing the square like Auberge St. Pierre. You will enjoy taking your pick of these handy restaurants.

Troglodyte dining options. Scattered around Grand Saumur are various eateries offering dining in a troglodyte *tuffeau* cave— an experience not to be missed. (Some venues are B&Bs as well.) My favorite cave venue, just a few miles from

downtown Saumur, is memorable **Les Caves de Marson** (http://www.cavesdemarson.com/cellars.html). If you visit one of the mushroom caves, many have restaurants or *cafés* where you can savor *galipettes* (juicy flat mushrooms stuffed with rillettes of pork), *escargot* (snails), or many other delicacies. Fifteen miles from Saumur is another favorite cave venue, **Le Pieds Bleus**, with a wonderful menu that includes mushroom *pâté* for spreading on their warm-from-the-wood-fired-oven breads. Be sure to try some of the Saumur wines with your meal. http://www.cave-aux-moines.com

Château Montreuil-Bellay*

In 1025 Fulk Nerra, Count of Anjou (and ancestor of the Plantagenet dynasty), erected a tower on the ruins of an iron-age Roman settlement. It overlooked the Thouet River as it flowed north to converge with the Loire in Saumur, about 25 miles away.

Nerra gave the settlement to his loyal vassal, Berlay. Berlay's name migrated to "Bellay"; and over three centuries, Bellay's progeny developed the estate to include ditches, ramparts, moats, a large underground complex, eighteen defense towers, and a large, garrison-style kitchen. It eventually became the impregnable fortress known as Montreuil-Bellay. The fortress, whose occupants were loyal to the Plantagenets, was unfortunately later destroyed by Phillip II of France when he finally vanquished the Plantagenet family and strove to punish their most ardent captains of war.

In the 1400s, owners Jacques d'Harcourt and his son adapted the fortress remains to create a sprawling, Renaissance style estate. They added a spiral staircase, updated the kitchen, installed pretty windows and elegant doorways, and decorated the oratory with frescoes painted by a pupil of Leonardo da Vinci.

After the French Revolution—during which the *château* was turned into a prison for female French monarchists—the *château* was purchased by a wealthy Saumur merchant. His daughter married Baron Alexander Adrien de Grandmaison, Officer of the guard of Charles X. Around 1860, an architect pupil of Eugène Viollet-le-Duc (the noted architect and visionary who famously restored Carcassonne in Southern France) further upgraded the estate with Italian-Renaissance influences. It is the descendants of the Grandmaisons who helm the estate today.

When I visited this arresting *château*—which wows by its mammoth width and height—I was struck by its strength of character particularly manifested in the many fireplaces, elaborate staircase, carved ceilings, splendid bedrooms, drawing rooms, and vaulted ceilings filled with the estate's own fine wines.

The kitchen is still filled with much of its 18th century cooking equipment. The dining room is a special treat, with carved beams studded with symbolic figures; I also liked the lyrical music room. The frescoes in the oratory have recently been restored. And of course there are massive tapestries and fine rugs throughout the *château*.

Plan some extra time at Montreuil-Bellay since the estate has a wine consortium and notable tasting room. It definitely makes for a full-service visit. You can naturally buy wine to take with you.

Outside, touring the massive ramparts will instantly take you back 500 years. There are 650 meters of these medieval marvels, plus thirteen towers. The views are stunning. You can almost imagine boiling oil being dumped on invaders down below. The barbican drawbridge tower, moats, and turrets almost made me want to put on chainmail and gallop out to the hinterlands with my flags flying. (This testosterone-heavy area works its magic that way.)

But there are some feminine touches, too, around Montreuil-Bellay in the graceful gardens that curl in and around the estate. Roses perfume the air, and a stroll beneath the lime trees and ancient yews is quite romantic. The friendly gift shop has souvenirs, wine, literature, and even ice cream to offer if you want to linger a little longer. The estate, by the way, is well known for its Cabernet France wines (Red Saumur Rosé and Cabernet d'Anjou) and Chenins (white and Saumur Brut Tradition).

At the feet of the *château* is the well-preserved medieval village of Montreuil-Bellay. The Place du Marche (Market Square) is ringed by some terrific examples of ancient *maisons* (houses) like the 15th century Maison de l'Apothicaire and the 11th century Maison des Remparts.

Wandering down the ancient streets, you'll run into picturesque Les Petits Augustins, a B&B with fragrant botanical gardens, as well as other dining and stayover options. Both castle and medieval village are well worth a visit. http://www.chateau-de-montreuil-bellay.fr

Abbaye de Fontevraud*

One of the Loire Valley's great landmarks, the 12th-century relic has played many roles over the years, from monastery to prison. It's now a cultural center and one of its priories is the setting for [an] ascetically luxurious lodging, restaurant included.
—Margot Guralnick, "Haunted Hotel," *Remodelista.com*

Founded in 1101 by the hermit Robert d'Arbrissel, Fontevraud Abbey, as it is known, is the largest preserved monastic site in Europe. It's unique in Europe, since it was designed to house both men and women. The Abbey encompassed five separate buildings accommodating priests, lay brothers, nuns, invalids, and lay sisters.

Each group led its own life with its own church and cloister, chapter house, refectory, kitchen, and dormitory. The head of the abbey was always to be a widow, and she served as General Head of the Order.

This very distinct religious complex was dubbed the "Royal Abbey," since many of the 36 abbesses were women of royal birth. From 1115 until the French Revolution (around 1792) these commanding abbesses led the double monastery of nuns (some of them were even cast-off royal mistresses) and monks. The abbey played a significant role for many centuries in the welfare of the local community, indeed all of France. It served both as a social services venue and political power recipient/broker.

The famous Plantagenets were significant benefactors of the abbey. Henry II, King of England, lavished money on the abbey, since he was a local boy with magnificent resources to fund it—and perhaps curry him favor in heaven. When Isabella d'Anjou (Duchess of Normandy) was Abbess in the mid 1100s, Eleanor of Aquitaine (now Henry II's widow) made Fontevraud her final home. In 1204 Eleanor died there and was entombed alongside Henry and other relatives in the nave of the abbey church.

It's quite stunning now to see Eleanor and Henry in effigy, lying side by side for eternity, after so much lust and conflict between them during their lifetimes. Nearby is the effigy of their son Richard the Lionheart, as well as Isabelle, wife of Richard's brother King John. *One bizarre note:* sometime during the Middle Ages or perhaps the French Revolution, the actual remains of these royals were removed from the abbey and scattered somewhere. Today, visitors see only the models. Eleanor and Henry lie elsewhere together— or perhaps gleefully apart.

If their ghosts are looking on, Eleanor and Henry are likely amused by the continued drama around them and their tumult. Film and book fanciers know that Henry and Eleanor figure prominently in several award-winning plays, movies, books, and television programs. Among them is Academy Award winning movie *The Lion in Winter,* starring

Peter O'Toole as Henry and the incomparable Katherine Hepburn as Eleanor. (Both actors seem to be practically "channeling" their famous namesakes.)

During the French Revolution, the abbey orders were unfortunately disbanded; the monks' priory was completely destroyed. After the Revolution, imperious Napoleon turned the property into a prison in 1804. This continued for more than a century and a half, until 1963. Between 1963 and 1975, the ravages of the Revolution and the years as a prison were meticulously scrubbed away from this religious enclave.

Today, the "Queen of Abbeys" is handsomely restored to her former glory—albeit repurposed for the modern age. Now she is known as the Centre Culturel de l'Ouest (Culture Center of the West), although most still call her Fontevraud Abbey. The entire complex has been converted into a cultural center and a very stylish hotel. Among other functions, the sprawling abbey is a museum. It's noted for its brilliant 16th century frescoes, as well as a uniquely octagonal Romanesque kitchen with a smoke room that rises to a high-pointed hood—the only surviving example from the medieval period in France.

All year round, the enclave is hopping with modern events: dance and music concerts, art exhibitions, interactive tours, guided hikes, overnight stays (in the former Priory of St-Lazare), and dining opportunities that maximize the abbey's regal beauty and locale. For kids, there's an iPad treasure hunt that takes them all around the abbey in search of "booty." During fair-weather months, I've witnessed huge light-show extravaganzas projected onto the Abbey's limestone walls, complete with pageantry, fireworks, and flying dancers that swirl through the air on trapezes.

But most unique, perhaps, is the hotel. L'Hotel Fontevraud (the Abbey Hotel) is a particularly trippy place in my opinion. When I say "trippy," I mean the French have a quirky way of shape-shifting ancient venues into modern-feeling "spaces." (*Cultural note:* After spending so much time in France, I have come to understand that whenever a town or area boasts a new "Space" or "Espace," it often means they've morphed a sometimes unused or dowdy location into a trendy hotspot. Nobody does this better than the French— so I'm a "tongue-in-cheek fan," especially since in the US we tend to "demolish" old buildings, whereas the French cleverly "morph" them.)

L'Hotel Fontevraud is a fun example of a trendy hotel with character *and* soul. "Spend the night with Eleanor" is how it advertises itself. (Since she loved troubadours and performed a little herself, Eleanor's ghost probably loves the spectacle.) But shape-shifting the abbey into a livable space was tricky. In order to create an in-house hotel, Canadian-born architect Sanit Manku and French designer Patrick Jouin had to overcome some hefty challenges. They could not deface the ceilings or walls, for example. They had to create modern livable space while maintaining the overall dignity of the abbey.

The clever result of their using something called "microarchitecture" is a streamlined hotel nested within the original limestone abbey priory. It features glass, chrome, *nouveau* lighting, modernist furniture, comfort accents such as blue-gray glazed stoneware, and cutting-edge techno-ware.

The 54 rooms have a variety of clever design features to make you modern-day comfy. These include built-in angled headrests, handsomely padded walls, high-end equipment for viewing Fontevraud TV, relaxing beds, modern shuttered windows, and French doors that open onto lovely garden vistas and orchards. (They provide woolen monk-like robes, though, if you want a little more of the religious experience.)

I laughed when I realized each guest receives an iPad upon their arrival so they can check out the Abbey and its offerings—and read their email. I enjoyed the minimalist iBar. Here, we enjoyed an *aperitif* while checking our social media feeds, since the place is a combo bar and "*digital mediatheque*" complete with touchscreen tabletops and built-in tablets. Radiant heat flooring warms your tootsies while you enjoy a tipple. The restaurant opens out onto the pretty courtyard; but the food, though plentiful, is a bit "monastic" for my taste. Still, I enjoyed my time here immensely—and could even get some writing done, since there was wonderful peace and quiet.

I decided not to dine at the abbey my last day, however, since I had some stellar recommendations about a couple of establishments nearby. About 10 minutes from the abbey by car is a wonderful cave-backed restaurant called **L'Helianthe**. My French friend Jean-Pierre swoons over its "amazing rabbit with prunes and bacon at prices so affordable that you will feel like going back every day." Of course I made a beeline for this popular French establishment, but instead I dined on the pikeperch fillet, creamed artichoke, and chestnut ice cream with orange hazelnut foam. (My dining companion had the casserole of "fried Loire River fishes"—in Marseille they'd call this *bouillabaisse*—and for dessert she had the roasted bananas slathered in white chocolate and caramel sauce. All of it was yummy.) http://www.restaurant-helianthe.fr

If you prefer an equally tantalizing option, try **La Licorne** (The Unicorn), is just up the road from the abbey in the village; it's an excellent dining choice. It's nestled in a lovely garden and features reasonably priced French food featuring local produce presented with considerable flair. http://www.lalicorne-restaurant-fontevraud.fr

But I have to share one last Saumur-area dining experience. One evening for dinner, I zipped over from Saumur to **Le Plantagenet** in the Hôtel La Croix Blanche, right at the gates of Fontevraud Abbey. My companion and I had a most marvelous evening, being taxied over and back so we could enjoy the evening without having to drive. We entered this darling hotel and were ushered into Le

Plantagenet like we were *Gourmet Magazine* food reviewers. My hotel, Hotel Anne D'Anjou, had booked our reservation and made sure the restaurant knew we should be taken care of like (near) royals. The

staff at Le Plantagenet did not disappoint. The chef has a Michelin star, and so each course was a delight. The service was also impeccable on all accounts. I'd highly recommend a meal at this stellar location. http://hotel-croixblanche.com

After your visit to the abbey and the wonderful dining options nearby, you might be ready for some fantastic wine tasting at the rustic *tuffeau* wine cellar at **La Grande Vignolle**. Also very close to l'Helianthe, you have one of the area's most interesting buildings carved in limestone. These "cellars" are usually a great opportunity to taste the local wine. http://www.ot-saumur.fr

As you travel further around Grand Saumur, you may come across some other fascinating venues. **Bioparc** is a wildlife preserve and zoo featuring more than 1000 animals from all parts of the globe. There's also the **Zoo de Doué**, where you can mingle with its animals in natural habitations formed in and around the caves and vegetation. This zoo is an exquisite preserve, since overgrown trees and foliage around the caves have been shaped into animal enclosures with waterfalls, streams, and grottoes. Here, the animals and birds happily roam nearly free. It lets you experience the wildlife in near-jungle-like settings. Many of the animals are part of international breeding programs, especially for endangered species.

Rose lovers will enjoy **Les Chemins de la Rose**, a truly exceptional 14-acre rose garden a short walk away. With more than 6,000 rose bushes and 950 varieties of roses, it's truly a rose lover's Eden. Windmill tours are fun here too. There are more than 200 windmills in the area, many of which are open to the public. Guides can take you through the mechanics of a working windmill and their interactive museums. Many of the windmills, by the way, still grind grain as in centuries past.

Ultimately a visit to Anjou, with its lively riverside city of Angers, its equestrian elegance in Saumur, its religious panache in Fontevraud, and its considerable charms of *tufa* caves nurturing not only mushrooms but fine food and drink, is an unforgettable experience. From views above and below, this land is steeped in history, religious fervor, and viticulture savvy. You can't go wrong spending a few days, weeks, or even months in this fascinating spot "with its heart in Anjou, its eyes in Touraine, and its arms full of treasures."

CHAPTER SEVEN

Touraine

(Tours, Amboise, Clos-Lucé, Chenonceau, Villandry, Azay-le-Rideau, Ussé, Langeais, and Chinon)

Quand le Touraine is known chiefly for the magnificent white châteaux strung out along the broad Loire and its tributaries. Added to these are its rich history and fertile landscape, making it the archetypal Loire Valley region. The rolling terrain and lush forests that once attracted the kings and queens of France continue to work their charm over visitors from all the world today.

—*Eyewitness Travel: Loire Valley,* Duncan Baird
Publishers/DK Publishing

How often have I returned to this royal Touraine, brimming with irresistible castles? How many hours have I lingered in Diane de Poitier's enchanting Chenonceau that arches like a lusty Cupid's bow across the River Cher? How many times have I stopped by Villandry's magnificent gardens to view the basket-sized eggplants and fairytale swans gliding on the mirror lake?

I admit I return again and again. I love Sleeping Beauty's castle at Ussé (even though I suspect the evil fairy's curse lingers in my GPS, since it sometimes leads me to a barbed wire fence instead of the enchanted castle). I'm drawn to delicate Azay-le-Rideau that floats on the water like a jewel. I pop into Amboise (pictured) where I buy tapestries. Or I linger in the castle seeking François I's secret passageway to Leonardo da Vinci's villa nearby.

Despite the delicate façade of today's Touraine, her history is filled with epic encounters—many of them with formidable women. These relationships tell tales of libidinous love, bloody clashes, and a fertile energy that birthed countless royals in the regal "Boudoir of France."

Previously, I described the Anjou region as masculine—forged through potent male energies save for one-of-a-kind Eleanor of Aquitaine and her ruthless resolve. Touraine, like Anjou, was a sometime battleground for the warring counts of Blois and Anjou. But in Touraine, it's the provocative nature of the feminine that dominates the land: a land of outward beauty, but one forged by iron-fisted women with steely resolves.

Joan of Arc, a mere Loire peasant girl, led an army against the English, for example. She bullied the vapid future King Charles VII into taking back the power of France. For this, Joan was lionized then burned at the stake. Yet there are more statues of this fearless lass throughout France than of almost any other symbol save Marianne, the face of the French Republic.

Diane de Poitiers, the beguiling mistress who enchanted King Henri II, drank gold daily and was admired as the Goddess of France. She sparred famously with ferocious queen Catherine de' Médici, yet remains a model for desirable women today.

It's rumored that Catherine de' Médici learned sexual techniques by watching her husband's liaisons with the divine Diane through a boudoir peephole. But she must have learned these lessons well. A battleax of a woman, Catherine at last conceived several sons after ten years of childless royal marriage. Three of her sons reigned as kings of France—with cunning Catherine behind their thrones and seer Nostradamus at her side.

Beloved Anne of Brittany married not one royal, but two! This shrewd lady was revered in her home territory as the royal protector of independent Brittany in western France. She was wary of the French monarchy, but she cannily took up her destiny to unite Northern France into one French empire. She did her best to produce males for her two spouses, kings both. But after 16 pregnancies and multiple miscarriages, her surviving children were girls—although one of them also married a notable king of France, François I.

The forces of love and fertility definitely shaped the Touraine. Yet these forces are still pulsating today. In its romantic *jardins*, lovers yet court. In the fecund kitchen gardens much of the bounty of the "Garden of France" is born. The lush wines of Chinon and Vouvray bring a lover's blush to the countenance of those who sip them. And the ripe psyche of the feminine fueled the themes of Charles Perrault's *Sleeping Beauty*, as well as favorite son François Rabelais's racy 16th century satires.

The Touraine has much to offer with her sensuous history and legendary allure. As a province, Touraine has similarities with Anjou nearby; warring dukes, invading armies, religious turmoil, and royal interference left their marks in both areas. The same Angevin (Plantagenet) dukes ruled Touraine until 1205, when the area was commandeered by French King Phillip II. Touraine then became a royal duchy. Yet it is the Touraine women who linger in the minds of visitors.

In July 1429, Joan of Arc led a French army to Chinon, where she facilitated the crowning of aforementioned King Charles VII at Reims. This event precipitated the gradual decline of English influence in the area, which in turn led to the eventual consolidation of France.

A succession of French monarchs associated with Touraine presided over the next 100 years, including Blois-born Louis XII of France. His second marriage to powerful Anne of Brittany (in Château de Langeais) produced no heirs. His cousin, François I, who was also reared in the Loire, therefore became king in 1515. It was tall François with the legendary proboscis and much-adored mother who cherished the Loire Valley so much he kept his royal entourage here for decades. The feverish *châteaux* building and renovations began to accommodate his court.

François's heirs furthered his love of the Loire—and also his ardor for women in general. These women were the power behind the thrones for centuries. Many of them ruled for their imprisoned spouses, still-young children, or inept lovers. Some of them saved the Loire castles from destruction. And some of them later worked in the French underground, subverting Germans and rescuing French soldiers during the World Wars.

Once the royals left the valley in the 1600s and 1700s when Versailles and Paris became favored habitats, Touraine rebirthed itself. It morphed into a bustling castle-centric tourist enclave, as well as a wine and agricultural Garden of Eden. Yes, a few telltale macho influences remained at fortress castles like Amboise and Chinon. But it is the abodes and lifestyles of the legendary mistresses, wives, and concubines that attract hordes of visitors today.

The Touraine is romantic, even sexy. The landscape is rich and supple. The produce is round and ripe. The wines are intoxicating, seductive. The castles are opulent and whisper of love and lust. Fertility manifests everywhere: in the lush gardens, the coquettish mazes, the lusty paintings, and the sumptuous castle furnishings. Plush fabrics, gilded ceilings, embellished tapestries, dainty glassware, feminine porcelain, juicy cuisine, wedding-ready locales, and erotic abodes proliferate. This is the terrain of love—and you'll feel the hormones undulating nearly everywhere you go.

I was amused to find in my research that local author Honoré de Balzac (1799–1850) felt the Touraine was memorably feminine as well. He wrote with fervor:

> Shame on he who fails to admire my joyful, beautiful, courageous Touraine and her seven valleys which flow with water and wine!
>
> —Honoré de Balzac

Touraine effectively is the heart center of the Loire Valley. As such, it makes a fascinating home base from which to explore the most famous *châteaux* and towns nearby.

Burbling waterways crisscross the land, inviting picnics or dreamy naps along their grassy banks. Most of the *châteaux* and towns sit prettily alongside these rivers: Langeais, Tours, and Amboise by the Loire; Ussé and Azay-le-Rideau on the gentle Indre; and Chenonceau straddling the lovely Cher.

When you arrive, it may be hard to choose amongst the bounty. My favorite Touraine destinations, however, are these: 1–Tours, the busy hub with a restored medieval quarter; 2–Amboise, with its royal castle and chipper commerce; 3–Château du Clos-Lucé, where Leonardo da Vinci lived out his days and which showcases his most interesting inventions; 4–Château de Chenonceau, the resplendent castle of six women; 5–Château de Villandry, a restored palace with the most ravishing gardens in France; 6–Château d'Azay-le-Rideau, the winsome manor on a lake; 7–Château d'Ussé, Sleeping Beauty's enchanted castle; 8–Château de Langeais, a rustic kingly fortress with a working drawbridge; and 9–Chinon, an active wine center on the banks of the Vienne.

Romantic Rolling Stone Mick Jagger owns a Touraine *château* near Amboise. He and Jerry Hall (another spectacular female) purchased La e Fourchette in the tiny village of Pocé-sur-Cisse more than 25 years ago. The estate was originally the property of the Duc de Choiseuil, Louis XVI's finance minister.

Jagger apparently loves visiting his *château,* and he spends a fair amount of time there. (Locals tell me he flies in to the Tours airport by private jet.) Since the French are nonplussed about celebrities (privacy is very important to most French people), they give him and his guests some breathing room. Jagger enjoys Touraine for mountain biking, cycling, fishing, and the local airshows. Jagger even plays cricket at the local club when he's around. The Stones have recorded some albums at the compound, and the band is sometimes spotted wandering happily around the area. Paul

McCartney, David Bowie, and many others have visited over the years. Jagger calls the Amboise countryside his "haven of peace in the Valley of Kings."

For the rest of us who visit Touraine without benefit of rock star power, however, there's plenty to ensure we have an awesome experience. The Tours Tourism Office is an excellent start. Located on Rue Bernard Palissy in Tours, the tourism office offers maps, brochures, guided tours, rides via *le petite train* and Segways, minivan trips, balloon flights, and information about accommodations and restaurants (http://www.tours-tourisme.fr). Amboise also has a perky tourist office that goes into overdrive to satisfy your needs. http://amboise-valdeloire.co.uk

So let's explore elegant Touraine with its tantalizing castles, tempting gardens, unconventional royals, and bodacious women. We'll look particularly at the feminine influences behind the throne since they not only influenced the character of their Loire consorts, but in my opinion, they shaped the very psyche of France as a provocative world power with a regal lust for living.

Tours**

> The city of Tours…is the very essence of what these palatial, aristocratic Renaissance homes are all about. The city has a long reputation for civilization, culture and refinement…There's a cheerful, bright quality to the light, and Tours is still, as Balzac described it, "a smiling city."
>
> —Andrew Sanger, et al., "Tours," *Drive Around Loire Valley*

"Tours? C'est le mini-Paris!" say the local *Tourangeaux* when describing their remarkable town on the Loire. Indeed, several times it's stood in for Paris as the capital of France during World Wars. Tours is often used as a base by many of the estimated nine million tourists who come every year to visit the Renaissance *châteaux*. Centrally located within an hour or so of all the most important *châteaux*, its modern TGV high-speed train transport links, plus its wide array of restaurants, hotels, and other amenities, make it a handy central location.

As a location between the Loire and Cher rivers, the town originally sat at an important crossing point in Gallic Times for the tribe known as the Turones. Later, the Roman Empire founded an important metropolis here. They christened it Caesarodunum ("hill of Caesar"). In the 4th century, the name morphed back into the Gallic term "Civitas Turonum"; this was later shortened to "Tours." One of the five largest Roman amphitheaters was built here.

One of the most acclaimed city figures, however, was Roman-soldier-turned-holy-man, Bishop Saint Martin of

Tours. He was famous for using his soldier's sword to cut his cloak in two and then giving half to a freezing beggar. The following night, Martin apparently dreamt he saw Christ wearing half of the cloak. He immediately awoke and dedicated his life to Christ. This religious motif of a soldier on horseback giving his cloak to a beggar can be seen all around Tours today; it lives as the symbol of the city many centuries later.

Among other accolades, Saint Martin is deemed an early conscientious objector, since he rejected military service as being incompatible with spirituality. He sallied forth with a soldier's zeal, however, to demolish pagan shrines and set up parishes all over France. He built the first monastery on Gallic soil. In 372 the people of Tours begged him to become their Bishop; he served faithfully until his death in 397.

Saint Martin was well known for freeing religious prisoners. He's considered the symbol of French Christianity, as well as the "spiritual bridge" for Europe. As such, visiting his shrine in Tours became a famous stopping point for pilgrims on the road to Santiago de Compostela in Spain. Stories of miraculous healings in his name proliferated. Over time, many of the royals even adopted St. Martin as their patron saint and invoked him in battles. (Some even carried the remains of his holy cloak into skirmishes as a talisman.)

Eventually, St. Martin's remains had to be transferred to a newly built basilica in Old Town Tours to accommodate the hordes of visitors. I will describe my visit to his holy remains in a moment.

But first, here are some Tours practicalities. When I last stayed in Tours, I really enjoyed the Hôtel Colbert in the heart of the medieval Old Town, Le Vieux Tours. From here I could walk to the Cathedral Saint Gatien, the Royal Château, the Musée Beaux-Arts and dozens of shops and eateries. If I hadn't had other venues to visit out of town, I could have simply whiled away a week in Tours and never gotten in a car! But I also had to remember this about the lifestyle in Tours:

> The easygoing approach to life in the Touraine has given birth to the expression *le quart d'heure Tourangeau*, which essentially means you shouldn't expect anything to start until 15 minutes after the scheduled time. Even the Loire [river] seems in no great rush to get to the sea, normally preferring to proclaim its existence in a pleasant purr rather than a threatening roar.
> —Todd Mauer, "The Lovely Laid-Back City of Tours," *France Today*

With my internal clock set on "chill," I set out to explore old Tours. The Hôtel Colbert actually sits in the medieval section that was originally part of the ancient Roman settlement. Some of the walls and cobbled streets follow the lines of the Roman amphitheater and 3rd century walls. Just beyond my hotel along some pretty cobblestone walkways, I found myself wandering through Cathedral Saint Gatien— one of France's most exceptional religious buildings. This marvelous stone cathedral was built gradually between the 3rd and 13th centuries. It offers visitors a unique chance to see the evolving styles of Gothic architecture. It basically morphs from Early Gothic at the chancel, to Middle Gothic in the nave and transepts, and later to Flamboyant (Late) Gothic with its intricate west façade. The stained glass windows and restored 14th century frescos are splendid. In one alcove, the infant sons of Anne of Brittany and Charles VIII are buried; their short lives marked the end of the royal Valois dynasty.

Although Tours is virtually the capital of *"châteaux country,"* it surprisingly has no grand *château* of its own. The Old Town's Château Royal de Tours, which I next visited near the cathedral, is more of a grand house than a castle. It served as a royal residence only briefly in the 13th and 15th centuries; today the castle hosts contemporary art exhibitions.

Also noteworthy is the Tours Musée des Beaux-Arts fine arts museum (shown). I spent time viewing the splendid paintings by Rubens, Rembrandt, Monet, and others, ranging from the medieval ages to more contemporary artists like Degas and Delacroix. There's also a rich collection of fine silks, *faience*, tapestries, and furnishings of the period. Two celebrated altarpieces by Andrea Mantegna are must-sees. Outside, I enjoyed the attractive formal gardens—and the quirky stuffed elephant that stands guard. "Fritz" was originally part of a Barnum & Bailey circus that came to town; but he "went rogue" and had to be put down.

Tours decided to keep him as part of its collection! This museum is quite elegant (despite the pachyderm), since the complex used to be the Archbishop's Palace from the 17th & 18th centuries. (Entry is free the first Sunday of every month.)

On the western side of the city, a religious community grew up around Saint Martin's sepulcher. Nowadays, the saint's tomb lies in the crypt of the later 19th century New Basilica. The stellar Museum of Saint Martin commemorates the life of the saint. After walking just a few minutes from my hotel, I was able to pay my respects to this legendary man. This saint's life truly means a great deal to the spiritual people of France. Notably, more than 450 towns in France bear his name.

Nearby is the hoppin' Place Plumereau. This animated square dubbed "Place Plum" for short (sounds like the feather, not the fruit) was once the hat market. It's lined with 15th and 16th century half-timbered and slate-clad townhouses and offers curbside dining in a party atmosphere. I could see immediately why my friend and guide Jeremy Kolbe makes this searing observation about Tours vs. Blois (near Amboise further east): "In Blois, the ladies wear nylon housecoats. In Tours, they wear miniskirts." I saw many a miniskirt in the square that day.

I spent a couple of merry evenings in Place Plum, jumping from café to café, seeing the gardens tucked into corners, and enjoying the local nightlife. Most of the people were worshipping the god of grape, I might add, rather than the piety of Catholicism. (Not surprisingly, I made lots of French friends that evening, especially at Café du Vieux Mûrier http://levieuxmurier.fr .)

Archaeology lovers will relish the Hôtel Goüin & Musée Archéologique nearby, which offers treasures from the prehistoric era through the 18th century. This early Renaissance building was destroyed in World War II but then was lovingly restored with a reconfigured ornamental *façade*.

Naturally, wine lovers delight in the vaulted cellars and 13th century cloisters of Eglise Saint-Julien that now houses the Musée des Vins de Touraine (wine museum). Early viticulture history is featured. On display are Gallo-Roman and Renaissance winepresses, plus winemaking tools dating as far back as the Middle Ages. In the same building cluster is the Musée du Compagnonnage, or craft guild museum. It's dedicated to ancient trades and artisans like rope makers, roofers, furniture makers, and more. Nearby, you can visit the Maison des Vins de Loire and taste wine favorites.

Afterward, I wandered along Rue Colbert back to my hotel and suddenly noticed No. 39 Colbert. This is the very shop where Joan of Arc bought her set of armor before setting out to liberate Orléans in 1429. (Yes, here is another French woman who knew how to dress for the occasion.) Notably, almost every move she made during her military exploits is documented in the Loire Valley. Don't be surprised when you round a corner and find a statue of Joan anywhere you go in the valley.

Despite its well-documented ancient past, modern-age Tours is very much on display as well. The city played key political roles in World Wars I and II, with American and Allied forces in evidence in many military camps and fortifications. German incendiary bombs caused fire and destruction through the city; many 16th and 17th century masterpieces were lost. After the wars, rebuilding began, starting with a conservation effort for the Old Town area, establishment of the François Rabelais University, and other commercial enterprises.

Beyond the Old Town, Tours is a bustling metropolis of sophisticated modern life. Since the building of the high-speed train station at Tours-Saint-Pierre-des-Corps, Tours has become a "suburb" of Paris for many professionals. Tours also is known as the "Cradle of the French language,"; 30,000 students flock here every year to learn "the purest French."

Travel note: It's possible to rent a car in downtown Tours or at the out-of-town train station, Tours-Saint-Pierre-des-Corps. Be aware there are two train stations associated with Tours. If you take the high speed TGV train from Paris to Tours, you'll arrive on the outskirts at St-Pierre-des-Corps station. You can then take a taxi or hourly shuttle from this train station to the in-town, smaller Tours station, which is located just off the Medieval downtown. This older station runs the slower trains that take you out to the countryside. (Check the https://www.raileurope.com website to book and download your tickets right from this website.)

You'll find plenty to do in Tours for a day, a week, or more. The little white train leaves from the Tourism Office every 45 minutes or so, although you might prefer a horse-drawn carriage. The Tourist Office also books helicopter and balloon flights over the Loire, as well as Segway and walking tours. Nighttime Tours is exceptional, since illuminations of both old and new structures are beautifully done. The giant sequoias inside Tour's Jardin des Prébendes are heavenly. The rest of the park offers swan-filled ponds and picnic spots.

In 2013 Tours was declared France's International City of Gastronomy. As such, it revels in its great variety of food and drink tours, featuring the best of the local Chinon and Bourgueil wines, as well as gastronomic specialties. Tours street markets occur almost every day of the week. Les Halles on Place Gaston Paillhou is the big covered market for daily produce shopping. Boulevard Béranger is where the aromatic, twice-weekly flower market is held. Rue Nationale is the big shopping street where you can purchase almost anything. Don't miss Place Jean Jaurès with its elegant fountains and floral beds; it divides the city into two distinct sections, with Vieux Tours (the medieval quarter) to the west and the cathedral quarter to the east.

Fairs and celebrations are popular in Tours. The Garlic and Basil Fair in July during the Feast of St. Ann on the Place du Grand-Marché in the Old Town is particularly fun. Pots of basil spread like a green sea along the streets, while garlic heads, garlic strings, and garlic piles six feet high greet your eyes and your nose.

Who knew that dancing is big in Tours? There are various dance halls and open air dance venues like Lulu Parc that provide "cut the rug" opportunities for young and older. But if you'd prefer to walk rather than dance, Tours is your place. An easy walk (even with strollers) of about 1.2 miles would start at the Cathedral in Old Town. From there you'd wander by the Musée des Beaux-Arts, then head toward the river and turn west on Rue Colbert. By walking this mainly pedestrianized street to the intersection of Rue Nationale, you can turn right for the Musée du Compagnonnage.

After viewing this marvelous structure, proceed west on Rue Colbert until it becomes Rue du Commerce. Head straight to Place Plumereau and spend some time in this pretty plaza, as well as the offshoot streets. From Place Plum, see Basilique Saint-Martin. Then retrace your steps down Rue du Commerce and turn south on Rue Nationale to enjoy an afternoon of browsing. Dine at one of the fabulous eateries listed later in this chapter or at a friendly pavement café where you can enjoy a *tarte Tatin* for dessert. I highly recommend it!

Boating, sailing, and canoeing on the Loire are popular activities near Tours, as are cruises with and without refreshments. "Loire by Velo," or cycling up and down the river or around the town, is a delight. There's an 800 km bike route from the Cuffy on the Cher all the way to Loire-Atlantique at the coast. Of course you can take part or all of this route at any time, although winter time may be a challenge. http://detoursdeloire.com

I'd like to add this gossipy note for those readers who are modern royal watchers. I was meandering by car outside Tours on my way to Château de Ussé (Sleeping Beauty's castle) when I happened by a small 16th century castle called Château de Candé. A memory sparked in my brain, and I recalled these fascinating factoids. First, the castle was bought in 1927 by millionaire industrialist Charles Eugène

Bedaux and his second wife, Fern Lombard. Bedaux was a Frenchmen with a rather checkered past who immigrated to America and became a US citizen in the early 1900s. His wife Fern was an American from Grand Rapids, Michigan. Bedaux made his millions enhancing employee productivity in manufacturing. He later became a big game hunter and famous explorer.

Second, Bedaux became enamored of the Duke of Windsor and his controversial American wife-to-be, Wallis Simpson. When the abdicated Duke gave up the British throne "to marry the woman I love," Bedaux offered Château de Candé for their nuptials. Thus, the Duke and Duchess were married in this out-of-the-way castle in 1937. Third, Bedaux became chummy with the Nazis when they occupied Paris during World War II. The Germans loved him so much, they appointed Bedaux economic advisor to the Reich, with the job of liquidating Jewish businesses in Occupied France.

Fourth, Bedaux graciously introduced the genial Duke of Windsor to Hitler—much to the horror of the British government. (This is one of the reasons the Duke was quickly shipped off to the Bahamas as governor—to keep him out of the way during the war.) Last, while in Algeria, Bedaux was arrested by Americans and transported back to the US. He died—by either suicide or murder—under dubious circumstances in FBI custody in Miami, Florida, while awaiting a grand jury investigation. Moral: you never know what skeletons may be rattling in these pretty castles.

Tours Accommodations

Les Hautes-Roches is a fabulous hotel with luxurious rooms, many of which are built into a cliff wall. It also offers river views and a seductive restaurant. http://leshautesroches.com
Hôtel l'Univers Tours is one of the most popular hotels in Tours. Located around the corner from the railway

station, it's adjacent to marvelous Place Jean-Jaurès. Quiet, comfortable, and professional, this accommodation books up fast, so make reservations well in advance. You'll find excellent dining at La Touraine restaurant (see later details). http://www.oceaniahotels.com

Hôtel Colbert is my little boutique hotel in Old Town, within walking distance of nearly everything, It's quiet and modest and has a helpful staff. http://tours-hotel-colbert.fr

Countryside Accommodations Near Tours

Château d'Artigny is a 19th century luxury castle hotel with rooms and apartments, plus a luxurious spa, on a 62-acre park. It offers an indoor pool and a Turkish bath and is located within minutes of Azay, Villandry, and Tours. http://grandesetapes.com/chateau-hotel-artigny-loire

Domaine de la Tortinière is a boutique hotel near Château d'Azay-le-Rideau. It's reasonably priced and has wedding facilities on a 37-acre park. It also offers an indoor pool and restaurant. http://www.tortiniere.com/en/

Tours Dining & Wine Bars

La Famille by Bardet is owned and operated by the son-in-law of famed chef Jean Bardet. This tasty restaurant's located in the heart of Old Town Tours' on Rue Grosse-Tour. http://www.restaurant-lafamille.fr

L'Evidence is a youthful establishment on Rue Colbert that offers market-fresh cuisine and good prices. Caviar, snails, and truffles are popular. http://restaurant-levidence.com

La Touraine, located at the Hôtel Univers (previously described), offers expensive, expertly prepared French cuisine. http://www.oceaniahotels.com

Le Petit Patrimoine is one of my favorite eateries along Rue Colbert in the Old Town Tours. It has simple classy dishes and reasonable prices; it offers some particular local specialties like *Tourte Tourangelle* (pastry with pork). http://www.lepetitpatrimoine.fr/en/

Charles Barrier is a classic gastronomic restaurant located about ten minutes from the city center. It has a posh interior with crystal chandeliers and wood paneling, and it pleasantly overlooks a relaxing garden. You'll particularly enjoy the seafood specialties and superb desserts. Yes, it's pricey, but worth it. http://www.charles-barrier.fr

Casse-Cailloux is Chef Hervé Chardonneau's tiny bistro on Rue Jean Fouquet. It provides inventive and superbly well-cooked dishes listed on a traditional slate chalkboard and offers excellent value for money. Try the warm salad of white beans and mussels, the steak in red-wine sauce with new potatoes, and the runny chocolate tart with caramel sauce and vanilla ice cream. http://www.casse-cailloux.fr

Les Hautes-Roches offers fine dining at its best, within this popular hotel that I can highly recommend. http://leshautesroches.com

Amboise***

It was eerily quiet as I floated above the shimmering Loire River. Gentle breezes whipped across my face. Below me, birds fluttered past. Then, sparkling in the Loire's reflection, a majestic citadel came slowly into view: royal Amboise.

My first view of this storied enclave, in fact, was truly a birds-eye one. I was flying over the Loire in a hot-air balloon about two thousand feet above the castle parapets From the air (balloon photo courtesy of Christy Destremau), the medieval town and picturesque Amboise Château with its flying flags looks like something out of the King Arthur legend. At the helm of our balloon was Nicolas Rodier of Balloon Revolution (http://www.balloonrevolution.com/en/).

I'd been invited to experience Amboise from above the trees with him—and I jumped at the chance. Nicholas is both a savvy balloon flyer but also a native of Amboise.

As we descended to land, the river came alive with lapping waves, while the fields of buttercups rushed up to meet us. As we dropped down to land, the striking turrets of the castle drifted past. I almost felt like Dorothy in the Wizard of Oz—and I soon realized I was about to meet a wizard of my very own in the royal bosom of Amboise. But before we meet my magician, let me offer you a little history about the beguiling, sometimes ruthless, Amboise.

The centerpiece of the busy market town of Amboise is the fabled *château*. It served as the pivotal residence for three French kings over 160 years: Charles VIII, Louis XII, and François I. Amboise Château was built on the foundations of an 11th century fortress constructed by the Count of Anjou at this strategic point in the river. In the 15th century, it began its conversion to a livable palace after seizure by Charles VII (1403–1461).

Charles VIII (1470–1498), who was born and died in this very *château*, added Renaissance decorations and gardens after his return from Italy in 1496. In Italy, young Charles was dazzled by the high artistic standards and lifestyle. He returned to Amboise with Italian furniture, fine fabrics, artwork, architects, sculptors, decorators, gardeners, and even a poultry breeder to maximize the chicken output. He hastily began work on the castle's Renaissance rebirth; hundreds of workmen labored continuously, many by candlelight, to meet the king's ambitious schedule.

Charles VIII perhaps had a premonition of his limited time on earth. He became monarch of the House of Valois at age 13. Not only was he young, he was considered slightly dimwitted; his powerful elder sister Anne of France ruled for him until he came of age. In a remarkable stroke of moxie at age 21, he married Anne of Brittany in 1491. Anne was already married, albeit by proxy, to the Habsburg Holy Roman Emperor Maximilian I. Nevertheless, Charles needed access to Anne's vast kingdom in western France, and so they married in Château de Langeais nearby.

Fortunately, Maximilian I failed to press his claim to Anne. Thus, with his hasty marriage, Charles successfully blocked the Habsburg incursion into France. Young Charles ultimately ruled over the vast Brittany territory to the northwest, as well as much of France and parts of Italy. But

Charles did not live long to enjoy his kingdom. At the tender age of 28 the king was on his way to watch a tennis match near the Château d'Amboise moat, when the unthinkable happened. Charles accidently smacked his head on a door lintel (beam). He died a few days later of head trauma. He never lived to see his finalized Renaissance designs for the great *château*.

His cousin Louis XII (1462–1515), from the Orléans branch of the House of Valois, succeeded him. Louis continued his cousin's Amboise renovations and even added a splendid new wing and additional formal gardens. Interestingly, when Louis XII (who'd been born nearby in Château de Blois) became king in 1498, he too moved swiftly to cement his sketchy powerbase by marrying. He had his current marriage to his sterile and handicapped cousin Joan annulled by Pope Alexander VI. Then he quickly married Charles VIII's widow, the reluctant queen dowager Anne of Brittany.

Thus Anne of Brittany twice became a queen of France based in Amboise. Anne, by the way, is considered a near-saint in her home province of Brittany. In childhood, she was betrothed six times as a pawn in the power wars. Her short seven-year marriage to young Charles VIII produced seven pregnancies, but none of the children outlived her and most were stillborn. Though she reportedly wasn't very fond of her next husband Louis XII, Anne nevertheless became pregnant nine more times. None of the male babies survived, but two of her daughters did. One of these daughters was Claude of France, who became François I's queen.

The stalwart Anne of Brittany unfortunately predeceased Louis, so that, when he expired in 1515, he still had no male issue. Thus the throne passed to Amboise's greatest champion, François I.

François I (1494–1547), the "Cavalier King," was the first King of France from the Angoulême branch of the House of Valois. Reared as a great patron of the arts, *François au Grand Nez* (François of the Large Nose) oversaw the Renaissance consolidation of the French monarchy. When he married Anne's daughter, Claude, he gained unquestioned power over Brittany. He continued to expand his kingdom into Italy and elsewhere.

François was a true Renaissance king. He was reared carefully by his savvy mother, Louise of Savoy. Louise was well educated, well read, and politically savvy. She had cultivated and maneuvered her son into position to take the throne, and she succeeded brilliantly. At 6'6", her son François was royal in all respects. He was tall, athletic, multilingual, well educated, and motivated by a lusty love of life. He was proficient in dancing, music, poetry, archery, falconry, horseback riding, hunting, wrestling, and jousting.

PORTRAITS DE FRANÇOIS Ier

François had a burning desire to make France the center of the Renaissance. As such, he oversaw the spread of humanism and Protestantism, as well as the beginning of the French exploration in the New World. Interestingly, he elevated the place of women in court. Until then, most women at court had been relegated to the Queen's service. But in François's reign and thereafter, women held public roles and became social focal points. He encouraged them to dress beautifully and develop cultural skills and elegant manners. He installed a code of courtesy for all at court.

As a contemporary of King Henry VIII of England (who looked short in comparison), François I rivaled Henry VIII as top Renaissance king. They each had splendid courts, elaborate entourages, stables of great artisans, and a hyper-sexuality coupled with a lust for war. The two royals once had a pow wow in 1520 near Calais to discuss an alliance. François I was desperate for a partner to help defeat his archrival, the Holy Roman Emperor Charles V. This *tête-à-tête* became known as the "Field of the Cloth of Gold," due to the gold-spun fabrics used over the many pavilions. The meeting lasted three weeks and nearly bankrupted both countries. It ended abruptly when Henry challenged François to a wrestling match. François promptly threw Henry to the ground, besting him. Henry got up and left in a huff; he then signed a pact with Charles V against François. Within a month, Francois and Henry were at war.

Wars and ego aside, François is remembered as the great champion of the Loire and of Amboise in particular. Though born at Château de Cognac, François was raised at Château Royal at Amboise; it had belonged to his sainted mother, Louise of Savoy. (He knelt whenever he spoke to her. She even ruled for him when he was away and while he was briefly imprisoned.) François grew up in his beloved Amboise castle from age 7 until he became king at age 24. After that time, he split his time between multiple palaces and oversaw the construction of his brainchild, Chambord—the grandest castle in the Loire.

François split most of his Loire time between Blois and Amboise. He lavished funds on renovations and new Renaissance construction at Amboise, even as he built Chambord. He also expanded Château de Blois, and rebuilt the Château du Louvre in Paris—transforming it from a dank medieval fortress into a Renaissance palace. At many of these locations, you can see his crest, the salamander, and his motto, *Nutrisco et extinguo* ("I nourish and I extinguish" or "I nourish the good fire and extinguish the evil").

During his 32-year reign, François expanded Amboise castle until it was six times larger than it is today. Despite his wars with Spain for control of Italy, François was mercurial and inconsistent in war as well as peace. He toured France often on horseback, showing himself to people who had never seen a king, lavishing largesse on the populace.

Yet he was also quite selfish, primarily amusing himself by enjoying hunting, playing at chivalry, holding artistic extravaganzas, and throwing lavish, pomp-filled parties. He particularly welcomed lovely ladies at court, saying, "A court without women is a year without spring and a spring without roses." (Modern Amboise regularly holds summer "La Cour du Roy" pageants to honor François at the castle. During these 90-minute extravaganzas, 450+ participants dress up in 1,000 costumes to show off the Renaissance dances, royal processions, cavalry exhibitions, and revelry that was typical in François's time. Enhanced by light shows, rock music, and fantastic fireworks, this is a spectacular event open to enthusiastic visitors. No reservation required.)

François is most remembered, however, for bringing Leonardo da Vinci to France. François met Leonardo in Italy around 1516; he convinced Leonardo to come to France and live out his life near him in Amboise. Leonardo assented and left Italy in late 1516, crossing to France via the Alps. He rode on a donkey with the Mona Lisa painting in his saddlebag. (The famous Mona Lisa, known in France as *La Joconde*, is actually rather small at 2'6" x 1'9", so you can see why it worked rather well as a carry-on.)

When Leonardo at last arrived, he was ensconced at Manoir du Clos-Lucé. The Clos-Lucé manor house is attached to Amboise Castle by a 500-meter-long underground tunnel. This allowed François to visit Leonardo unseen whenever he wanted. François gave Leonardo a pension of 700 gold crowns a year (about $46,000 a year in today's dollars). His roles were philosopher, architect, engineer, painter, and party planner. By this time, however, Leonardo wasn't painting a great deal; but he did seem to relish being the event overseer for François I's many parties and pageants. I would also suggest Leonardo's most famous occupation for the last three years of his life was sorcerer and seer—as famous as Merlin. He conjured up some remarkable inventions that foretold the future, including the tank and a flying machine. Leonardo is the wizard I "commune with" whenever I visit Amboise.

A first project for Leonardo's royal patron was the design of a mechanical lion. This lion could walk, stop, rear on its hind legs, and open its chest to present a cluster of lilies. Letters of the day note that Leonardo also enjoyed coming up with games made specifically for François. François and

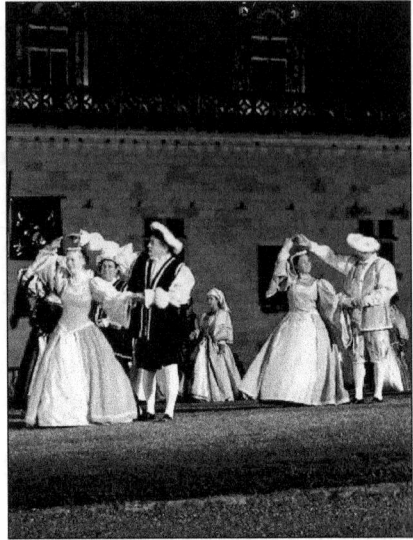

Leonardo became inseparable friends during the final years of the great master's life.

Upon Leonardo's death, the Mona Lisa was inherited by his assistant, Sala. François then bought it from Sala for 4000 écus (or about $270,000). He kept it at the Palace at Fontainebleau, where it remained until Louis XIV moved it to the Palace of Versailles. During the French Revolution, the Mona Lisa was moved to the Louvre in Paris ever after, although it allegedly spent a brief period in Napoleon's bedroom in the Tuileries Palace. (Some even say it was kept in the bathroom above the commode.)

Upon François's death from syphilis and other ailments at age 52, Amboise was home to subsequent royals, including François's son Henri II and his wife Catherine de' Médici. The pair raised their children along with Mary Stuart, the child queen of Scotland, who was promised in marriage to the little future French King, François II. Amboise Château became a family haven in which the royals housed their wives and children—so they could dally with their mistresses in castles nearby.

Henri II (1519–1559) was first introduced to sex at age 15 by the lovely Diane de Poitiers at François's urging. Diane, a pretty widow, had been a fixture at court and a sometime mistress of François I. Post-coitus, Henri remained madly attached to Diane, despite his marriage to fierce Catherine and his dalliances with other mistresses. When he became king in 1547, Henri kept Queen Catherine at Amboise and naturally had to find Diane a worthy abode nearby. He found it just eight miles from Amboise at Château de Chenonceau—arguably the loveliest castle in the valley.

Henri II died tragically in 1559 when an arrow pierced through his eye during a jousting tournament. The tournament was held in Paris in what is now called the Place de Vosges in the Marais district, just beyond the Louvre complex. (I've often strolled between the two locales and then sat in the beautiful Place de Vosges Park, trying to visualize poor Henri galloping along. Henri's demise, by the way, marked the end of the court's fascination with jousting tournaments.)

Catherine de' Médici promptly booted Diane out of Chenonceau and made it her own. Her sons, who became kings in succession, ruled from Amboise, Paris and elsewhere. But the Renaissance peace in Amboise was ultimately shattered with the Wars of Religion.

In 1560 a terrible vengeance was wreaked against the Protestants who'd plotted against Catherine's young son François II: more than 1,200 of the Protestants were disemboweled and then hung from the Amboise castle walls overlooking the river, as harbingers for those who dared cross the crown. (The court allegedly had to vacate Amboise for a time due to the smell of the corpses.)

Still later, Amboise was inherited by Gaston d'Orléans (Louis XIII's brother), who involved himself in conspiracies against the crown; the huge *château* was largely demolished in 1631 as punishment. The French Revolution saw the demolition of still other parts of the old extended castle.

In the 19th century, the temporarily restored monarch King Louis-Philippe began restorations on what was left of Amboise. His non-royal descendants today operate the much smaller castle as a much-loved tourist attraction and part of the Loire

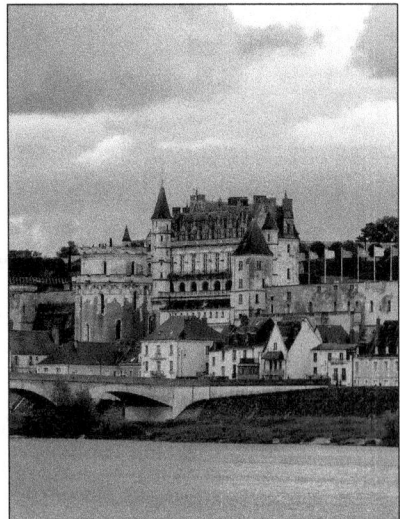

UNESCO World Heritage Site.

Amboise castle (shot courtesy of France Off the Beaten Path Tours) today is a somewhat spare but remarkable *château* complex. Some attractive furnishings have been brought in from other locations, with restored gardens, stellar views of the valley, and a quirky town at its feet. It's open all year round, and visitors are free to roam the royal apartments (the only part left intact through the centuries), as well as the chapel and the surrounding gardens. Parts of the castle's underground passages can be accessed only on guided tours at restricted times. I find the underground tunnels and spiral passageways particularly interesting, since the spirals were built large enough to accommodate men on horseback as they ascended and descended to and from the *château*.

The Flamboyant Gothic Chapel of Saint-Hubert greets you as you first enter the grounds. It is particularly ethereal, with artful decorations and beautiful stained glass windows. The chapel (shown here with pageant players and Christy) is also advertised as the burial place of Leonardo da Vinci, although the exact location of his remains is unknown. Around the grounds, there's a memorial to Leonardo, as well as mechanical depictions of his discoveries. There are numerous Renaissance-style pageants and light shows; the castle also hosts large group

parties, weddings, holiday celebrations, corporate groups, and a variety of romantic venues.

It's often said that Amboise the town has the most Italian flair of all the Loire Valley cities. Amboise is certainly one of those French locales that maximize its tourist opportunities. The tourist-friendly town is mostly pedestrianized areas with cute shops and reasonably priced eateries. Remember that Amboise has three famous AOC wines: Amboise Blanc, Amboise Rosé, and Amboise Rouge. You'll also find some excellent Amboise B&Bs and hotels to use as a base to see the area *châteaux*.

You can download a free app from the aforementioned website that offers tips for wandering the city. Don't miss the fantastic open-air markets every Friday and Sunday morning. (Get there early, or those crafty French housewives will have snapped up the best vegetables, fruits, and cheeses.) Families might especially enjoy the Parc des Mini-Châteaux; this is an unconventional five-acre park with miniature models of the Loire castles, plus mini carts and mechanical horses for children. Amboise Segway tours are quite fun at http://www.freemove.fr, as are bike trips around the town. See the handy Amboise tourism office

for rental companies. And, of course, the little white train is an enjoyable way to get around Amboise for an overview of the town and its many offerings.

I sometimes stop in Amboise for dinner if I'm in the area or, as I stated previously, to buy tapestries. (Even Joan of Arc passed through the town for reinforcements on her way to defeat the English in Orleans in 1429.) And I most highly recommend taking a balloon ride over this fantastic area via either Balloon Revolution with my fun friend Nicholas (http://www.balloonrevolution.com/en/) or Touraine Montgolfiere http://www.touraine-montgolfiere.fr. You haven't really seen the Touraine until you've viewed it from above the treetops.

Amboise Accommodations

Château de Pray is a well-preserved Gothic and Renaissance mansion of the 13th and 14th centuries. Rooms are lovely with period touches; the grounds are wonderful, with swimming pool and fab views of the rolling river. The restaurant—which also serves vegan dishes—is gorgeous (and I had a riotous dinner there one evening with friends). The Orangerie offers breakfast. http://www.chateaudepray.fr

Hôtel Pavillon des Lys is a friendly mansion-turned-hotel owned by my hotelier friends Guillaume (shown with Christy and me) and Julia Jouvin. It's a lovely property in town near the castle. Beautiful rooms abound. Experience a little bit of luxury at reasonable prices at this lovely property. http://pavillondeslys.com

Hôtel Le Fleuray was created from several

vintage farm buildings by a friendly Anglo-French family. This 24-room hotel offers a tranquil setting in the country just outside Amboise. Spacious rooms are named after flowers, and many have private terraces overlooking the gardens. There's also a terrific restaurant and heated outdoor swimming pool. http://www.lefleurayhotel.com

Hôtel Le Manoir les Minimes is a charming monastery-turned-hotel with pretty grounds and well-appointed rooms. Unparalleled views of both the Loire and Château Royal. Serene terraces, romantic breakfasts, and accommodating staff. Has a bar and on-site concierge services as well. http://www.manoirlesminimes.com/en/

Amboise Dining & Wine Bars

La Brache is called "heaven on a plate" by some diners. Located at Logis La Breche hotel, this is the number one dining choice in Amboise via TripAdvisor—and it's worth every euro. http://www.labreche-amboise.com

Château de Pray is slightly out of town (mentioned in the Accommodations section) and offers charming, delicious fare. It has the best vegan menu, which is offered on request. Chef Frederic Brisset does not disappoint and the service is crisp. http://www.chateaudepray.fr

L'Echanson is a family restaurant with a quirky *décor*. It's more of a wine bar with small plates, but it does have some innovative dishes. http://echanson-amboise.fr

Chez Bruno is a fun and friendly bistro and wine bar run by a young local couple from the region. He also has a fabulous wine shop on the same street corner in front of the castle. This place is great for small plates and wine tasting. It's modern and reminds me of a small Paris wine bar. http://www.bistrotchezbruno.com

L'Epicerie. Jim Lockard, wine tour leader and expert (http://deluxewinetours.com) remembers learning something special at L'Epicerie in Amboise. "Following a wonderful first two courses and a nice bottle of 2008 Olga Raffault Chinon, Les Picasses, a tray of cheese, was brought to our table. We were invited to select any five of the fourteen cheeses—a very difficult decision, but we forged ahead anyway. When the cheeses were on the table, the server dipped a small spoon in a clay crock in the center of the tray and spread the contents over some of the cheeses. It was golden raisins marinated in Armagnac. It was absolutely delicious with the cheeses. We always keep a container in the refrigerator now." I love stories like this. Go to this fun eaterie for a fine evening. http://www.lepicerie-amboise.com

Château du Clos-Lucé*

From the balcony of Amboise castle, you can look across to some pretty park lands set with a red-brick manor house. This is Château du Clos-Lucé. Clos-Lucé is where Leonardo da Vinci spent the last three years of his life with a generous pension and the freedom to pursue his marvelous inventions.

Legend has it that François recognized Leonardo's considerable genius immediately. The two became fast friends and spent a great deal of time together. By the time Leonardo arrived in France, he was considered a true Renaissance Man, with mastery in painting, sculpture, architecture, science, music, mathematics, engineering, anatomy, geology, astronomy, botany, history, paleontology, and more. He's sometimes credited with inventing the parachute, helicopter, and tank.

In François's beloved Chambord, Leonardo is very much present because he reportedly designed the double helix staircase in the middle of the castle. Leonardo also created the spiral marble staircase in Blois Château.

François and Leonardo each held great power and influence. Perhaps in each other, they found their intellectual soulmate. Reportedly, François held Leonardo's head in his arms as he died at age 67. This is depicted in romantic paintings by Ingres, Ménageot, and other French artists.

The house today, located within walking distance of Amboise castle, is a museum dedicated to Leonardo's life and inventions. The first floor is Leonardo's studio and the bedroom where he died. The basement houses the museum of Leonardo's 40+ fantasy machines. The grounds have more inventions, including a helicopter, a water mill, and a two-level bridge. I highly recommend a visit; it offers a glimpse into the heart and soul of this seer into the future. You'll also find a copy of the Mona Lisa at Clos-Lucé, painted by the master himself.

I will end with my favorite quote from historian and painter, Giorgio Vasari, who wrote about Leonardo in *Lives of Artists* in 1568:

> In the normal course of events many men and women are born with remarkable talents; but occasionally, in a way that transcends nature, a single person is marvelously endowed by Heaven with beauty, grace and talent in such abundance that he leaves other men far behind, all his actions seem inspired and indeed everything he does clearly comes from God rather than from human skill.

Everyone acknowledged that this was true of Leonardo da Vinci, an artist of outstanding physical beauty, who displayed infinite grace in everything that he did and who cultivated his genius so brilliantly that all problems he studied he solved with ease.

Château de Chenonceau***

The Château de Chenonceau, shrouded in aristocratic dignity, exudes a strangely suave atmosphere...It can be glimpsed at the end of a wide avenue...surrounded by woods, framed by a vast park boasting fine lawns. Built on rippling waters, it rears its pretty turrets and square chimneys into the skies. The Cher runs beneath it, swirling at the foot of its arches, whose pointed features break up the sparkling current. The general feeling is one of gentle peace, elegance, and comforting strength. Its stillness is not remotely boring and its melancholy is never conducive to remorse.

—Gustave Flaubert, *Parles Champs de les Grèves* (1847)

The Château de Chenonceau is aptly called "the Ladies' Château." It stretches romantically across the Cher River and is considered by many to be the loveliest in the Loire. As you approach the castle (depicted here by France Off the Beaten Path Tours) from the car park, you'll find yourself entering a palatial kingdom. I call Chenonceau a "kingdom" because it's second only to Chambord with its comely grounds, burbling waterways, lavish gardens, architectural sophistication, and intriguing backstory.

When I first went to the Château de Chenonceau near the small village of Chenonceaux (with an *x*), I was struck by

a couple of things. First, was the exceptional busyness of the village near the castle. Second was the immense size of the Chenonceau parking area. I soon learned that Chenonceau is indeed a massive estate, with so many romantic nuances it's the most visited *château* in France except for Versailles. Nearly 800,000 visitors arrive every year, so keep this in mind when visiting. Go early or late to avoid the crowds in the parking area and the village.

As you begin your walk through the outer grounds, you'll find yourself surrounded by 173 acres of absolutely gorgeous parklands. There are graceful fountains and a trickling creek, as well as the rushing Cher River. Multiple gardens abound—some for flowers and some for produce— plus some elegant eateries, a zoo and a wax museum.

But the queen of the place is the enthralling *château* arching over the river. As you approach along a gravel pathway, you'll first see side buildings that contain the kitchen and flower gardens (plus an on-site bouquet factory where a team of on-site florists create new arrangements for every castle room twice a week.) After a few hundred feet along the hedgerows, you'll come to the pure Renaissance castle itself, flanked by two extraordinary gardens.

One garden is the winsome Le Jardin de Diane de Poitiers, designed by the king's favorite mistress. The other is the Le Jardin de Catherine de' Médici with its beautiful Renaissance walkways, shaped hedges, and Italianate fountains. Here, Queen Catherine outdid her nemesis Diane after she finally booted her from Chenonceau and took possession of the comely *château* for herself.

Facing you will be the beautiful "Château des Dames." This bewitching Chenonceau structure has a remarkable history of more than 500 years, due to the oversight of several notable women. They loved, lived, fought, and sometimes died here—but through the ages, they all nurtured this enchanting sight that we get to visit today.

First came Katherine Briçonnet, wife of Thomas Bohier, the busy royal chamberlain for King Charles VIII. Bohier purchased what was a modest *château* and fortified mill from the Marques family in 1513. He quickly demolished the little castle but retained the Keep (tower). While he was building an entirely new residence between 1515 and 1521, his wife, Katherine Briçonnet, supervised most of the work, since Bohier was often away with the king. It was she who hosted the nobility in the new castle, including François I.

Then, in 1535, François I seized the *château* from Bohier's son due to unpaid debts to the crown. When François's son Henri II came to power in 1547, Henri gave it to his favorite, Diane de Poitiers. Diane, twenty years his senior, was the most powerful woman in France during her roughly 25 years as Henri II's main mistress until his death in 1559. Dubbed "the everlasting beauty," Diane retained her looks well into her 50s.

Well educated, multilingual, and well schooled in dancing, music, manners, and sex, Diane made a superior consort for young Henri. Despite performing his connubial duties with arranged wife Catherine de' Médici, he was nevertheless devoted to Diane for all of his life. Among other gifts and honors, he gave her Château d'Anet and entrusted her with the Crown Jewels of France. And Diane made the most of her exceptional power over him.

With vast wealth and royal sanction, Diane immediately commissioned architect Philibert de l'Orme to build an arched bridge joining the Chenonceau *château* to its opposite bank. Diane loved to swim and hunt; with this installation of a winsome bridge that seemed to float above the water, she could bathe in the Cher and hunt on both sides of the river. (This is one of the reasons many of the paintings show her depicted as Goddess Diana, the huntress.) She then oversaw the planting of exquisite flower and vegetable gardens, plus a number of fruit trees.

She furnished her love nest with paintings and busts of herself, many in the nude. Massive fireplaces warmed the various bedrooms and parlors of Diane's estate. Outside, almost every view gave glimpses of the Cher lapping the shore or the gorgeous flower gardens perfuming the air.

Diane was disciplined as well as dazzling. Her portraits highlight her creamy skin, ripe breasts, and kissable neck. She apparently started each day with a cold bath at 6 a.m.

Then she climbed onto a horse for a three-hour ride to maintain her youthful figure. She kept to a strict diet, often swam in the Cher River like a swimming pool, had regular massages, bathed in asses' milk, treated herself to perfumed oil wraps, and drank gold bouillon as a form of beauty elixir. As a widow, she chose to be adorned perpetually in black and white; such was her power of Henri that he showed allegiance to her by often wearing the same color scheme.

Yet Diane was no featherbrained beauty. She had a sharp, managerial mind. She was intensely interested in maximizing the income of her and the king's estates. She learned how to turn the Chenonceau farm into a profit-making enterprise; then she wisely propelled the proceeds into beautifying and expanding the estate. Diane was so politically savvy that the king trusted her to write many of his official letters; she even signed some of them jointly with one name, "HenriDiane."

When it came time for the young king to marry, Diane approved the choice of Catherine, who was actually a much younger distant relative of hers. Catherine had had a harrowing upbringing in Italy, which may have contributed to some of her paranoia and violent leanings. Catherine came to the marriage as a pawn and struggled to make a life for herself at court. (Interestingly, she is credited with bringing the Italian dinner fork to France; until that time, the French basically ate every meal with their hands. Catherine also introduced to France many new foods: parsley, the artichoke, lettuce, broccoli, the garden pea, pasta, Parmesan, turkey, and the tomato.)

Once Henri ascended to the throne, Diane was part of Henri and Catherine's court; she knew full well that part of her duty, however, was to be sure royal heirs were produced. She's reported to have nursed Catherine when she was ill and to have given her seduction lessons in order to ensure offspring.

After ten years of childless marriage, there was discussion of a divorce from Catherine. In desperation, Catherine tried every trick for getting pregnant, such as placing cow dung and ground antler stags on her genitalia and drinking mule's urine. (This next part may be more than you want to know about royal genitals, but it was Dr. Jean Fernel who originally noticed that Henri unfortunately had a major penis deformity. Diane seemed able to work around the problem, but Catherine benefited from the doctor's very specific positional coaching.) At the relief of everyone at court, Catherine finally began producing regal offspring. While Catherine and her offspring lived at the official residence at Amboise, Diane and Henri regularly enjoyed the sensual comforts at Chenonceau.

Diane was seen as the woman behind the throne, while Catherine appeared only to be a royal breeder. Over time, Catherine's seething jealousy grew toward the ageless Diane, especially as Catherine's sons prepared to become kings. When Henri lay dying in 1559, Catherine took her revenge. She forbade Diane access to ailing Henri, despite his calling repeatedly for her. Diane was even barred from the funeral once the king expired—and then from Chenonceau for life.

Catherine sent Diane to Château de Chaumont. But Diane bypassed it, choosing instead to live out her days at Château d'Anet. She died there at age 66 after a fall while horseback riding; she was buried at a nearby chapel. During the French Revolution, Diane's tomb was opened and her skeleton thrown into a massive grave. However, French authorities dug up her remains in 2009 and found high levels of gold in her hair. They speculate that the "drinkable gold" she imbibed regularly to preserve her youth may have ultimately hastened her death.

Meanwhile, Catherine became unfettered regent; she ran France from the green study in *her* Chenonceau, which she'd taken possession of with gusto. Since her sons were still young enough for her to rule for them for decades, Catherine made the most of her newfound power as top royal.

She spent a fortune on her new favorite abode, Chenonceau. She added a two-story, Florentine-style walking gallery on top of Diane's arching bridge. (Psychologically, I'd suggest there's a significant message in that architectural move.) Catherine built a massive service wing and several more rooms. On the opposite side of Diane's *jardin,* she installed an Italianate garden set in buttressed stone terraces, with pretty fountains and magnificent flowers. Beyond it she installed extensive kitchen gardens. She upgraded the castle furnishings to royal palace level. She also imported silkworms and began producing a legendary fabric so fine it was dubbed "the Queen's cloth."

She also expanded the vineyards and upped the wine-producing capacity.

Catherine ultimately made Chenonceau the party spot of the valley. She hosted lavish nighttime parties, complete with naked nymphs and mock river battles. To her credit, Catherine seems to have been a ferociously protective mother who went to great lengths to protect her children and future kings in a time of great religious unrest. She even employed seer Nostradamus to cast horoscopes for her sons to divine their political moves. When her son François II ascended the throne in 1560, the first-ever fireworks display launched from Chenonceau.

When Catherine died in January 1589, Chenonceau passed to her daughter-in-law Louise of Lorraine, wife of assassinated Henri III. Henri III was the last of Catherine's sons to rule France; as I mentioned previously, a Catholic fanatic assassinated him eight months after his mother died. By all reports, his poor widow, Louise, suffered major depression once she learned her husband had died. She spent her days wandering aimlessly along Chenonceau's corridors, dressed in mourning clothes amidst dark tapestries stitched with skulls and crossbones.

The estate then passed to Françoise of Lorraine, wife of Cesar de Vendome, who was the son of Henri IV, the new ruler. It remained with her descendants for more than a hundred years. By that time, the Bourbon French kings had long ago left the valley and seldom visited, except during hunting expeditions. Louis XIV was the last royal to visit in 1650. Chenonceau was then bought by the Duke of Bourbon in 1720; over time he sold off most of the castle's original furnishings. Many of the original statues ended up in the collection at Versailles.

In 1733 a wealthy squire named Claude Dupin bought the *château* for 130,000 livres (about 1.3 million dollars). His famous wife, Louise Dupin, was well known in France, since her father was financier Samuel Bernard and her mother was famed actress Manon Dancourt. Louise established a famed literary salon at Chenonceau in the 1740s, which attracted the great Enlightenment leaders of the day. Voltaire, Montesquieu, playwright Marivaux, and many others came to visit. Jean-Jacques Rousseau was Dupin's secretary and tutored her son. The later-widowed Louise saved the property from destruction in the 1780s during the French Revolution by proving how essential it was for travel and commerce as "being the only bridge across the river for many miles." She smartly saved the chapel by turning it into a wood store.

A rich heiress, Marguerite Pelouze, acquired the castle in

1864. She commissioned changes in the structure that ended up leaving her bankrupt. In 1891 a Cuban millionaire, José-Emilio Terry, bought Chenonceau from Pelouze. Terry sold it to a family member, and later in 1913, it was sold to Henri Menier, a member of the Menier family (known for their chocolates). The family still owns Chenonceau today.

During World War I, Chenonceau's two long galleries functioned as a makeshift hospital and surgery center for 2,000+ soldiers. Simone Menier acted as head matron of the hospital operation; it was completely funded by the generous Menier family and their chocolate business. In 1940 during World War II, the Germans bombed the *château,* but the structure remained relatively unharmed. It also served as a means of escape, since the gallery bridge's southern door provided access to the unoccupied Free Zone, while the castle's main entrance was in the Nazi occupied zone. Simone Menier herself played a key part in all this by facilitating escapes via the French Resistance. By 1944 the Germans were occupying Chenonceau, and on June 7, 1944, the castle was bombed by the Allies. Luckily, only the chapel was hit, and its windows were blown out.

In 1951 the Menier family entrusted the *château*'s restoration to Bernard Voisin. Voisin brought the dilapidated buildings and gardens (which had been ravaged by the Cher River flood of 1940) back to their former grandeur. Though the Menier family still retains ownership of the *château*, their chocolate empire is now owned by Nestlé. Nevertheless, Chenonceau today is a beautifully marketed venue, finessed by a legion of savvy marketeers. They've maximized the historical sheen of the castle's 500-year-old history while making it a comprehensively modern experience for 21st century visitors.

> The very name of this site evokes music; the vision of it, pure enchantment. Here charm transcends beauty. The majesty and simplicity of Chenonceau touches the heart and the soul.
>
> —Laure Menier, Château de Chenonceau

When you visit Château de Chenonceau, give yourself time to enjoy all the beauties of this sumptuous estate. As you enter, the perfume of fresh flowers wafts over you. This is because Chenonceau is one of the few Loire castles that has gorgeous

fresh floral displays in every room! Unlike some of the other Loire *châteaux*, Chenonceau is fully furnished and warmly decorated. (In winter, the fireplaces are also lit to give visitors the feeling that they are guests.)

I'll now explore some of my favorite rooms in detail. Diane's boudoir, with the blue bed and the handsome white and gold fireplace, is especially inviting. Catherine de' Médici's bedroom and the nearby Five Queens' Bedroom offers stunning floor-to-ceiling tapestries and superbly carved wooden ceilings.

Catherine's Green Study is a tranquil room with pretty windows, handsome tapestries, and another grand fireplace. The Gallery makes for a lovely stroll, with its arched windows overlooking the burbling river, tiled and slate flooring, exposed-joint ceiling, and pristine walls inlaid with sculptures. François I's bedroom is a wood-paneled masculine room with regal furnishings and famous paintings of Diane as the Huntress and a nude of the Mailly-Nesle Sisters—all three of whom were royal mistresses.

The Louis XIV red living room, with its curves and elegant baroque fabrics, evokes the memory of Louis when he visited on July 14, 1650. The stone staircase is amazing, with its caissons of human figures, fruits, and flowers leading downstairs; it's one of the first straight staircases built in France on the Italian model. One section leads down to the wonderful kitchen, which is festooned with copper pots used in medieval cooking. I particularly love the pantry.

Chenonceau has an exceptional museum collection of the Old Masters' paintings: Murillo, Le Tintoret, Nicolas Poussin, Le Corrège, Rubens, Le Primatice, and Van Loo, as well as some very rare 16th century Flanders tapestries. There's also a wax museum—but it's rather underwhelming.

Outside the *chateau* itself, you'll find a marvelous opportunity to walk along the bloom-filled gardens, shrubbery maze, verdant pathways, and kitchen gardens. More than 40,000 flowers are grown on the estate; they're replanted twice a year—in spring and summer. The entire estate is quite massive at 173 acres, which includes the gardens, *château,* and eateries plus a 16th century farm along with a wooded park along a creek with a picnic area and zoo.

You absolutely must wander through Diane's photogenic garden with its pretty terraces, aromatic flower beds of hibiscus, climbing iceberg roses, alternating grasses, and glorious fountain. Overlooking it is the steward's house and dock onto the Cher River.

On the opposite side of the walkway you'll be delighted by Catherine's Garden. The forecourt features climber rose trees and a wonderful alley of orange trees. Then you'll enter the lyrical flower gardens that are the main supplier of the splendid floral arrangements you'll see all around the estate. Five lawns are positioned around an elegant circular pool surrounded by sphere-shaped boxwood bushes. Alongside is the Cher, where ivy trellises form a pretty border. Nearby are the farm buildings and floral workrooms. Beyond them are absolutely enormous vegetable and flower gardens—which help to supply not only the *château* but the tourist eating venues. A team of ten gardeners tends this lush paradise.

You'll find a handy snack consortium set up in the old Royal stables with perfect views of the castle. But my favorite of favorites is the L'Orangerie Restaurant. This elegant dining venue is a restaurant and teahouse. It has a fantastic menu and stellar collection of wines. Every time I enjoy a meal here, it lasts 2–3 hours; we're having such a lovely time, we hate to leave. I've included a picture here so you can see how you'll be spoiled in this pampering eatery. (Be sure to book reservations well in advance.)

The man and woman at the far right and left of the photo are my great friends Julie and Jeremy Kolbe, who live in the heart of the Loire and offer *gîte* (cottage) rentals called "Les Bocages." These are available for rent usually on a weekly or two-week basis, though shorter stays are possible in the off season. Julie and Jeremy have sympathetically restored what was formerly a wine producer's property, over two centuries old. They welcome travelers the world over, mainly English speaking. I can highly recommend them. Jeremy is also available as a local guide. http://www.loirevalleygite.com

At the entrance just off the car park to the whole Chenonceau estate, you'll enter and exit through one of the best boutiques of all the Loire castles. You'll find trinkets, souvenirs, books, clothing, wines from Chenonceau's own vineyards, and, of course, tapestries.

A few tips about visiting. The *château* provides multilingual iPod guides; but if you're really smart, you'll go to the website and look at the 360-degree views of each room on each floor of the castle to get oriented. There is also helpful information on all the activities at the site—one of the best websites of the Loire. http://www.chenonceau.com

Chenonceau Accommodations

Hôtel la Roseraie is a famed French *auberge*, a vine-covered 18th-century stone house, converted into a 15-room hotel. The rooms are lovely, along with the outdoor pool (in season), a bar with wood-burning fireplace, and a good restaurant that serves big salads for lunch. A great-value 29-euro *prix-fixe* (fixed-price) menu is available in the evenings. Winston Churchill and some Rockefellers have stayed here. http://www.hotel-chenonceau.com
Le Bon Laboureur is a long-established inn and eatery with delightful ambiance for visiting Chenonceau and surroundings delights. http://www.bonlaboureur.com/en/

Chenonceau Dining & Wine Bars

L'Orangerie. This eatery at Chenonceau is one of my

favorite dining venues in the Loire. It oozes charm with lovely surroundings, a great menu, and fine wines. Do make reservations in advance. http://www.chenonceau.com
Auberge du Cheval Rouge. After working at Le Meurice in Paris, young chef Jacques Guillaumat recently took over this auberge down the road from Château de Chenonceau featuring modern French cuisine. It's a delight. http://auberge-duchevalrouge.com

Château de Villandry***

> The Château de Villandry is the last of the great châteaux of the Loire built during the Renaissance in the Loire Valley. The sober elegance of its architecture combined with the charm of its outstanding gardens make this one of the jewels of world heritage.
>
> —*http://www.chateauvillandry.fr*

The Amboise-based royal entourage scrambled to follow François I's lead by erecting Renaissance palaces near him. Château de Villandry might be one of the finest examples of these. The estate has a sturdy, well fashioned Renaissance castle, but its fame stems from its palatial gardens—some of the finest in France, save Versailles and the Paris Tuileries.

The estate was constructed by Jean le Breton, Minister of Finance for François I. Breton was a savvy builder by the time he built his own grand estate at Villandry. Having been the construction supervisor of several grand *châteaux,* including Chambord, Breton was armed with an exquisite plan for a stylish castle with spectacular gardens for himself. When he first arrived at the Villandry site in 1532, he had the old feudal fortress razed to the ground except for the keep. In its place he constructed a multistoried manor with genteel arcades, mullioned windows, and ornate rooms, all framing an elegant courtyard. Despite Azay-le-Rideau and Chenonceau's being nearby, Villandry rejected the Italian influences and medieval splashes. Instead, it has a pure, French style absent the turrets, pinnacles, and decorative machicolations of the nearby estates.

Breton was a fervent garden lover. He set out to depict romance in greenery, planting exquisite Renaissance gardens and an ornamental moat in harmony with the River Cher and the natural surroundings. The *château* remained in the Le Breton family for more than two centuries until the Marquis de Castellane acquired it in 1754. Castellane "warmed up" the castle by installing wood paneling for soundproofing and thermal insulation, as well as a fine Louis XV staircase. During the French Revolution, the property was confiscated; in the early 19th century Emperor Napoleon acquired it for his brother Jérôme Bonaparte.

In 1906 the estate was acquired by Spanish nobleman and physician Joachim Carvallo and his wealthy American wife, Anne Coleman. The pair spent much of their lives and fortune on restoring Villandry. When the couple began renovations, the *château* looked a lot like a barracks, with dark windows and a crumbling exterior. Over a decade, and with the help of a team of 100 stonemasons, however, they lovingly restored the *façades* to Renaissance beauty. The Carvallos fully refurbished the interior, playing up the mullioned windows, high-sculpted dormer windows, and horseshoe courtyard. Then they filled it with lavish furnishings and a celebrated art collection that impresses even today.

Soon, the Carvallos turned their attention to the overgrown grounds, which were a tangled mess of English style lawns with an overgrown forest overtaking the estate. They pulled out the forests of cedars, pines, and magnolias, as well as the boring lawns. Then Dr. Carvallo used his scientific mind to begin recreating the original Renaissance environment from centuries before.

Using old architectural plans from the 17th and 18th centuries, plus the foundational remains of walls and pipes around the property, Carvallo slowly rebuilt the decorative kitchen gardens and Renaissance "outdoor rooms" that had once grown at Villandry. The classical water garden at the top of the property was based on the original plans of the Marquis of Castellane.

When it came to the second-tier salon gardens, Carvallo

brought in modern help. He smartly called on painters and landscape architects to craft "salons" or rooms with specific themes. These included the salon of the crosses, the salon of love, and the salon of music designed by Carvallo himself. The Carvallos continued until Villandry had the grandest *jardins* in the valley.

The Carvallos are still much loved in the Loire Valley. In 1924 Joachim Carvallo founded the "Demeure Historique," the first association of castle owners of historical residences. He pioneered the opening of monuments to the public. Villandry today remains in the Carvallo family; I believe the grandson and his family still reside at the estate. (I think I even ran into some family members one morning in the *château*. I have a habit of arriving very early to these estates, then studying a room or a portrait all by myself for a long time; sometimes one of the staff or *château* owners wanders along and lingers to chat. I've had this happen to me in many of the most famous places in France, by the way. This is one of the reasons I seldom travel in large groups; when I am by myself or perhaps with only a couple of other people, I often am invited to meet the owners or management personally.)

When you visit this modern-day "Garden of Eden" today, you'll find that the Villandry Gardens are laid out in seven distinctive enclaves ringed by 1,015 lime trees. First is the Ornamental Garden, where the four symbols of love are found: Tender

Love (hearts separated by small flames), Passionate Love (hearts broken by passion laid out in a *farandole* to evoke dancing), Fickle Love (fans of volatility and horns of jilted love), and Tragic Love (daggers and swords used in duels of rivalry).

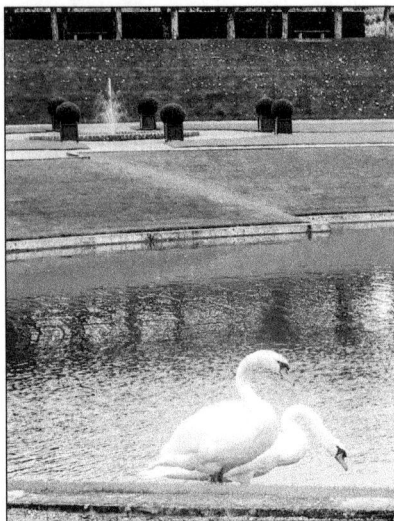

Second is the Woods area, with its pretty walkways, greenhouses, and pavilion. Third is the meditative Water Garden, with a mirror-shaped reflecting pool and marvelous white swans. The water irrigates all the other gardens as well as the ornamental moat. (I don't mind telling you I spent half an hour making friends with these swans and coaxing them out of the water for a photo. You can see they finally posed prettily.)

Fourth is the Sun Garden, with its "Cloud Room" of blue and white shrubs, "Sun Room" with bright orange and yellow flowers and bushes, and "Children's Room" with peaceful apple trees and plenty of running space. See this happy shot by Maureen Beals of the children's enclave that is delight for young and old.

Fifth is the Maze, symbolizing man's path on earth. Children adore this maze, especially since they can climb up into the middle platform and shout down to others racing through the maze.

Sixth is the Herb Garden, devoted to aromatic, cooking, and medicinal herbs. Last is the glorious *Potager* (Vegetable Garden), made up of nine squares laid out like a chessboard.

It's planted with alternating colors of vegetables and roses, plus fountains and arbors. In total, there are more than 115,000 flowers and vegetables. The flowers are replanted twice a year. In 2009, Villandry moved to organic gardening methods. It takes four full-time tree trimmers to prune the lime, pear, and boxwood trees yearly. Additionally, ten full-time gardeners labor all year round to keep this Eden blooming. I might add that this spectacular garden has some of the biggest vegetables I've ever seen in my life! It's bursting with giant eggplant, robust melons, head-sized artichokes, soldierly asparagus, and soccer-ball sized cauliflower. The ornamental cabbages dotted throughout for year round color are also quite extra ordinary. As a visitor, I've spent hours just sitting or wandering through various parts of the gardens. I particularly like watching the gardeners who are so expert at what they do!

Villandry is one of the top three destinations in the Loire—so it is absolutely a must-see for the whole family. There are well-run tours here, or you can simply wander the *château* and the gardens at your leisure. The Villandry app is handy to help guide you through the estate. In the modern age, Villandry has also become a gardener's destination; an entire gardening culture has sprung up around it.

Along with a handy tearoom called La Doulce Terrase, there's a snack shop and an exceptional garden shop where you can buy gifts and paraphernalia from the estate. I came away with a bag full of treasures including some seeds I planted in my garden in California.

The Villandry website gives you a detailed tour of the estate and gardens. There's also gardening advice written by head gardener, Laurent Portuguez, on a variety of topics such as rose pruning, topiary care, and handling such garden pests as aphids. You can order products from the mail-order shop or book receptions or seminars at the estate. The gardens, by the way, are open year round. http:// chateauvillandry.fr/en/

Villandry Accommodations

Le Haut des Lys. Tranquil hotel, relaxing gardens, lovely breakfast. http://lehautdeslys.com/fr/
Auberge Le Colombien. Short walk from Villandry, it's a charming family-run hotel and restaurant in the center of the village. http://www.hotel-villandry.com/fr/ColombienHotelF. htm

Villandry Dining & Wine Bars

L'Etape Gourmande. This is a fantastic farmhouse restaurant with delicious food, and it's located right near Villandry (just up the road from the village of Villandry). I spent a charming afternoon here (and plan to go back). Madame Béatrice de Montferrie, owner and delightful cuisine expert, was especially accommodating. Sitting by the fire, dining on her exceptional cuisine in this farmhouse haven of Loire cuisine, I thought I had died and gone to heaven. Most tourists would miss this place, but if you want to have a truly country-French experience, make reservations and enjoy! http://www.letapegourmande.com

Le Cheval Rouge. Here you'll find down-to-earth French cuisine at reasonable prices. http://www.lecheval-rouge.com

Château d'Azay-le-Rideau***

> A faceted diamond set in the Indre.
>
> —Honoré de Balzac

Azay-le-Rideau is a tranquil little village with a very big calling card: the bewitching Château d'Azay-le-Rideau. The first time I drove into the Azay area through winding fields edged by quiet cottages, I soon found myself in a rather ordinary French village that obscured the graceful castle moored at the end of a dainty lane.

After I parked and strolled through the medieval wall leading to the *château*, however, I entered some beautiful parklands edged with enormous trees. Then I crossed a stately bridge across the River Indre and stepped onto the castle grounds proper. In front of me was a radiant castle that floated like a Renaissance vessel in the middle of a serene lake. I was about to enter the ethereal Château d'Azay-le-Rideau—another one of the Loire's cherished destinations.

Though similar in elegance to Chenonceau, much-smaller Azay is a graceful example of early Renaissance architecture with some unique features. Azay is a rather compact castle, sturdily built in gothic style. It looks like it's floating like the Lady-in-the-Lake, but it's actually built on a small island with parts of it sitting on stilts driven into the mud. Its unique embellishments—the slender pencil turrets, the dainty windows, the façade's symmetry, and the creamy lake reflection—make it a mesmerizing abode.

I can say frankly that you can't take a bad photo of Azay; it's so storybook pretty that I've spent hours setting up my camera at different points around the outside and snapping photographs (and selfies). Even more, I've posed and had others pose, in front of its picture-perfect windows that overlook a burbling stream so verdant and fanciful, it makes me want to write a fairytale book every time I visit.

Azay was begun on the ruins of a former feudal castle in 1518. It was semi-completed in 1529 by Gilles Berthelot, the mayor of Tours and Treasurer-General for François I. Later François I confiscated it due to Berthelot's alleged embezzlement of royal funds. It was owned through the centuries by various parties who completed the original plans with the assistance of the Swiss architect Pierre-Charles Dusillon. (Dusillon also worked on the neighboring Château de Ussé.) Azay was finally bought by the French state in 1905 for 200,000 francs (about $34,000), and it was listed as a Historical Monument. During World War I, it became the relocated home for the Education Ministry when they had to withdraw from Paris.

Today, this much-visited, fully restored castle with a peaked roof and delicate bright blue spires is enchanting. Inside is a meticulously maintained *château* filled with lavish Renaissance furniture, magnificent artwork, and handsomely staged remnants of Renaissance life. Of particular note is the galleried stairwell and straight grand staircase with its three floors of twin bay windows and landings. This was particularly innovative at the time, since most of the staircases at the other *châteaux* were curved. (It's

the oldest surviving staircase in France.) Also notable are the opulent drawing rooms and stately apartments with wood floors and etched marble fireplaces; additionally, visitors will find 15th century brocaded canopy beds, 17th century credenzas and tables, and floor-to-ceiling 16th and 17th century Flemish tapestries.

Don't miss the topless portrait of Henry IV's haughty mistress Gabrielle d'Estrées; it's painted in the style of François Clouet and features d'Estrées in the same pose as Diane de Poitiers years earlier. You'll also find François I's salamander crest carved above the doors and fireplaces; this was done to please the king. (But it didn't help Berthelot when he was evicted by the king.) I love to linger at the windows and in the bedrooms of Azay; I can say with complete candor this is the only public *château* in the Loire where I would love to spend the night.

The last time I was there, they were preparing for a Renaissance string concert inside Asay. Sadly, I couldn't stay for the performance—but the feeling I had, as they rehearsed in this Renaissance abode, was the closest I've ever felt to actually "time traveling" to the 15th century.

If you can, bring a picnic to enjoy on the riverbank. If you're visiting with children they might like the miniature golf course nearby or the Musée du Jouet toy museum. Best of all is the nighttime Azay's "Son-et-Lumières" show "Les

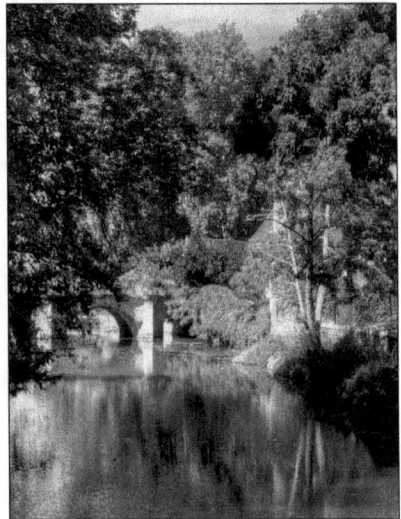

Imaginationaires d'Azay." I'd also recommend a visit to the Azay village for a meal. http://www.azay-le-rideau.fr/en/

Azay Accommodations

Le Grand Monarque is a tree-shaded 25-room French country chic hotel, created from an 18th-century coaching inn and a mansion. Here you'll find a lovely garden, reasonably priced rooms, and a cozy bar with a fireplace and limited-menu eatery. http://www.legrandmonarque.com
La Petite Loge. These *chambres de hôtes* rentals have a fully equipped kitchen and a garden with barbecue. http://lapetiteloge.free.fr
Hôtel des Châteaux has small but attractive rooms and brasserie-type food. http://www.hoteldeschateaux.com

Azay Dining & Wine Bars

L'Aigle d'Or features Jean Luc Fèvre's contemporary French cooking. Try the goat's cheese tart garnished with cooked and raw vegetables and duckling glazed with strawberry vinegar. The desserts are terrific too. http://www.laigle-dor.fr/aigleor/
Auberge du XIIe Siècle is one of the finest dining opportunities in the valley; it's located just a few miles from Azay and offers gourmet French. Also a favorite of Balzac. Phone +33 2 47 26 88 77.

Château d'Ussé**

I had almost reached the top of the dim, spiral staircase when I heard soft music floating through the castle's turrets not far above. It was music from Disney's film *The Sleeping Beauty*. Immediately it awoke the child within me, transporting me back to

the world of fairytale castles, beautiful princesses and
handsome princes.
—Don Townshend, "About Sleeping Beauty and
Ussé," *The Sidney Morning Herald*

A scant nine miles from Azay lies the tiny hamlet
of Rigny-Ussé. Populated by just a few hundred intrepid
souls, the looming presence for them all is the spellbinding
Château d'Ussé. It's known far and wide by another name,
however: "Sleeping Beauty's Castle."

In the 17th century, Charles Perrault's stay at Ussé
prompted him to use the castle as inspiration for one his
most enduring fairytales, *Sleeping Beauty*. Interestingly,
the actual history of Château d'Ussé echoes the story of a
malevolent fairy who threatens the forever love of a prince
and princess and then dooms the princess to slumber for
a century in an ancient castle surrounded by mysterious,
foreboding woods.

In a faraway land, long ago, there lived a King and his fair Queen. Many years they had longed for a child, and finally their wish was granted. A daughter was born, and they called her Aurora. Yes, they named her after the dawn, for she filled their lives with sunshine. Then a great holiday was proclaimed throughout the land, so that all of high or low estate could pay homage to the infant Princess. And our story begins on that most joyful day...

—Narrator, *Sleeping Beauty*

Ussé began as an 11th century stronghold at the edge of the Chinon forest, overlooking the Indre Valley. Fortified by the Norman *seigneur* (Lord) Gueldin de Saumur, who in some French archives is referred to as "the devil" for his vicious tactics, the fortress was ultimately sacked and left in ruins for hundreds of years.

In the 15th century the Bueil family, who had distinguished themselves in the Hundred Years War, gained the property. In the 1440s, Jean V de Bueil, Captain-General for Charles VII and the new Lord of Ussé, began rebuilding upon the old ruins a residence castle in cheerful white *tufa* stone. His son, Antoine de Bueil, married Jeanne de Valois in 1462, daughter of Charles VII; needing money, Antoine sold the castle to Jacques d'Espinay in 1485.

The Espinays were a fine Breton family who had been chamberlains to the Duke of Brittany, Louis XI, and Charles VIII. Espinay further refurbished the castle, making it warm and livable. His son, Charles, completed the chapel and other expansions, mixing Renaissance motifs with Flamboyant Gothic style. Entry to the castle was made across a drawbridge spanning a broad moat. The result was a majestic estate of round towers and battlements, pointy turrets, and steel-dark slate roofs in perfect harmony between Gothic and Renaissance elements.

In the 17ᵗʰ century, Louis de Valentinay, Comptroller for the king, became Marquis of Ussé. Desiring to open up the view, he demolished the northern buildings to make way for some formal French gardens. He had a dream for a beautiful representation of Versailles-like elegance.

Along the terraces and newly tilled acreage, the famous gardener André Le Nôtre (who designed the Versailles gardens) was hired to create a masterpiece *jardin*. Le Notre drew up the plan that manifested in the beautiful garden terraces and *orangerie* that still exist today.

Around this time, author and Académie Française member Charles Perrault (1628–1703) came to visit. Perrault was a man of letters and an esteemed part of Louis XIV's administration. It was he who loved the fables of Aesop and convinced Louis to include 39 fountains with animal heads, representing Aesop's animal characters in the gardens of Versailles. After his forced retirement in 1686, Perrault decided to dedicate himself to his children. He began by writing fairytales. Among them are *Tales of Mother Goose*, *Little Red Riding Hood*, *Cinderella*, and *Sleeping Beauty*. (The Brothers Grimm borrowed heavily from Perrault a century later to create their Grimm's tales.)

In the time of Perrault's visit, the dense Chinon woods abutting Ussé castle were teeming with wild boar, howling wolves, and startled deer. It seemed a mysterious place—and legend claimed it harbored fairies, evil witches, and forest sprites that sometimes dabbled in the lives of the humans nearby. Sometimes the sprites were dark-natured creatures bent on destruction.

> The princess shall indeed grow in grace and beauty, beloved by all who know her. But...before the sun sets on her 16th birthday, she shall prick her finger on the spindle of a spinning wheel... and DIE! A forest of thorns shall be (her) tomb! Borne through

the skies on a fog of doom! Now go with the curse, and serve me well! 'Round Stefan's castle, CAST MY SPELL!

—Evil Fairy Maleficent, *Sleeping Beauty*

But sometimes there were loving fairies in the forest whose happy aims were to bring goodness to the land:

Sweet princess, if through this wicked witch's trick, a spindle should your finger prick...a ray of hope there still may be in this, the gift I give to thee. Not in death, but just in sleep, the fateful prophecy you'll keep. And from this slumber you shall wake, when true love's kiss, the spell shall break.

—Good Fairy Merryweather, *Sleeping Beauty*

It was in this mystical setting where Perrault germinated the idea for a fairytale love story where true love's kiss could save the day. *Sleeping Beauty*, or *La Belle au Bois Dormant* (The Beauty Sleeping in the Wood), was first published in 1697. Most know it as one of the most beloved stories ever written. It's been reproduced again and again in poetry, film, cartoons, books, coloring books, opera, ballet, and more.

In 1802 the Duc de Duras purchased Château d'Ussé. Politicians came to conspire for a possible restoration of the monarchy. Diplomat, writer, and historian François-René de Chateaubriand often stayed at Ussé; it was he who gifted his hosts with the cedars of Lebanon that still stand on the grounds today. Chateaubriand even worked on his *Mémoires d'Outre-Tombe* at Ussé as the guest of Duchesse Claire de Duras.

In 1885 the Comtesse de la Rochejaquelein bequeathed Ussé to her great-nephew, the Comte de Blacas. In 1931 Ussé was classified as a *monument historique* by the French Ministry of Culture. Today the *château* belongs to his descendant, Casimir de Blacas d' Aulps, the 7th Duke of Blacas. Born in 1943, the current duke still occupies the private quarters of the castle with his family. He keeps the estate "fairytale ready" at all times.

As a recent visitor to Ussé (once my GPS system got me at last to the castle), I can share it is truly a unique visit. The *château* is quite extraordinary at first glance. It backs up majestically to a cliff at the edge of the Chinon Forest, while its lyrical gardens overlook the bubbling Indre.

The estate is a marvel in contrasts. Its bulky fortified towers meld dreamily with the creamy white stone foundation walls that climb to handsome roofs, towering turrets, quirky pointed dormers, and chimneys rising up against a backdrop of pines and cedars.

Inside, the castle unfolds in stages that mirror its history. First, the military outer walls belie its fortress past. But as you enter the courtyard, elegant inner chambers rise in Renaissance splendor. When you pass through the entrance, you're greeted by beautifully furnished halls of white stone and wood. Then you wander on through salons and apartments with magnificent tapestries and furniture depicting the various centuries. The Grand Gallery linking the east and west wings are hung with floor-to-ceiling Flemish tapestries depicting country scenes. A regal 17th century wrought-iron staircase leads to the library and apartments on the second floor.

The Chambre du Roi (King's bedroom) is quite exceptional—although no king ever slept here. Its white and gold columns and grand red-silk bed is truly fit for a royal. The library and antechamber is exceptional, containing a startling Italian 16th century cabinet with 49 drawers. The Dining Room boasts Louis XV furniture and crested silverware. (*Secret tip:* the present owners still dine there.)

The Salle de Jeux, or Keep, houses a recreation room with china dinner services, as well as toys and miniature furniture. The old chapel functions as a splendid salon, set with a Mazarin desk fashioned from lemon-tree wood, as well as other notable furniture. The guardroom boasts a 17th century *Trope-l'oeil* ceiling that looks like real marble; there's also an extensive collection of ornamental weapons.

Unlike many of the other *châteaux*, Ussé has mannequins stationed in the rooms to provide a human flavor of what it would have been like to

live here in centuries past. I particularly enjoyed the estate's Costume Exposition; each year it selects an era to display a collection of the styles of the period. When I attended, it featured the Belle Époque depicting the 1900s. And, if you squint your eyes a bit, you can almost see these wax figures come alive with tales of the past. Walt Disney is rumored to have based his *Sleeping Beauty* castle for Disneyland on Ussé—and most certainly his movie mirrors it.

But it's in Ussé's enchanted tower where young and old alike will find Perrault's *Sleeping Beauty* staged in living color.

Here [is] the beautiful Princess Aurora in her richly adorned bedroom, the dashing Prince with his long fair hair and a feather in his cap, the wicked dark-shrouded evil fairy Carabosse (Maleficent) with her black raven, bright-eyed Good Fairies, and the old spinster (disguised Carabosse) with the spinning wheel that led to the princess pricking herself and falling asleep for 100 years.

—Don Townshend, "About Sleeping Beauty and Ussé," *The Sidney Morning Herald*

Outside, back in present day, I found the rest of the offerings equally fun. I had a grand time roaming the grounds, taking photos of the castle and chapel, and of course visiting the Disney-like shop where you can buy your heart's desire in fairytale souvenirs. Even the stream of families with little girls racing to see the "real home" of Princess Aurora was fun to watch. They practically knocked me down getting to the Sleeping Beauty paraphernalia in the well-stocked shop!

I confess I bought a copy of *Sleeping Beauty* (in French) to take with me on my journey. I hope to give it to my granddaughter some day. Because as hokey is it may seem, I believe there lives in all of us—young, old, male, female, or transgender—the hope that love is still the greatest power in the universe. As such, I want to add one quick story that illustrates the power of a place like Ussé, with its dream of everlasting love.

On one of my milestone birthdays, I said I wanted to see the movie *Enchanted.* So we hopped in the car—my husband, me, my 30-something daughter, and her platonic friend, "Daniel." Daniel had tagged along because he was feeling low; his wife had just divorced him for another man. Soon we were seated at *Enchanted* and watched, completely absorbed, until the movie-musical was over.

Most know that *Enchanted* is based on a wacky Hollywood confabulation of story elements from *Sleeping Beauty, Snow White,* and (maybe) *Buffy the Vampire Slayer.* It has a cartoon princess, prince, and evil stepmother who are at odds in the magic kingdom of Andalasia. The trio soon flees Andalasia, but they resurface through a manhole cover in New York City as real live humans. Giselle (Amy Adams), the princess, ultimately decides her cartoon prince (James Marsden) is an idiot. She instead falls in love with New York divorce-lawyer Patrick Dempsey (McDreamy from *Grey's Anatomy*), who is her actual one true love.

Dempsey kisses Giselle awake after she eats a poisoned apple, but then Giselle has to grab a sword to defend him against the evil stepmother who morphs into a gigantic dragon. (Susan Sarandon must have had a ball playing this role). In *Enchanted,* the *princess* is the one wielding the sword and saving her prince so they can live happily after.

As the movie ended and the lights came up, we clapped our hands and laughed uproariously at this zany fairytale mash up. Well, all of us except one. I looked over and saw Daniel sitting there with tears streaming down his face. His divorce was just too fresh. And by watching *Enchanted,* he somehow felt that true love would never be his again. It took him several minutes to come around. We made sure to be extra supportive the rest of the evening.

> Wait, Prince Phillip. The road to true love may be barred by many more dangers, which you alone have to face. So arm thyself with this enchanted Shield of Virtue, and this mighty Sword of Truth, for these weapons of righteousness will triumph over evil.
> —Flora, *Sleeping Beauty*

And, like Prince Phillip, there actually *is* a happy ending to Daniel's story—just as in the fairytale. I am a Facebook friend of Daniel's. He ultimately met a lovely woman a few years ago. And they now have their own little curly-haired princess who's about three years old as of this writing. Never have I seen a man post so many adorable photos and videos of his cherubic child and beaming wife. I can tell by the wide, wide grin on Daniel's face these days that he has likely found true love at last. I suspect he probably gives his little princess (and her mother) true love's kiss every day. I hope Daniel takes them to Ussé someday. I think they'd love it.

As I got in my car and drove across the river away from Ussé (https://www.chateaudusse.fr), with the castle turrets reflected in my rearview mirror, I recalled Daniel's encounter with the power of love—and *Sleeping Beauty's* fervent words:

I know you, I walked with you once upon a dream. I know you, the gleam in your eyes is so familiar a gleam. Yet I know it's true, that visions are seldom all they seem...But if I know you, I know what you'll do: you'll love me at once, the way that you did, once upon a dream...
—Princess Aurora,
Sleeping Beauty

Château de Langeais*

Smack dab in the middle of a tiny medieval river town sits the swarthy Château de Langeais. I say "swarthy" because Langeais hasn't been power-washed to blast the 500-year-old soot away. It hasn't been prettified and overly embellished with floor to ceiling tapestries or great bowls of fresh flowers. Langeais is raw, rough, rather masculine, and real (although another powerful woman plays a major part in its history). Langeais has a working drawbridge that looks like a 15th century cavalcade could still pass over it carrying 600 pounds of cannon balls. And it's the only *château* in the Loire that I "stumbled onto," not even knowing what I was looking at until I was inside.

For some reason we'd decided to stay for a few days near Villandry in an off-the-beaten-path B&B in a non-touristy town called Cinq-Mars-la-Pile. Cinq-Mars-la-Pile is a tiny "suburb" of Langeais, if you can call a few streets of houses a suburb. Cinq-Mars is only a few blocks from a most stately castle that wasn't even on my radar the week I was visiting.

In retrospect, my whole visit to this still-medieval Langeais area was a series of unexpected encounters with "ancient France." It felt "ancient" in the sense that my days weren't tourist-burnished and they weren't necessarily comfortable. But this is one of my best France experiences simply because I was in a "real" locale where kind French people were cheerfully integrating their internet-savvy lives amongst a thousand-year-old relic.

Let me explain. Langeais (a tiny town) and Cinq-Mars-la-Pile (an even tinier village) are definitely in *château* country backwater. That is, Langeais Castle and surroundings are typically not in the top-10 *châteaux* favorites. Yes, expansive Villandry with its ethereal gardens and floating Azay-le-Rideau are only a few miles away. But castle lovers don't often visit Langeais because it has more of a working-town vibe with a medieval castle fortress "plopped" down in the middle of it.

I arrived in Cinq-Mars-la-Pile from Paris in a rental car one Sunday morning in November. It was foggy, damp, and a bit dark. My primary destinations were Villandry and Azay, but my spouse had selected a B&B from the Michelin Guide that I hadn't read anything about. And so the GPS took us through the fog to our abode: La Meulière, a *chambres d'hôtes* in Cinq-Mars-la-Pile. (The name of the village derives from the ruins of a Roman brick tower that's now mostly a pile of French rubble.)

Our proprietress was supposed to be Claudine Manier. But it was her non-English-speaking husband who greeted us, handed us our keys, and directed us to Langeais proper for a quick castle tour before lunch. He was a kind, elderly gentleman. But since he spoke no English, he had that rather terrified look on his face that many English-only speakers get when they encounter French people. We got by on my fractured French and headed back out for sightseeing.

We found the castle easily, since it towers above tiny Langeais; the town itself doesn't look like it's had much new construction in 400 years. Château de Langeais began in the 10th century when formidable Foulques Nerra, count of Anjou, built a fortress poised on a critical promontory overhanging the Loire. Since it lay between Anjou and Blois, it was a coveted locale. The often-sieged fortress therefore passed back and forth between the rival counts of Blois and Anjou for years. (Even Richard the Lionheart owned it for a time; he added still stronger fortifications.)

In the 1206, however, Langeais became part of the French Crown lands of King Philippe Auguste. During the Hundred Years' War, armed bands sometimes occupied the fortification. Charles VII (of Joan of Arc fame) finally had enough of the fight for Langeais and ordered it destroyed except for the *donjon* (Keep). That Keep is still standing today (and, yes, you can walk right up and touch it). It is the oldest Keep in France.

In 1465 devious King Louis XI (who inherited the title from his father, Charles VII) decided to flex his royal muscles and build a new castle on the Langeais ruins. Today you can clearly see the remnants of the old fortress while inside is a 15th century residence with all the comforts of royal medieval life.

This confused me when I first saw the castle misted in fog on that November day. On the town side, where you enter, the *façade* has all the attributes of a fortress: huge towers, working drawbridge, and a parapet walk on machicolations.

Inside on the courtyard side, however, the structure is a comfortable castle residence, opening to friendly gardens. There are some stunning rooms with remarkable windows and finely crafted chimneypieces. Construction lasted two years. In July 1466, Louis XI gave the *château* to his cousin, Dunois, the son of Joan of Arc's companion.

Louis XI died in 1483 and was succeeded by his son Charles VIII who was just 13. When Charles came of age, he wed Anne of Brittany at dawn on December 6, 1491 in one of the great halls of Langeais. As I mentioned when discussing Amboise castle, this marriage finally incorporated the duchy of Brittany into the French kingdom. The castle today actually has a wax tableau of this momentous event—and I practically bumped into it when I was wandering around the castle. (The benefit of seeing Loire castles in November is that there are very few tourists; when I stepped into this room, I was virtually by myself!) Anne's wedding chest is also on display.

After this time, Langeais was given little or no royal attention, since subsequent rulers like François I were busy expanding the royal seat at Amboise and designing Chambord—or embellishing castles like Chenonceau for their mistresses. After the end of the 15th century, the Château de Langeais was owned by various people and underwent little maintenance.

In 1886 Jacques Siegfried, an active businessman and a great lover of Middle Ages art, acquired the castle. He spent nearly twenty years of his life restoring and refurnishing it, thus reconstructing the living environment of the nobility at the end of the Middle Ages. In 1904 he donated the castle and its rich collection to the Institute de France, which is still the proprietor today.

I enjoyed visiting Langeais because it's regally furnished but still raw. The gardens help offset the masculinity of the castle. The royal apartments accurately depict life for the wealthy in the Middle Ages: canopied beds with sumptuous coverlets, polished furniture, and massive tapestries to help warm up the ancient rooms. The guardroom morphed into a handsome dining room with a hand-carved fireplace; places

are set for a royal banquet.

By the way, a French historian came into one of the royal apartments as I was scrutinizing the furnishings. He turned to me and began explaining the room's particulars in rapid-fire French. (He thought I was French.) He seemed so impassioned about his topic that I didn't want to interrupt his train of thought to reveal I spoke mainly English. At the end of his recitation, he bade me farewell and I said goodbye in French. (Sometimes it's wonderful to be taken for a local.)

My other "raw" experience in Langeais was trying to find food on a Sunday afternoon. I knew full well that if I wasn't seated somewhere for lunch before 2 p.m., there would be nothing open. France closes tighter than Tupperware on a Sunday afternoon, friends. Many Francophiles know the French religiously guard their Sunday afternoons with family. These traditional family Sunday events go on for hours. They eat many courses with many wines, take a nap, and then eat some more. (This is one of the reasons I think many shops are closed on Mondays in France—they are recovering from their Sundays!)

It follows, then, that few restaurants are open in France on a Sunday evening except in major cities like Paris or Tours. As such, eateries in a small town like Langeais will be closed, closed, closed by 2:15. Any tourist wandering around for luncheon around 2 p.m. therefore is a complete fool. Unfortunately that day, I was the fool.

At five minutes before 2 p.m., my starving husband and I wandered out of Langeais castle to the bistro across the street. Closed. We moved to the café next door. Closed. We stepped over to the final *pâtisserie* on the teeny street and found the door open. We slid inside and looked over the *patisserie* counter to the inviting empty tables. We begged to be seated. At first the proprietress said no. Then she looked at our faces and took pity on us. She informed us we could sit down for ten minutes or so but then we had to be gone as her family was waiting for her.

I need to explain that she was not being insensitive. She was merely setting French boundaries—something the French are very good about. (They are not a culture that likes to be pushed around—and they will tell you at length about this.) We sat down and quickly asked for anything that was available to eat. She said there was no cooked food left—but she said she could bring us some cheese and a baguette and some French beer. We shouted, "Oui, merci!" She scuttled away and was back in a flash with her meager offerings.

She stood at a discreet distance as we wolfed down the food and gulped the beer. I could tell she was very anxious to leave; by 2:10 we were ready to go. We paid, thanked her for her extraordinary kindness, and slipped back outside. We wandered around Langeais knowing that that was it for food until the next morning.

By 5 p.m., we returned to Le Meulière (which offered only breakfast, not dinner) and retired to our third-floor bedroom, the Balzac suite. We had met Madame Claudine Manier when we first entered, and her English was exceptional! (She so reminded me of my dear mother, who passed away last year, that I liked her at once.)

As we prepared for bed, we could smell the wonderful aroma of chicken roasting. Madame Manier must have been preparing dinner for friends or family. A short time later, I could hear guests arrive. Soon I heard the pop of a champagne cork, then the clinking of champagne glasses. We weren't eavesdropping *per se*—but our suite was just above the salon and dining room—and since we were hungry, our growling stomachs were keeping us awake.

Soon, the aroma of roasted chicken and savory potatoes probably swimming in goose-fat wafted up the staircase as they tucked into dinner. More corks popped. A little later, I thought I smelled the appley goodness of a *tarte Tatin*. We went off to sleep giggling like naughty children with empty stomachs. But I have to say I had a wonderful night's sleep in Madame's hefty guest featherbed.

The next morning, we packed and loaded our bags in the car in preparation for heading over to Villandry. But first, we were more than ready for breakfast! It turned out that we were the only guests who stayed for *petite dejeuner*. I can barely describe the delightful spread Madame had laid out for us when we entered the dining area. She had her finest china and stemware on display. She'd piled fresh brioche and warm baguettes on great French platters; next to them were plates of cheeses and meats, as well as bowls of delicious fruits. In hefty French pitchers, Madame had poured *chocolate au lait* (hot chocolate with milk) and steaming coffee with tiny French carafes of warm and cold milk nearby. Both Madame and her husband joined us for breakfast—a rarity, as far as I can tell, for a *chambre d'hôte*.

And what a wonderful breakfast we had! Soon Madame was passing me her homemade pomegranate and plum jelly and was chatting up a storm in English. (Her husband was a sweetie too, and I kept trying to speak French to him—but he seemed mostly content to watch his wife chatter on.) She was so open and warm. She spent nearly an hour telling us (in excellent English) how she'd been born the eldest of 15 children and how she'd inherited this 15-room *maison* (house) when her parents passed. They'd turned the upper floors into a B&B and were enjoying a fine reputation in the Michelin guide.

She had so much energy for someone in her 70s, and she seemed so happy to talk with us that she even invited us to linger for a few hours more. When we finally arose to be on our way, she handed us a little care package of goodies to take along for the drive. She kissed us goodbye and warmly expressed her wish that we would come back someday to learn more about Cinq-Mars-la-Pile and the Loire. I promised her we would love to return one day.

This is another one of my favorite experiences in France—where the rawness of Loire history assails me wherever I go, but where the warmth of marvelous people makes me want to return again and again. (Just book your Sunday luncheon reservations well in advance!)

Chinon**

A scant eight miles from Sleeping Beauty's castle at Ussé and fifteen miles from Fontevraud Abbey is the ancient city of Chinon. Nestled in the midst of an extraordinary wine district, the royal Château de Chinon hosted not only English kings, French kings, and the Knights Templar, but also a young upstart named Joan of Arc.

Chinon is definitely the stuff of legend. In ancient days, Chinon was the coveted center of the main river trade route between the Poitou and the city of Limoges. Since it sat at a high point along the Vienne River just before it joins the Loire, it was prime real estate. First the Gauls and later the Romans built fortifications on the main hill in Chinon. Chinon was later expanded by the clergy, who constructed a monastery complex, and it was expanded again by Plantagenet royals who saw Chinon as their seat of power.

In the 10th century, Theobald I the Deceiver, Duke of Blois and Lord of Chinon, erected a sturdy fortress on the Roman ruins. Nearly two hundred years later, the fortress passed to Henry Plantagenet, the future Henry II, King of England. Henry loved Chinon—it was his original home and his wellspring of power.

Henry was of course a "Frenchman" by birth, but he became an "English" king by primogeniture (the passage of a crown to the next available male). As such, he ruled from both England and the Loire, since at this time English might dominated much of Northern France, including the Loire. (*Psychological note:* Henry had to fight his younger brother Geoffrey for rights to the throne. It shouldn't have been a surprise when Henry's own sons fought him *and* each other for the right to rule once they were grown. We call this "multigenerational transfer" in family systems therapy. In modern speak it means, "What Dad does, the kids most likely will do." Henry's family squabbles plagued him all of his life. Parents, take note.)

King Henry extended the fortress beginning in 1156 and crafted a splendid royal Chinon citadel. He made it his administrative center during his 35-year rule—and it was always his favorite residence. During his lifetime, Henry fought off his ambitious sons and his wily wife, Eleanor. Exhausted, Henry finally expired at Chinon in 1189.

Upon his death, Chinon passed to Richard the Lionheart and then to John Lackland, who lost it to French King Phillip II Augustus in 1205. From that point forward, Chinon became part of the royal duchy of Touraine. Unfortunately, the French kings occupied the residence only intermittently. (As you've already read, they preferred Amboise and elsewhere.) The castle served as a prison when Philip IV the Fair ordered the Knights Templar arrested in 1307. They were eventually executed.

Chinon played a critical role during the Hundred Years' War (1337–1453) between the French and the English who sought to "reclaim" their land. The young French Dauphin Charles, who was heir to the French throne though disinherited by his father, relocated in Chinon in 1425 with his small court after being pushed out of Paris by the Burgundians. The Burgundians were allied with the English to take over the French crown. (You can see why even today England and France have a love-hate relationship.)

The Touraine province supported Charles's efforts, however. While the shaken Dauphin contemplated his chances of subduing the Burgundian forces, he was visited at Chinon on March 8, 1429 by a 17-year-old girl with a divine mission. Her name was Joan of Arc, "The Maid of Orléans." *Jeanne d'Arc* (in French) claimed to be an instrument of God sent to help him, directed by the Angelic voices of the Archangel Michael and Saint Catherine.

Escorted by six men-at-arms, Joan traveled from Lorraine to Chinon to ask Charles to supply her with troops to break the English siege at Orléans. Despite the armed gangs roaming the countryside, she met no resistance—and many whispered this was a sign of her divine protection. She spent two nights at an inn in the lower Chinon, fasting and praying before her audience with the Dauphin.

But Charles didn't make it easy for her. He wanted her to prove her God-given powers. So he lit 50 torches in the great Chinon castle hall and assembled 300 courtiers dressed in fancy dress. He disguised himself as one of his courtiers, put one of the courtiers in his own royal garb, and then the Dauphin stood in the crowd. Joan entered and promptly walked past the royal imposter to Charles. She bowed low and embraced his knees, exclaiming, "The King of Heaven sends word by me that you will be anointed and crowned in the city of Reims, and you will be Lieutenant of the King of Heaven, who is the King of France."

After a private conversation with Joan, who also revealed many secrets known only to the king, he was convinced of her mission and gained strength. Yet, she went through an additional tribunal with experts who peppered her with questions until they deemed she was legitimate. Ultimately Joan secured arms, men, and able commanders. She returned to Orléans and routed the English in a few days. Singledhandedly, Joan had turned the Anglo-French conflict into a mighty religious war.

Charles was finally crowned king at Reims Cathedral (the traditional crowning venue) in 1429. The Burgundians ultimately captured young Joan in 1430 and then cheerfully handed her over to the English. She was tried and then burned at the stake on May 30, 1431. She was only 19 years old. But her name lives on—while young Charles VII's legacy has mostly faded in French history. In 1803 Napoleon Bonaparte declared Joan a national symbol of France. She was beatified in 1909 and canonized in 1920.

As king, Charles occupied Chinon for a time, but gradually the castle fell into disuse. Much of the stone was used for other projects—especially by Cardinal Richelieu (of Musketeers fame) who confiscated much of the building material to build his namesake city of Richelieu about 10 miles away.

At the end of the 15th century, Chinon was the birthplace of the writer and humanist François Rabelais. His works, including his racy, satirical novels about two giants, Gargantua and Pantagruel, are part of some of the most prized works of French literature.

Apart from townhouses and convents that were built on the banks of the river and around the ruins, Chinon changed little up to the Revolution. But the vineyards grew at a mighty pace. In the 1820s, the old fortifications were pulled down, and the banks of the Vienne River were opened up to the outside. Chinon spread out in the late 19th and 20th centuries to both sides of the River Vienne. In 1968

Chinon was registered as a conservation area and has been undergoing restoration in order to respect and preserve its historic and architectural identity.

Most important to today's wine connoisseurs, Chinon is the wine haven of some of the most famous AOC appellations in France. As my friend André says, "It's hard not to like the sharp, dry Chinons with their hint of strawberry. Goes with everything!" Wine cellars are carved into the banks of the Vienne River all around Chinon. These make for wonderful wine visits to sample the delicious Cabernet-Franc vintages. By the way, you'll find far fewer tourists in this pretty town, since the castle isn't on the top-ten list. However, if you love wine, you'll relish the uncrowded streets, plentiful wines, and excellent edibles.

Your visit to Chinon (which can be done on foot in a day) most likely starts with the 2000-year-old *château*. It consists of three castles separated by moats. The middle castle, or Château du Milieu, has an interesting 14th century clock tower. West of the gardens, another moat bridge leads to the Fort du Coudray, which is situated on the spur of a rock and offers spectacular views. Its Keep housed the imprisoned Templars; you can see their carved graffiti on the north wall. The Tour de l'Horloge details the dramatic life of Joan of Arc.

The Royal Apartments sit above the great hall on the first floor, where Joan picked out the Dauphin in the crowd. Only the fireplace and west wall remain, unfortunately. The guardroom on the ground floor displays a large model of the castle. In the summer months, this very royal center taps into its kingly past and presents a royal light show around King Arthur. See http://www.forteressechinon.fr. (*Trivia note:* Chinon castle is the setting of the *Lion in Winter* movie based on Henry and Eleanor's conflicted marriage. But because Chinon lay in rubble in the 1960s when the film was being made, stand-in locations included the Abbey de Montmajour in Arles France, Pembroke Castle in Wales, and Château de Tascon in Rhone Valley France.)

La vieille ville (the old town) is sandwiched between the *château* on top of the hill and the river Vienne. The charming streets, which run parallel to the river, are lined with pointy-roofed manor houses and medieval half-timbered buildings with stone gables and sculpted doorways. Many date back to the 1400s.

The main street at Rue Voltaire is cobbled and lined with houses, shops, and restaurants in the beautiful old buildings. In fact, there are nearly twenty streets of medieval wood frame houses in the pedestrianized part of the old town. On Rue Jeanne-d-Arc, a plaque marks the well where Joan of Arc dismounted her horse to go and meet the Dauphin.

Hidden at the end of a cobbled alleyway off Rue Voltaire lie the Caves Painctes (Painted Cellars). These former quarries were converted into wine cellars during the 15th century and were written about by Rabelais. A brotherhood of local winegrowers dedicated to the Rabelais and the "Sacred Bottle" runs tours in summertime. This group meets four times a year, by the way, to celebrate Rabelais's humanism as well as the divine Chinon wines. (Nothing beats reading the French classics by firelight while sipping a great Cab.)

Don't miss the extraordinary Caves de Pierre Plouzeau. These wine cellars stretch for more than a hundred yards under Chinon castle and are wide enough for a car to drive through. The 150,000 Chinon wine bottles stored here take up only a fraction of the space. You can taste, buy some bottles, or both.

Chapelle Sainte-Radegonde is half built into the rock-face just outside the town. An underground natural spring at the back of this lovely chapel was a site of pagan worship, which became Christian in the 6th century. Behind the 12th century frescoed chapel are ancient hermit caves (now displaying traditional crafts.) The chapel contains two exceptional naves, one carved directly out of the rock. Don't miss the colorful paintings, including the "Royal Hunt" that depicts five riders, two with crowns; it's said the painting shows members of the Plantagenet family at "play." The churches of Saint Maurice and Saint Etienne both have some wonderful vaulted Gothic ceilings similar to Sainte-Chapelle in Paris. The Romanesque monastery of Saint-Mexme is Chinon's oldest building.

If you like shopping you won't find any large stores in Chinon. However charming boutiques are dotted around Place Victoire and the pedestrianized Rue du Commerce. Try the wine jam—it's particularly good on a baguette!

Other points of interest are the Musée du Vieux Chinon (Chinon History Museum) and the Maison de la Rivière (river museum). The Musée Animee du Vin et de la Tonnellerie has a dozen mechanical dolls depicting the ancient wine-making art from start to finish. The Jardin Anglais nearby is a breath of fresh air; it's amusing to see flourishing plants and palm trees like you'd see in California or the Bahamas—a testament to Loire's balmy climate

Chinon is a hotbed of festivals and events. April hosts the Salon des Vins (wine fair), and in late June and August are the horse races. In summer there's the Festival of Musical

Comedy. A yearly "medieval market" features characters in period dress and gives shoppers a chance to experience a true "Renaissance" extravaganza. The state forests outside Chinon and Loches offers acres of beautiful countryside in which to camp, picnic, hike, or laze the day away. See the Chinon Tourist Office for more details and information. http://chinon-valdeloire.com

A few miles from Chinon proper is La Devinière. Here, Rebalais' homestead has been turned into a museum. Rabelais is much loved in France as a true Renaissance man and searing farcist. He was born to a lawyer, and then studied to become a monk. During his studious childhood he fell in love with Ancient Greek and humanism. He transferred to the secular clergy, studied medicine at Montpellier, and became a famous doctor. By 1532, his bawdy side had emerged and he became a much-loved satirist who elevated the common man and regularly harangued the elites.

You may enjoy a visit to Château du Rivau nearby, a quirky addition to the list of should-see Loire *châteaux*. Owner Patricia Laigneau has created a fantasyland of gardens and castle fun for young and old alike. Rivau has a several unique offerings: famous stables, fourteen fantastical gardens, and a castle peppered with mythical characters and storybook creatures. The stables once supplied stallions not only to the royals but to Joan of Arc, who picked up a few steeds for her army. The beautifully restored castle (with a stag's head in a queen's costume and teddy-bear-festooned hunting heads) overlooks the many gardens.

The gardens themselves are a wonderland of giant-sized produce and extraordinary flowers interwoven with fanciful art. Rivau maintains its link to Rabelais's *Gargantua* where he wrote about the gentle giant offering Château du Rivau as a reward to the valiant captain Tolmère. The motif that a giant lives here appears particularly in the enormous, multi-hued pumpkins, squash, cabbage, lettuces, artichokes, and

outsized gardening tools. I particularly like the giant's huge gardening boots.
www.loire-castle-rivau.com

Around the Chinon countryside, you'll have the extraordinary chance to drop in on some of the finest Cabernet Franc and Cabernet Sauvignon wine estates. You can visit their wine consortiums in Chinon or stop in at such estates at Charles Joguet, Baudry-Dutour, Domaine de la Chevalerie, Couly-Dutheil, or several others. (Call for reservations first.)

Finally, a few miles north of Chinon proper, is the much-revered wine haven of Bourgueil. Bourgueil is one of those famous little villages that produce some of the most famous wine in France.

As I explained in the wine section, Bourgueil produces superb violet-scented wines with a hint of strawberry and slightly more tannins than what is produced in neighboring Chinon. While you are in Bourgueil, try the local specialty, *La Galette Bourgueilloise,* a divine vanilla custard-filled *brioche* that is a little bit of heaven in your mouth. It was created by Monsieur Anceline, owner of the Bourgueilloise *Pâtisserie,* and this is the only place where these heavenly *brioche* can be purchased.

Chinon Accommodations

Hôtel Agnès Sorel. This charming, homey hotel with ten rooms is located not far from the town center on the banks of the river. It has no restaurant, but picnic lunches are available, plus bikes for hire. www.agnes-sorel.com

Hôtel Diderot is a beautiful 15th century building filled with quirky furniture and antiques. It has a lovely garden for enjoying an apéritif. The hotel offers yummy breakfasts and is within walking distance of several popular Chinon eateries. www.hoteldiderot.com

Chinon Dining & Wine Bars

Auberge de la Route d'Or is a darling *auberge* serving local produce. http://www.tables-auberges.com

Restaurant l'Océanic is a highly regarded eatery specializing in seafood and other Chinon specialties and wines. http://www.loceanic-chinon.com

Diane de Méridor offers gourmet French food in a rustic setting in nearby Montsoreau. Delightfully different. http://diane-de-meridor-restaurant.zenchef.com

La Crémaillère. This is an unusual long, narrow restaurant in town. (No website.)

La Maison Rouge is a half-timbered eatery located in the medieval quarter. http://fr.maisonrouge-chinon.com

Les Années Trente offers *chambres d'hôtes* accommodations and enjoyable and delicious food on Rue Voltaire. http://lesannees30.com

Overall, a visit to the Touraine area is a memory-making experience from border to border. Added to the magnificent *châteaux* strung out along the Loire and its tributaries, the scintillating history and fertile offerings make this a Loire domain not to be missed.

CHAPTER EIGHT

Orléanais and Blésois

(Orléans, Blois, Vendôme, Chambord, Chaumont, Cheverny, and Sully-sur-Loire)

The two closely linked regions [of Orléanais and Blésois] are excellent starting points for an exploration of the central Loire Valley. The area's forests and marshlands have attracted nature lovers for centuries. During the Renaissance, magnificent hunting lodges were built by kings and nobles throughout the area, including the great Chambord, the sumptuously furnished Cheverny and the charming Beauregard.

—*Eyewitness Travel: Loire Valley*, Duncan Baird
Publishers/DK Publishing

Orléans and Blésois (the Blois region) are some of the most illustrious parts of the Loire Valley. They are monarchial and historic, yet some of the wildest parts of the valley. Horticulture predominates; a proliferation of greenhouses dots the land. Orchards and vineyards flourish on the southernmost slopes. The thick Orléans forest teems with rabbits and hares, deer and wild boar. The mysterious Sologne is a secretive expanse of small villages and brick farmhouses nestled on shrubby heaths and marshy lakes (*étangs*). The Sologne is a hunters' and fishermen's paradise. To the west is the Petite Beauce, the "granary of France," where wheat fields spread for miles. And at its most southern point flows the pretty River Cher, burbling through dreamy villages on its way west to exotic places like Chenonceau and Chambord (photographed here by Christy Destremau).

Yet the northern stretch of the Loire spills through strategic towns like Orléans and Blois, whose pivotal bridge points made them military, political, and commercial darlings. It was at Orléans where teenager Joan of Arc lifted the English siege in 1429, galvanizing the spirit of the French army. Blois's royal *château* served as a regal hub for several monarchs, but sank into political intrigue; today it's a busy bedroom community on the Loire. In the western section, the smaller River Loir (no *e*) tributary flows through the gothic town of Vendôme. Vendôme is home to one of the finest cathedrals in the area, La Trinité.

And scattered across the region are some of the most famous *châteaux* of France: Chambord, the greatest castle in the Loire; Chaumont, the comely stronghold with the valley's famous Garden Festival; Cheverny, the symmetrical *château* with world-famous hounds and a link to cartoon character Tintin; and Sully, the seigneurial residence with fine tapestries and 17th century furnishings.

The Orléanais and Blésois area is one often traveled by those who want an adventurous experience coupled with a few prestigious castle visits. It's rugged, grandiose, and famed for treachery; but it's also notable for divine courage, then and now. Joan of Arc saved a nation here. François I built a massive legacy. The Wars of Religion tested the faith of many.

Yet, 600 years later after the political *sturm und drang* dissipated, this rugged area beguiles— especially for the locals who, in my opinion, underplay its beauties so they can keep it to themselves!

Orléans and Blésois have less sheen and more raw power than the Touraine and Anjou enclaves. Things are bigger here. Life is chewy, flavorful, aromatic. The smell of the hounds and the scent of the earth and the damp of the oak-tinged waters linger in the air and wines. Visions of François on the hunt flit through your daydreams—especially as you stand atop mighty Chambord. Joan and her divine angels hover in the shadows. Yet the cacophony of modern commerce at Orléans, less than an hour from Paris, reminds you that royal testosterone fertilized this land—but it's the modern heartbeat of today's commoners that propagate it now.

In this region, power rumbles under your feet. You can lay your hand on 600-year-old stone that whispers many stories. You can climb the turrets for a king's eye view of the Loire. A visit to Orléans and Blésois is simply an adventure through some of the most untamed, yet civilized areas of the Loire. It's here where Paris-west spreads out as a burgeoning enclave for students, nature lovers, industrialists, techno wizards, and castle fans. Thus I am happy to share my favorites in this seminal area: 1–Orléans, Joan of Arc enclave now high-tech ready; 2–Blois, residence of multiple kings; 3–Vendôme, a city among the islands; 4–Château de Chambord, the largest *château* of them all; 5–Château Chaumont-sur-Loire, grand estate and International Garden Festival home; 6–Château de Cheverny, a classical French castle with famous hounds; and 7–Château de Sully-sur-Loire, the castle-fort.

We'll explore this diverse collection of towns and castles in the pages to follow. I trust you too will be mesmerized by this earthy land of history and heart.

Orléans*

> At an age when most of us were baby-sitting or bagging groceries for minimum wage, 17-year-old Joan of Arc was donning armor and helping to defend the city of Orléans, France, from invading British armies....But don't think that Orléans is stuck in the past. The warren of cobbled streets and half-timbered houses there holds everything from upstart wine bars to a new Michelin-starred restaurant to alternative night life. And it's all an easy one-hour train ride from Paris.
> —Seth Sherwood, "36 Hours in Orléans, France,"
> *The New York Times*

The Joan of Arc connection is certainly a highlight of this strategic town within minutes of Paris. Since Orléans sits at the most northerly point of the Loire River, warring factions prized the municipality as the epicenter of the ancient Loire Valley.

Orléans, "the city of roses," began as a stronghold for the Celts, then became a Druid assembly locale. Still later it served as a mighty Roman nerve center under Emperor Aurelian, who named it after himself. "Aurelian" naturally morphed into the French word *Orléans*. Attila the Hun even besieged the valuable city without success.

The Merovingians used Orléans as their capital, and the Capetians later used it as the center of their Valois-Orléans duchy in the 1100s. During the Middle Ages, few bridges existed over the treacherous waterways of France; thus Orléans, Rouen, and Paris became France's most coveted cities as gateways and transportation pivot points.

It was at Orléans' Royal Bridge (Pont George V) that Joan of Arc (shown above by Christy Destremau) broke the siege of the English Plantagenets in 1429 during the Hundred Years' War. Her valor set France on a path to self-determination that still exists today. She is revered here as *La pucelle d'Orléans* (the Maid of Orléans); every May the city pays homage to her in great parades and festivals.

From 1453 to 1699, Orléans recovered its prosperity. The mighty bridges across the River Loire brought in tolls and taxes, and merchants thrived on the busy Orléans streets. In the mid 1470s, King Louis XI greatly contributed to its economy, revitalizing agriculture in the surrounding area (particularly within the exceptionally fertile land around Beauce) and by relaunching saffron farming at Pithiviers. Later, during the Renaissance, the city benefited when it became fashionable for rich *châtelaines* (castle commanders) to travel to along the Loire Valley—a fashion begun by François I himself.

The University of Orléans contributed to the city's prestige. Specializing in law, it was highly regarded throughout Europe. John Calvin was received and accommodated here; he wrote part of his reforming theses during his stay. In return, Henry VIII of England, who'd relied on Calvin's work in his separation from Rome, offered to fund a scholarship at the university. Many other Protestants were sheltered by the city. Jean-Baptiste Poquelin, better known by his pseudonym Molière, studied law at the University; he was expelled for frivolity, however, for attending a carnival contrary to university rules.

From the 1700 to the early 1900s the French colonization of America evolved. France's American territory spanned the entire breadth of the Mississippi River from its mouth to its source in Canada. The busy capital at the southern end was called La Nouvelle-Orléans (New Orléans) in honor of Louis XV's regent, the Duke of Orléans. France settled the French military (and later their families) here to forestall the threat of the British incursion into the American northeast. The French dukes seldom visited their city on the Mississippi, however, since they were required at court. The duchy of Orléans was the largest of all the French duchies at this time. In 1870 Orléans became strategic once again, when the Prussians occupied it that year.

During World War II, the German army made the Orléans railway station one of its central rail hubs. The Germans also built a transit camp for deportees at Beaune-la-Rolande nearby. The American Air Force heavily bombed the station and the city, and many historic buildings were unfortunately destroyed. Luckily, the city was one of the first to rebuild after the war. The restored old quarter is now a delight to visit.

Since it lies only an hour by TGV train to Paris, today's Orléans of around 250,000 people attracts big business and industry that want to reduce Paris-area real estate costs. Modern trams (photo by France Off the Beaten Path Tours) thread through the city neighborhoods, old and new. Auto routes zip around and through handy Orléans to many destinations. It's also a popular university town, as well as an important regional administrative center.

I can attest to the fact that there's much to enchant visitors in Orléans. Start off with a visit to the tourist office near Rue Jeanne d'Arc, however. They'll provide an itinerary for the main sites of interest.

You'll notice there's a sense of timelessness about Orléans. It has ancient as well as modern relevance. Some of the key points of historical interest for visitors, however, include the following locales. The Maison Jeanne d'Arc is the re-creation of Joan of Arc's house on Place General-de-Gaulle. Joan's house is a fascinating family visit, but explain the history to your children first so they can get oriented. (The original house, on the same site, was destroyed in World War II.) Touch-screen computers and a short film recount her birth in Dorémy, as well as her teenage visions from God directing her to fight against the English. The film details her victorious campaign in Orléans in 1429, the failed campaign to retake Paris, and ultimately her capture, trial, and martyrdom.

http://jeannedarc.com.fr

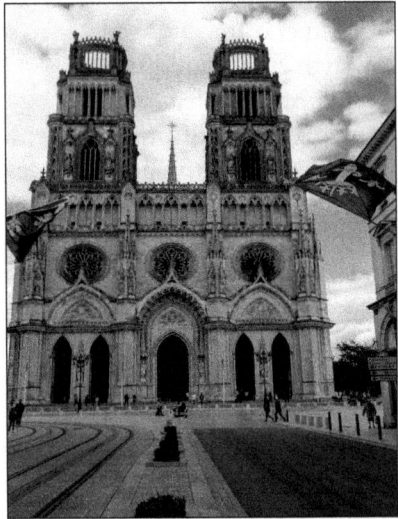

Later you can stroll to the monumental Cathédrale Ste.-Croix d'Orléans (snapped by France off the Beaten Path Tours), where Joan of Arc prayed during the Orléans campaign. The circular towers are popularly likened to a wedding cake decoration. The cathedral is quite light and airy, both within and without, compared to other French cathedrals. The soaring neo-Gothic cathedral features stained-glass windows showing scenes from Joan's life.

Place du Martroi is the busy central plaza that acts as the social crossroads of the town. On Friday evenings the open market (with its monumental 19th century statue of Joan of Arc in the middle) is crammed with dozens of stalls selling everything from pungent cheese to socks. Nearby is the Rue Royale shopping street with its elegant arcades; handsome

18th and 19th century *façades* front the private buildings and museums. This stately avenue leads down to the river at the Royal Bridge (Pont George V). On the other side of the bridge is the Quai Fort-des-Tourelles square. Here you'll spy a commemorative cross that marks the spot where Joan and her forces captured enemy combatants, which lead to the defeat of the English. Quai du Châtalet provides a serene walk along the river.

Rue de Bourgogne is the grand Orléans shopping street. It's lined with arresting antique stores like Antiquité de la Préfecture and Patrick Lidon. But there's plenty of other shopping too for comestibles, clothing, shoes, and souvenirs. You'll find a surprising ethnic diversity among the eateries; the wine bars are quite fun too.

At the Musée des Beaux-Arts d'Orléans, you can head directly to the top floor, where you'll see Italian Renaissance masterpieces by Correggio, Tintoretto, and Veronese. The lower level is home to some Gauguin work (he grew up partly in Orléans before he set sail for Tahiti). Additionally there are some quirky pieces like Jean Hélion's still life of two Pop Art umbrellas on a stool. In the Lower Mezzanine, a vaulted red salon with 19th-century academic paintings stacked to the roof houses William Etty's 1846 canvas of an armored figure in a plumed helmet riding a white horse. Yes, it's that heroine of France, Joan of Arc.

Don't miss the covered stall market at Les Halles-Châtelet on Place du Châtelet. A plethora of eateries beckon nearby. But for pure serenity, take a 20-minute ride on Tram Line A from Place du Général de Gaulle to Parc Floral de la Source. This is an idyllic green space unfolding over 86 acres. The grand park is home to everything from a 950-species iris garden to Le Jardin des Formes with trees trimmed into unusual shapes. See the fantastic butterfly house, where exotic species come from as far away as Indonesia and Madagascar. http://www.parcfloraldelasource.com

From the end of April to the first week in May, the city celebrates the anniversary of the liberation of Orléans by Joan of Arc. This is a multi-week extravaganza that includes a medieval festival and market, concerts, exhibitions, sound and light displays, and various processions commencing with "Joan" entering the city through the Port de Bourgogne. Here's an interesting factoid by the way: There are an estimated 40,000 statues of Joan of Arc throughout France. Yes, *40,000!*

But if you're a jazz lover, the Orléans Jazz Festival is your ticket to music heaven. This popular jazz fest hails the start of summer with concerts at venues across the city. For full program details, check the festival website. http://jazzorjazz.fr By the way, you may be interested in how jazz got started in France. Here's a nice recap:

The love affair of France and jazz is a long one, dating back to World War I. Black musicians came as soldiers to fight in France and brought their new music to a Europe where dance music was still pretty staid. At first it was thought too American... but the popularity of the music spread. The 1920s saw musicians like Sidney Bechet then Archie Shepp settling permanently in France. In 1934 the Quinetette du Hot Club de France, one of the greatest and most influential jazz groups was formed, with Django Reinhardt as the principal guitarist. Very soon France was jazz crazy.

The first jazz festival in France was in Nice in 1948 with Louis Armstrong as the headline act. Today you'll find jazz festivals all over France, from small villages to large cities. It's a roll call of the great and the good and during the summer months, the top jazz players make their way around France.

—*http://gofrance.about.com*

Orléans Accommodations

Hôtel de l'Abeille offers Old World charm in 30 antiques-filled rooms inside an early-20th-century grand house. The ground floor salon, done up like an English drawing room, serves teas and refreshments, while the top-floor garden offers rooftop views. www.hoteldelabeille.com

Hôtel d'Orléans is business oriented but handy to downtown attractions. www.hoteldOrleans.com

Hôtel Archange is located mere steps from the train station and the city's historical core. Rooms are done in fun colors with kitsch and Pop Art touches. http://hotelarchange.com

Hôtel des Cèdres affords a quiet location and has a pretty breakfast veranda. http://www.hotelcedresorleans.com

Le Lièvre Gourmand is a town-house restaurant that serves French, Asian, and fusion courses. Since Chef William Page is Australian, he's sometimes known to whip up roasted kangaroo. It's a good idea to book ahead. http://lelievregourmand.com/en/

Chez Jules, with its quaint *décor*, has top-notch traditional cuisine and an agreeable bargain three-course lunch. http://chezjulesorleans.fr

La Parenthèse. Here, youthful Chef David Sterne turns fresh produce into old-fashioned, family-style French cuisine. Book well ahead. http://www.restaurant-la-parenthese.com

La Dariole offers French cuisine and delicious specialties, including beef simmered in sauce *Bourguignonne* (Burgundy-style red-wine sauce) and desserts such as rum-flambéed-and-caramelized pineapple with vanilla butter and coconut ice cream. There is no website, but see Michelin for information. http://www.viamichelin.com

Le Lift is where a white horse sculpture sits atop a long table in the glass-and-steel dining room, setting the stage for a quirky dining experience. Le Lift offers a modern take on international cuisine. The Angus beef dish is quite a production. http://www.restaurant-le-lift.com

Blois**

> In the heart of the French region of Centre-Val de Loire, not far from Paris…Blois is the gateway to the kingdom of castles. Here, between the Cher and the Loire, stand some of the most elegant Renaissance buildings in the world, in such abundance that their grace and beauty are almost overwhelming.
> —*The Green Guide: Châteaux of the Loire*

Blois is steeped in history as a locus of intrigue and royal incubation. In the Middle Ages, the counts of Blois were powerful lords with two key estates: Champagne to the east and Blois/Chartres. One of the counts of Blois married the daughter of William the Conqueror; their son, Stephen, became King of England in 1135. Under Stephen's son, Theobald the Great, Blois reached its zenith. After Theobald's death, the family concentrated their efforts on Champagne and abandoned Blois (and England) to the Plantagenets in 1154. (If you are keeping track of all of this history, you'll recall that as King of England Plantagenet Henry II shifted the Loire power base to Chinon.)

In 1392, the last count sold the county to Louis, Duke of Orléans and brother of Charles VI, King of France. Louis was assassinated in Paris in 1407, and his son, Charles d'Orléans, inherited. Charles, the "aristocratic poet," spent some of his youth at Blois but was later imprisoned in England for 25 years after his capture at Agincourt. He wrote copious amounts of poetry to pass the time. When he finally returned to France in 1440, he married Marie de Cleves and lived at Blois.

In 1462, Louis XII was born at Blois, and it became the main Loire royal seat rather than Amboise through the time of François I. François became king when popular Louis XII, "the father of the people," died without an heir. François expanded Amboise considerably, as I mentioned previously, but he liked to go back and forth between Amboise and his more intimate Blois. The royal *château* at Blois is therefore less expanded than other sights, since François had his hands full with Renaissance redos or expansions at Amboise, Chambord, the Louvre, and Fontainebleau.

However, François wasn't content to just hunt and erect. He felt he was a language savant as well. Christy Destremau offers up this tidbit: "Blois castle is where François I wrote the first 29 pages of the language we know today as French (Français). François called it after himself when he created it, *naturalment*. He then passed the 192-page Ordinance of Villers-Cotterêts in 1539. This legislation required the new language 'François' to be implemented across the kingdom, particularly for all legal acts, notarized contracts, and official legislation. This meant the discontinuation of Latin in official documents. Hence we're speaking French, not Latin."

Blois continued as a royal hotbed after Francois's demise. It acted as the royal seat of court for his son, Henri II, and later Catherine de' Médici (Henri's wife) and their sons when they were not in Paris at the Louvre palace. Their son Henri III drew up the first code of etiquette here; he also introduced the title "His Majesty," taken from the Roman Emperors. (The linguistic gene didn't fall far from the apple tree with regard to coining regal words.)

Blois palace had to have plenty of room for the royal retinue, of course. Henry's queen and her mother had, between them, over a hundred ladies-in-waiting! Catherine acquired a "Flying Squad" of pretty girls who spied for her and assisted with her intrigues. More than a hundred pages acted as messengers to the king, in addition to dozens of servants, over fifty clerks, twenty-three doctors, and fifty chambermaids. The King's suite accommodated two hundred gentlemen-in-waiting and more than a thousand archers and Swiss guards. Thus, even from François I's time, the royal entourage numbered about fifteen thousand people. And when the court was on the move to yet another palace, twelve thousand horses and hundreds of carts and wagons were needed to move this massive clump of French humanity with all their home furnishings and royal duds. Once the royals moved away from the Loire, Blois became a busy market town.

During the 18th century, the castle slowly deteriorated, as maintenance had become too costly and the royals favored Versailles. In 1788, Louis XVI put the Blois estate up for sale. Sadly there were no buyers; the Comtois Royal Regiment (king's infantry) subsequently set up their quarters on the premises. While the military men's work caused some further deterioration (not to mention the infusion of sweat, boot black, and horse excrement), they concurrently maintained the castle and pursued renovation of the classical wing.

In 1810 the buildings reverted to the town of Blois, but they were still occupied by the army. The François I wing was restored in 1845 from designs by Félix Duban; a museum was installed therein. In 1867 Blois castle was the first historical monument outside Paris to be restored for the French state. It then served as a restoration model for others.

During World War II, Blois was occupied by the German army, which took the city on June 18, 1940. American soldiers finally liberated Blois during the last two weeks of August 1944. On both occasions, the city withstood several days of intense bombing. France again set out to restore the *château*, particularly to refurbish the 19th century restoration colors, flooring, and *façades*.

In present day, riverside Blois is an active municipality capped by the grand *château* at the top of a graceful crest. The castle—the best in-town *château* in the valley—is pitched on a tree-shaded esplanade that was once the farmyard of the *château*. Slightly below the castle itself are peaceful terraced gardens that offer a serene view of the bridge spanning the Loire beyond the rooftops. To the right you can see the spires of the church of Saint Nicholas, as well as the huge Cathedral with its Renaissance tower to the left.

Upon entering the *château* grounds, you'll find that the vast Royal Château of Blois is an intricate structure ringing a pleasantly expansive courtyard. It has many arresting elements since it was remodeled frequently between the 13th to the 17th centuries. The *façade*, described by author Henry James as "one of the most beautiful and elaborate of all the royal residences in this part

of France," is rife with architectural detail.

Blois castle's architectural wealth is an echo of the diversity of all of the different *châteaux* built in the Loire Valley from the Middle Ages to the 17th century. Notably, its wings are built in four different styles. Around the courtyard, dominated by the majestic François I staircase, a whole range of French architecture is represented, from Gothic and Renaissance styles to Classicism. The style of open-air staircase, by the way, is unique in the valley. This tour-de-force stairway is enclosed in an octagonal well and has intricate carvings throughout. It allowed the royals to watch the proceedings in the courtyard from its open balconies.

In 1845, the Château de Blois became the first of these historic residences to be restored; it served as a model for the restoration of numerous other Loire castles thereafter. The Flamboyant style gateway is particularly interesting, as it's surmounted by an alcove containing an equestrian statue of Louis XII. The window consoles are adorned with carvings.

As a residence of seven kings and ten queens of France, the *château* interior invokes regal grandeur, as well as daily life in a Renaissance court. This is evident from the royal apartments that are furnished and embellished with magnificent polychrome decorations. It's one of the most well-maintained royal abodes in the Loire, with beautifully authentic furnishings—absolutely a must-see visit. Additionally, since the castle was built in four discrete sections, visitors can see the architectural evolution from one century to the next. You'll note two main royal crests: the crowned salamander, emblem of François I, and the royal porcupine, crest of Louis XII.

Many of the rooms or wings have historical significance as settings for royal intrigue. For example, the queen's chamber is where Catherine de' Médici passed away in 1589. The *Studiolo* was set up by François I as a traditional Italian study dedicated to reading, poetry, medication (sometimes poisons), and collections. The *décor* consists of 180 sculpted, painted and gilded oak panels that dissimulate four small cabinets, often with concealed doors, which contained small artifacts or, it's whispered, where Catherine de'Médici kept her potions and jewels. (The cabinets could only be opened by pressing a lever concealed in the skirting board.)

The King's Chamber on the second floor was where Henri III surrounded himself with effeminate men and limited access to most everyone else. It was here in this room that, on orders of Henri III (with his mother's blessing), the Catholic Duke of Guise was assassinated. This assassination took place after the Duke had spent the night with one of Catherine de' Médici's ladies in waiting, who was doing double duty as a spy.

After the Duke of Guise, a potential usurper of the throne, had entered a narrow passageway on his way to see the king, twenty of the king's guards descended on the unwitting Duke with swords ready. Twelve hacked at the poor man from inside the King's Old Cabinet room. When the Duke turned to retreat, eight more assassins were ready for him from the King's Chamber. An exceptionally strong man, the Duke of Guise apparently put up quite a struggle (and wounded five of his assailants). He fought the entire length of the Kings Chamber until he collapsed right next to the King's bed. Henri III then popped out from behind a curtain where he'd been lurking. He cautiously bent over the dead Duke. He then slapped him to be sure he was dead. The King murmured, "He's such a large man… even in death!" Henri then raced down to his mother, Catherine de' Médici, and exclaimed gleefully, "My comrade is no more, the King of Paris is dead!" Conscience clear, he went on to mass.

This same cadre of assassins also murdered the Duke of Guise's brother Louis II the next day. Callous Henri III, however, didn't live long to enjoy his triumph. He himself was assassinated one year later in Paris by rabid Catholic Jacques Clément, who sought revenge.

At the end of the François I wing, I find the huge Salle des Etats-Généraux particularly fascinating; it was the original meeting place of the medieval French Parliament and survives from the original fortress. Later it served as the gym for the army billeted here. However, today it's as cavernous as any modern ballroom—but with handsome floors, walls, and pillars. If you have time, also visit the Musée Archeologique located in the *château* kitchens.

Elsewhere in the castle, there's a spectacular collection of 35,000 works of art, including sculpture, portraits, friezes, gargoyles, and tapestries. They're presented in the Royal Apartments in the François I wing, the Fine Arts Museum (Musée des Beaux-Arts) housed in the Louis XII wing, and also in temporary exhibitions housed along the tour route. This is one of the best collections outside the Louvre in Paris. The nighttime sound and light shows are especially good, since the courtyard setting offers a 360-degree "screen" to project the images—plus there are spectacular acoustics! http://chateaudeblois.fr

Blois as a town is quite vivacious. From across the river, the elegant buildings in pale and dark gray step up in pleasant terraces to the grand *château* at the top. Since there are varying levels of elevation in the town, I find it quite charming to wander the streets that seem both modern and old. (I once saw a bridal party screeching through downtown Blois in top-down sports cars with their horns blaring; it was a comical contrast between ancient and modern Blois, like something out of a movie. I could imagine James Bond lurking nearby.)

The cute boutiques and street markets, traffic-free streets, and flower-bordered stairways make this a charming place to stay. And the handy pavement *cafés* and tasty restaurants make this a keen locale for overnighting, then touring Chambord, Amboise, Cheverny, and Chaumont. There's train access as well.

If you stay in Blois, you'll have many reasonably priced accommodations to choose from. Along the streets are dozens of delightful *brasseries* and *bistros* for your dining pleasure within walking distance. I highly recommend Rue du Commerce, the main shopping street. The thrice-weekly street markets are fantastic. The produce is gorgeous—and the people hawking them are priceless!

There's even more quirkiness and fun. For example, the Maison de la Magie situated opposite the Château de Blois takes visitors on a surprising voyage through the universe of the famous Blois conjurer, Jean-Eugène Robert Houdin. (Yes, American-reared magician Erik Weisz borrowed his name and added an *i* when he became known as "Harry Houdini.") The fun starts even before you enter! As I stepped toward the building one morning, these dinosaur-like beauties suddenly popped out at me from the windows. Inside is the fascinating magic museum the whole family will enjoy. The underground Théâtre des Magiciens stages family-friendly magic shows three times a day as well.

From the castle you can take a tour of the town via carriage ride or on foot with a map and/or guide. The tourism office across from the castle provides lots of colorful details for your stay. Don't miss the church of Saint Nicholas with its flying buttresses or lunch in an eatery on Place

Louis XII. Two websites refer you to details about visiting the town and *château*, plus nearby castles. They have a variety of turnkey packages (visits and accommodations) and tickets for sale. The low-priced all-in-one ticket *Pass Châteaux* is well worth the expense. These all-in-one-tickets come in a variety of formats and prices, by the way. http://en.blois.fr and http://www.bloischambord.com

Boat rides from Blois are delightful. Biking from Blois is very popular. Cycling out to Chambord, for example, is on a level, two-hour ride along a well-marked 13-mile route. It's a lovely cycle route, mostly along the river. You can then loop back after seeing Chambord, connecting with a slightly different bike route back to Blois if you choose. See the free Le Pays des Château á Vélo bike map handed out at the tourist office.

Blois Accommodations

Hôtel Anne de Bretagne is a reliable hotel near the train station and not far from the *château*. It has a pretty terrace, too. http://hotelannedebretagne.com
Le Monarque is a well-equipped hotel near the *château*. Its French restaurant is very good. http://hotel-lemonarque.com
Hôtel Mercure Blois is modern and a bit pricey, but it has a riverfront location within walking distance of the *château*. You can always count on a Mercure establishment anywhere in France for reliable accommodations. http://www.mercure.com/gb/hotel-1621-mercure-blois-centre-hotel/index.shtml
Domaine des Hauts de Loire is a fabulous Relaix & Chateaux property with fine dining. It's grand but expensive (my top dining choice in the area) but have your credit card ready. http://domainehautsloire.com/en/
Gîtes (houses or bungalows to rent) are offered by Jeremy and Julie Kolbe. Called "Les Bocages," these self-catering cottages can be rented daily, weekly, or monthly. Les Bocages

are restored from a former wine producer's property. http://
www.loirevalleygite.com. office@france-tours.net, mobile +33
6 19 07 05 98, phone +33 2 54 70 20 52.

Blois Dining & Wine Bars

L'Orangerie du Château is a 15th century *château* restaurant
with classic, elegant food. It's fantastic and quite romantic.
http://orangerie-du-chateau.fr

Au Rendezvous des Pêcheurs is helmed by decorated Chef
Christophe Cosme (with whom I've enjoyed cooking lessons,
as detailed in the food chapter). This is one of the best-
ranked restaurants in Blois and offers fresh fish, wild game,
and delectable desserts, as well as a fantastic wine selection.
It's a local favorite. Christophe also now offers "take-out" of
his culinary creations made fresh daily of everything from
sweets to appetizers. http://rendezvousdespecheurs.com

Le Médicis is where I had the hilarious cheese lesson
from my pig-toting Michelin-starred chef friend, Damien
Garanger (photo by
Christy Destremau).
This is a fine restaurant/
hotel (with ten hotel
rooms) within minutes
of Old Town Blois. You
can dine fabulously on
a variety of cutting-edge
dishes. Damien also offers
gourmet "take-out" meals
that include a selection of
appetizers, main courses,
and desserts, available
for order on his colorful
website. Everything is
prepared fresh prior to

pick-up. The restaurant and hotel have recently also been completely renovated. http://le-medicis.com

Vendôme**

At the foot of the hillside, the Loir divides and its narrow branches glide unhurriedly under the stone bridges; then after the outskirts of the town, they rejoin one another and the widened river flows, with long meanders, across opulent meadows. The town is full of large gardens with rustling greenery, from which emerge uneven rooftops, gables, turrets of old dwellings, church bell towers and the superb tower of Trinity Abbey. In the distance, the horizon disappears in fine undulations. This has not yet either the grace of the Touraine, or the elegance of Anjou, but a welcoming, intimate landscape, adorned with vineyards, woods and a charming river...

—André Hallays, French writer and traveler

The flower-bedecked town of Vendôme (photo by France Off The Beaten Path Tours) is gracefully built over a group of river islands in the Loire Valley. The rushing river divides itself at the entrance to Vendôme, then splits into multiple arms. The result is a striking group of river islands below a castle-topped cliff called La Montagne. With its many bridges, water gateways, and ancient stone structures, Vendôme is a pleasing tableau town ready for Instagram. And now that it's just 45 minutes from Paris by train, it's become a popular weekend retreat for visitors and Parisians alike.

Historically, Vendôme has been a hotspot of power. It was a prized locale during the Gallic period when it was dubbed Vindocinum, "the white mountain." The Romans fortified the town, since its locale made it a comely but sturdy stronghold on the rushing Loir (no e). In medieval times, Vendôme sat between the French and English feudal territories. As such, it was a power pawn passed back and forth between factions. During the Hundred Years' War, it passed to the Bourbons in 1371; in 1515, it became a duchy. Held by the Holy League during the Wars of Religion, it was recaptured by King Henri IV in 1589. (His fiercest enemies' skulls are on display at the Musée de Vendôme.)

The Vendôme of today, with its population of more than 30,000, is a beauteous place to sojourn for a weekend or a week; ignore the surrounding industry and residential areas

and concentrate on the town center. The old town's features include the old abbey cloisters that morphed into the Musée de Vendôme, in which reside remnants of wars past, plus a Marie-Antoinette harp, earthenware furniture dating from the 16th to 19th centuries, and some remarkable frescoes.

The star of Vendôme, however, is La Trinité, the abbey church founded in 1034 by Geoffroy Martel (photo by Christy Destremau). The bell tower is more than 260 feet tall, and the church's florid Gothic *façade* was designed by Jean de Beauce; he also designed the spire of Notre Dame in Paris. Place Saint-Martin is the shopping square lined with shops and cafés. Keeping watch over modern day visitors and locals is General Rochambeau, hero of the American War of Independence.

The best view of the town's old fortifications is from Belot Square. From here you can glimpse the old gate Porte Saint-Georges and the ancient hospital of Saint-Jacques. The old hospital became a Collège des Oratoriens, where 8-year-old Honoré de Balzac first entered as a student. Though later an acclaimed historical novelist, Balzac the boy was an absent-minded student who complained about the strict teachers and bullying classmates. Clever even then, he sometimes purposely got himself into trouble so he could go to detention and read in peace. He took up writing as a 30-year-old and eventually penned more than ninety novels. Many of these richly detail the quirks and foibles of contemporary society. Balzac's caricatures are priceless; psychologically, it makes sense that a bullied boy would become a satirist with a biting wit. Balzac eventually worked himself to death from an addiction to writing and coffee. In modern day, the stern oratory has become the chipper administration offices for the town.

The tourism office is located nearby in the gardens of Parc Ronsard. Free tour information is available, as well as recommendations for restaurants, accommodations, and guide services (http://uk.Vendome-tourisme.fr). Vendôme's ruined *château* stands on a bluff above the town; its picturesque Promenade de la Montagne gardens are worth a wander (though you may want to drive up to it rather than walk, as it's rather steep). The markets are fun and fruitful— many are focused on organic products; the main markets are held each Wednesday, Friday, and Saturday.

During the summer, "Les Rendez-vous de l'été" are open-air concerts in the cloister of the Abbey; the St. Jacques Chapel also mounts revolving exhibitions. In October, the "Rockomotives" present a whole week of alternative fringe/music concerts (rock, pop, electronic music). December brings the return of the Vendôme Film Festival, a national and European competition for the best short- and medium-length films.

Vendôme Accommodations

Hôtel le Vendôme is the number one hotel in Vendôme; it's classy and centrally located. http://en.hotelVendome.fr
Auberge de la Madeleine offers unpretentious comforts and an affordable restaurant downtown. Although it has no website, it's reviewed on Michelin and elsewhere.
Le Saint Georges is a trendy, three-star hotel in town center. http://en.hotel-saint-georges-Vendome.com

Hôtel Capricorne is an excellent, unfussy overnight venue. http://www.hotelcapricorne.fr

Vendôme Dining & Wine Bars

Restaurant Pertica offers romantic French dining. http://www.restaurantpertica.com
Auberge de la Madeleine is part of the hotel of the same name, mentioned previously; it has very good food.
7e Sens. This eatery is a family-run charmer with decent French food. Phone +33 2 54 77 35 32
Restaurant du Pont is Michelin reviewed and offers good value. http://laurentcoucaud.wix.com/hoteldupont

Château de Chambord***

> For full-blown *château* splendor, you can't top Chambord, one of the crowning examples of French Renaissance architecture, and by far the largest, grandest and most visited *château* in the Loire Valley. Begun in 1519 as a weekend hunting lodge by François I, it quickly snowballed into one of the most ambitious (and expensive) architectural projects ever attempted by any French monarch. This cityscape of turrets, chimneys and lanterns crowns some 440 rooms, 365 fireplaces and 84 staircases, including a famous double-helix staircase, reputedly designed by the king's chum, Leonardo.
>
> *—http://www.lonelyplanet.com*

Young monarch François I was just 25 years old in 1519 when he initiated the immense construction of the Château de Chambord (photo by France off the Beaten Path Tours). Fresh from his victory in Italy, his mind was set on a hunting-lodge-cum-palace like no other. It had to be grand

and expansive. It had to incorporate the essence of Italian verve coupled with French finesse. And it needed to match the masculine profile of a 6' 6" hunter king who was the master of his universe—and everyone in it.

The castle—designed as a grand hunting and hawking retreat—began construction in the swampy Sologne lowlands at the edge of a huge game preserve in the Forêt de Boulogne. Hunting and hawking were the foremost pastimes of the royal court during the 16th century. Chambord was therefore meant to be the ultimate locale for grand hunting events. (At one time there were more than three hundred falcons on the estate.) François personally oversaw the construction of a twenty-mile wall surrounding the hunting grounds and forest to contain his potential prey of deer and wild boar.

The castle was not intended as a permanent residence in and of itself. But it was meant to be the architectural jewel François could show visiting heads of state as evidence of his regal prowess. Over twenty-eight years, 1800 workmen and 2 masons labored to bring François's vision to reality. Some say the grand architectural plan was modeled after an Italian church; but in this case it was designed not to worship God, but to worship royalty. Interestingly, Chambord was built while the pope was erecting the new St. Peter's Basilica in Rome; a few historians suspect François was rivaling the Vatican.

Slowly the extravagant structure of sturdy *tuffeau* stone rose to 183 feet high by 512 feet long. Its design was the shape of a classic Greek cross with a central keep flanked by four large towers and two massive wings surrounded by stables. Inside, there was to be a complex system of multiple floors with high ceilinged chambers and salons separated by fifteen main staircases and seventy smaller stairways.

In the middle, the king wanted an enormous central concentric spiral staircase. Most likely the staircase was the design of royal favorite Leonardo da Vinci, although da Vinci died before it was built. This unique double helix staircase allowed two people to use each staircase at the same time without passing each other; however, they could speak through side openings as they passed.

Over the decades, construction was repeatedly halted due to financial problems (not to mention the king's imprisonment by his cousin Charles V of Spain after the

French loss at Pavia). But François was determined it would be his crowning construction despite the obstacles. The king's crest is found more than 700 times within and without. Yes, it's the crowned salamander with the motto *Nutrisco et exstinguo.* Ever master of his world, François even considered rerouting the entire Loire River for a "moat"; but instead he opted to redirect the tiny Cosson tributary.

Over the years, François enjoyed still-unfinished Chambord for numerous hunting excursions. Each time, however, he left it completely devoid of furnishings. The royals—with an entourage of 10,000 people and 20,000 horses—would leave Paris with everything in tow: furniture, linens, tapestries, cooking utensils, clothing. It reportedly took them a full day to get to the Loire. This is another reason each *château* in the valley had to have a "royal chamber" ready for the king if he happened to stop in on his way to and from Paris or elsewhere. When the king departed a castle, even Chambord, he took everything but the stones with him.

In total, François stayed at Chambord for only about 2 months during his entire reign from 1515 to 1547. Ironically, François found his elaborate Chambord too drafty in the end; he preferred the comfy royal apartments in Amboise and Blois. When François died in 1547, Chambord was still incomplete.

Work on the chapel wing continued under the reign of Henri II but was again interrupted upon his death in 1559. Until the reign of Louis XIV, kings came rarely to the great *château.* The permanent residents of the vast estate were mostly the stewards and men responsible for its upkeep.

Fortuitously, Louis XIV, the Sun King, was a great fan of hunting and enjoyed Chambord particularly. Louis finally finished the massive estate in the late 1600s. Areas around the *château* were built up. He constructed stables for twelve hundred horses, which were used for riding and hunting within the grounds. And the small River Cosson that cuts through the park was partly retained in canals to improve the site. All told, there are over four hundred twenty-five separate rooms, three hundred sixty-five fireplaces, and a chapel, plus massive dining and kitchen facilities. Chambord ultimately became the largest castle in the valley—six times larger than any other single *château.*

The Sun King held grand hunting parties at Chambord, and entertainment flourished. In 1669 and 1670, the playwright Molière traveled with the king to Chambord. He had two new plays given for the first time there, *Monsieur de Pourceaugnac* and *The Bourgeois Gentleman.* These were performed in a theatre temporarily set up in a hallway on the first floor of the keep.

Chambord was relatively spared by the French revolution, although any furnishing remnants were either sold or plundered. In the 19th century, various would-be royal family members or Napoleon's minions stayed at Chambord. Ceilings were lowered to increase their comfort level in the drafty rooms; smaller fireplaces were often inserted into the massive fireplaces of François's day.

Chambord officially became state property by right of pre-emption in 1930. Shortly before the outbreak of World War II in 1939, the art collections of the Louvre and Compiègne museums (including the Mona Lisa and Venus de Milo) were stored at Chambord. An American B-24 Liberator bomber crashed onto the *château* lawn on June 22, 1944, but didn't damage the structure. A massive restoration program began in the 1970s. Today, Chambord is a major tourist attraction, and more than 700,000 people a year visit the castle.

As you step onto the grounds as a modern tourist, Chambord will wow you. It's so vast it looks a little like Buckingham Palace on steroids. As Henry James said of it, "Chambord is truly royal—royal in its great scale, its grand air, and its indifference to common considerations."

Note that there are two ticket offices. One sits just inside the grounds as you enter from the huge parking lot. This one is usually glutted with tourists. The second one is just inside the front of the castle itself; this is a far easier place to pay for tickets. Upon entry, you'll receive a handout offering directions through the castle. For better details, however, rent the audio guide or iPAD mini guide now on offer for a few euros if only to avoid getting lost around the endless rooms and corridors. Several times daily there are guided tours as well.

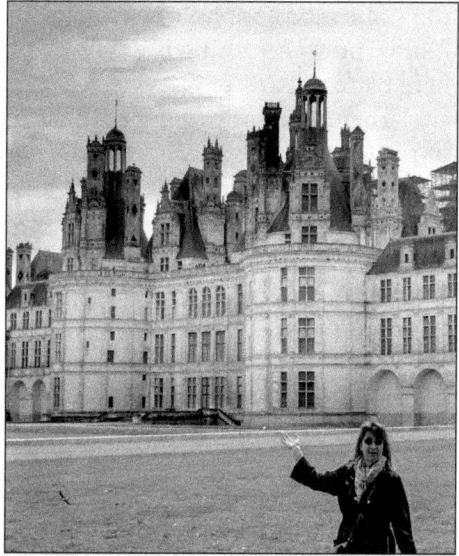

The ground floor has reception rooms. Start at the film room, where you'll find a multi-language film that relates the history of the castle's construction. Don't be surprised at the lack of furniture; the furnishings are on the next floor. The double helix staircase is probably the most stunning element in the castle. It's especially fun to send your partner down one set of stairs and for you to take the other and pass each other without touching!

The first floor up houses the royal apartments. Start with the king's wing. Here you'll pass through the grand bedroom of Louis XIV and his wife Maria Theresa. Her chamber is hung with Parisian tapestries. Next you'll enter the sumptuous boudoir of François (with salamander motif). Notice how everything is designed for easy dismantling to haul back to Paris or elsewhere.

There's an entire wing devoted to the thwarted attempts of the Comte de Chambord to be crowned Henri V after the fall of the Second Empire. Henri d'Artois, the last of the French Bourbons, was brought back out of exile ostensibly to take the crown again. (This always stuns me because the French Revolution rid the French of their haughty royals once and for all—but in one moment of insanity they nearly reinstituted the monarchy save for one sticky detail: Henri wouldn't accept a tri-colored flag, insisting instead on a white one. The French senate said a resounding "Non!" and he was banished once again; the rigid man died in exile. *Moral:* be careful of your color palette choices in France.)

The wing called the "Musée du Comte de Chambord" has some stunning elements from Henri's life: coronation outfits and souvenirs from a coronation that never was; his boyhood collection of petite guns and other weapons; and stunning portraits of the man-who-would-be king and his family. (I find it fascinating and disturbing at the same time; he came very close to sending France back centuries politically. But here he is in a glorious tribute. The French love to cherish their royals—but they definitely don't want

them back in the flesh.)

The second floor up presents a series of ballrooms for hunting-party events and entertainments. Today, these large rooms house temporary exhibits like the Museum of Hunting with its copious displays of weapons and hunting trophies. From this level you will climb to the top of the castle via the double spiral staircase that winds up to the great lantern tower and the rooftop. (Be sure to lean over the center of the staircase and look down its spiral). Out on this most regal "deck," you can look out across the valley over a hodgepodge of cupolas, domes, chimneys, and sculpted gables. From a distance, this topsy-turvey roof skyline looks a bit like a gigantic chessboard.

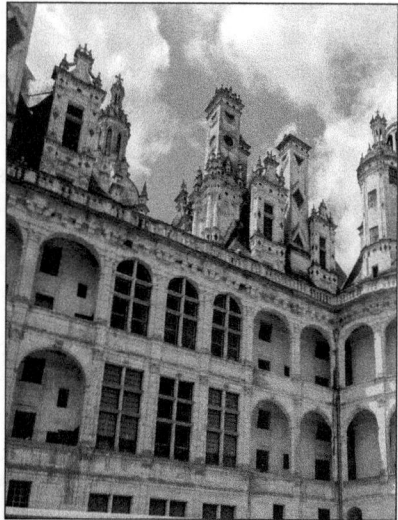

The rooftop is where the royal ladies ogled their lovers and husbands. On hunting days, the king's beaters went to the ends of the forest at the wall and beat the bushes to send the boar and deer toward the king's hunting party (in full view of the ladies). François and his hunting hounds would then ride full tilt into the oncoming herd of game and kill as much as possible.

After you come down from the lofty heights of the rooftop, you'll have access to a courtyard café, a carriage room, a lapidary room, and the Chambord "store" selling Chambord books and paraphernalia. You can also scoop up bottles of Chambord, the 16.5% proof raspberry liqueur.

Outside the *château* proper, there are a variety of exciting things to do, see, and sample, so plan on spending at least a half day, if not a whole day, at Chambord. (Many visitors come and stay for days or weeks.) You can cycle or walk the grounds via the marked paths, but even the shorter walks can take over an hour. (Be sure to wear sensible footwear and take plenty of water.) You can also ride horses or take a horse-drawn cart from the stables where, during the summer months, there is an equestrian show. Boats are also available for riding the pretty waterways.

Along the little village you'll find gift shops, eateries, wine-tasting venues, a newsagent, and a cash dispenser. Each evening in July and August, the *château façade* is lit up in a way that blends the building to the forest through a sound and light show. May through October there's also a Medieval Pageant on Horseback Show that can be fun, but it's mostly for children. More elegant is the Chambord Festival that takes place in July, offering classical and contemporary music concerts given for a wide audience in this extraordinary setting. But the grand show is the Royal Fireworks of Chambord offered in July; it features the music of Handel, coupled with a stupendous pyrotechnical show that can be seen for miles (and probably from space).

The best photographic points are these: in front of the castle entrance, up close and back at a distance at the edge of the lawn; at the back of the castle across the riverlet; from up top on the roof with all the chimneys; and sipping a drink on the terrace of the Hôtel du Grand St. Michel.

Chambord Accommodations

Hôtel du Grand St. Michel lets you wake up with Chambord outside your window if you stay here, and you can roam the grounds anytime you want. This is a hunting style hotel with a masculine, trophy-lined dining room. www.saintmichel-chambord.com
Chambre d'hôte la Giraudière is a hotel nestled in a rural wooded setting. It's pretty, and reasonably priced. http://www.chateaudelagiraudiere.fr
Restaurant La Maison d'a Cote is a hotel and restaurant operated by Michelin favorite, Chef Ludovic Laurenty. At the helm now is savvy Christophe Hay who trained under Blois' Christophe Cosme at Rendezvous des Pecheurs (where I learned about *macaron*-making). This is the best place to dine when heading to the expansive Chambord area. http://lamaisondacote.fr

Chambord Dining & Wine Bars

Le Restaurant du Château de Chambord (restaurant in the castle) is pedestrian but handy.
Restaurant La Maison d'a Cote offers hotel rooms and fine food in a charming setting; see preceding text. http://lamaisondacote.fr

Château de Chaumont-sur-Loire**

Château de Chaumont contains more legends than many [of the *château* in the area]. It once housed a

queen and her husband's mistress under the same
roof.

—Hubrecht Duijker, *Touring in Wine
Country: The Loire*

From a tranquil village called Chaumont ("*chaud mont*"
meaning *hot mountain* or *volcano*) nestled on the south bank
near Blois, a steep path leads up through verdant parklands
to a majestic cliff top castle. Château de Chaumont-sur-Loire
boasts massive round towers of white *limestone* capped by
pointed slate peaks that herald the castle's prestigious role as
guardian of Blois.

In fact, a defensive castle has been located at the
Chaumont spot since the 11th century. Why? This will be
apparent as you make the climb up from the village below.
The castle stood in ready defense to repel the many attacks
on royal Blois. As you crest the hill, you'll be charmed,
however, not by armed guards with crossbows, but by a

patchwork of glorious gardens. Chaumont is now the Loire home for the yearly International Festival of Gardens. I can attest this is one of finest venues in the valley.

But before we step through this medieval marvel nestled in the midst of a garden paradise, let's explore a bit of history. The crude original castle passed to the Norman knight Gelduin after the 10th century; Gelduin consolidated all the fortifications. His great-granddaughter, Denise de Fougère, brought it as a dowry to her new husband, Sulpice d'Amboise. The castle stayed in the hands of the Amboise family for five centuries. After Pierre d'Amboise rebelled against Louis XI, however, the king angrily ordered the castle's destruction. Later in the 15th century, Château de Chaumont was gradually rebuilt by Charles I d'Amboise starting in 1466.

After the death of King Henri II in 1559, Chaumont was bought and lived in regularly by his wife, Catherine de' Médici. Catherine had lived off and on at Chaumont for nine years when her husband died of a lance through the eye. Upon his tortured demise, Catherine evicted Henri's mistress, Diane de Poitier, from Chenonceau and forced her to swap Chenonceau for this very castle at Chaumont.

Diane, ever the diva, stayed only a short time. Instead she ended her days at her own *château* in Anet. Diane naturally added her personal touches to Chaumont while she was there, however. You'll see evidence of them both within the furnishings. But it was a much later woman of power who turned Chaumont into a show palace.

Marie-Charlotte Say, seventeen-year-old heiress to the Léon Say sugar fortune, saw Chaumont one day. She fell instantly in love and demanded that her father buy it for her in 1875. Later that year, she married Prince Amédée de Broglie—and thus became Princess de Broglie. With his taste (and her money), they beautifully remodeled the *château* and parklands into a show palace.

They refurbished the residential apartments, added fine furniture and brilliant tapestries. The pair paved the floors with 17th century majolica tiles taken from a Sicilian palace. The portrait medallions on display were made in the 18th century by the Italian engraver Nini, who maintained a workshop in the palatial stables on the estate. The Prince and Princess de Broglie introduced an exceptional sense of modernity and high society to the locale. Esteemed visitors came in droves.

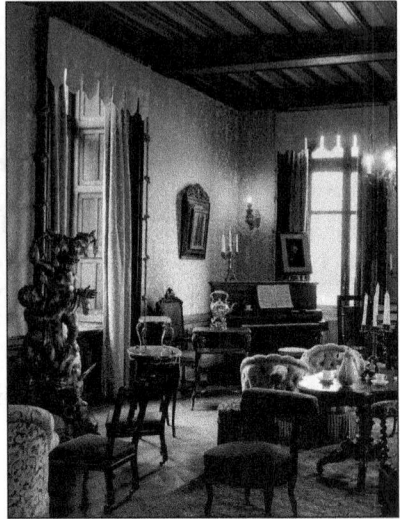

Anthony Peregrine of the *Telegraph* had this to say of the Princess in "*The Best Châteaux of the Loire Valley, France*":

> Marie began to set new standards in unreason-ableness and party-giving. Everyone—maharajahs, actresses, our (British) Prince of Wales—came to her *fêtes*. She'd ship the entire Comédie Française down from Paris specially. She would always rise at 2 p.m. sharp, and be late for dinner at 8 p.m. Kitchen staff prepared four different meals, so that one would be ready whenever she was. She also moved nearby village houses and the church; they interfered with her garden plans.

The Prince is famous for commissioning the luxurious stables to be rebuilt using 1877 designs by Paul-Ernest

Sanson. These stables include deluxe padded horse stalls complete with bins and bowls for hay, oats, and water, plus a handy drainage gutter for "download." Unheard of in the day, the stable had running water, electric-arc lighting, and a Horse Kitchen (Cuisine de Chevaux), which produced French mash twice weekly for the lucky brood. One of the finest tack rooms in all of France, it shows off the extraordinary horse paraphernalia of yesteryear. Today, the stables have morphed into an extraordinary riding center. Nearby is the *château*'s farmhouse that is now home to the Conservatoire International des Parcs et Jardins, which manages the annual Garden Festival.

The estate was donated by the elderly princess to the French government in 1938. It now functions as a museum and home of the April–October Garden Festival, where contemporary garden designers display their work in resplendent individual gardens. When I first visited, I was stunned by the sheer size of this enchanting place. Vast parklands surround the splendid castle that sits like a medieval fairytale abode overlooking the Loire. The stable complex sits a distance away, while a village-like enclave at the center of the estate includes a bee barn, donkey stables, a greenhouse, *café*, and conference hall. Along the path to the Garden Festival area are two restaurants, a gift shop, and a garden shop. But the *piece de resistance* is the vast collection of

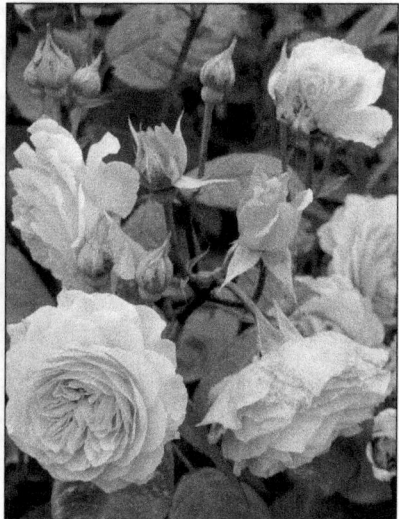

Festival Gardens that extend hundreds of acres across one whole side of the estate.

Chaumont makes for a pretty visit. But there's no public transportation here. During the summer season, you can drive up and park near the castle. In off-season, you can drive up behind the *château* in the direction of Montrichard from the river, then take the first hard right turn following the *Stade du Tennis* signs; park in the lot beyond the soccer field.

When you arrive at the castle, you'll be in good company, since Louis XVI, Marie-Antoinette, Voltaire, and even Benjamin Franklin all spent time here. You'll quickly see that Chaumont is an exceptional example of a feudal Gothic fortress, but it has the quirky feature of a fantastic collection of modern art sprinkled within and without. The feudal elements include a dry moat, large and small drawbridges with ramparts, loopholes for archers and their bows, and "windows" from which to dump hot oil on interlopers.

Modern life teems at the estate, however, with the fantastic contemporary gardens that are more outdoor art installations than *jardins*. Each year a theme is selected, and artists from around the world apply for spots in the 27 festival plots. The winners go wild with splendid outdoor installations. You may see ground-up tires, smashed bricks, broken glass, or rusted metal with soft flowers and topiaries curling around them.

You'll want to stroll through the park towards the *château* initially; quirky art peeks out from among the flowers and greenery as you stroll toward the castle. Inside the grand structure, signs will direct you through the *château's* three wings. Catherine de' Médici festooned her digs with Italianate touches, of course. (Her astrologer Ruggieri had a room next to hers.) Particularly note the grand salon, the billiard room, and the library, which presents several stunning 16th century Flemish tapestries. A spiral staircase takes you up to the guardroom above the drawbridge and then through several chambers with more tapestries in each chamber. The small chapel is a delight, with its fantasy garden infiltration that reminds me of the movie *Avatar*.

Unlike most other Loire *châteaux*, there are plenty of dining options at Chaumont. These include a high-end French restaurant with white tablecloths and crystal, a café, and my favorite, a fast-French-food cafeteria. This place makes me laugh, since you can eat wonderful French food off a tray, plus your favorite wine—plus dessert and coffee for one low price. Who knew fast food could be *haute* delicious?

Chaumont Accommodations/Dining & Wine Bars

Hôtel Château des Tertres is located across the river from

Chaumont-sur-Loire, in the charming village of Onzain. The hotel is owned and operated by personal friends Bernard and Christine Valois; both are natives of the region and speak fluent English. They enjoy offering guests suggestions, and assisting with logistics to make the most of their stay in the region. Local wines produced by Christine's family are on offer to enjoy on the hotel terrace. They have a very loyal clientele, so reservations are highly recommended. The hotel also offers bicycle storage facilities for guests who need them. http://www.chateau-tertres.com

Espace 108, a new and inviting concept in the region called "an artistic experience in the Loire," is a an art-deco rental property designed and realized by Bernard and Christine Valois, owners of Château des Tertres (described earlier). Espace 108 is located also in Onzain, a charming village located across the river from Chaumont-sur-Loire. The couple's new venture is a completely new concept of accommodation in the region. Consisting of twenty bedrooms each with private en-suite bathrooms, each suite overlooks a central common space that features a living room, meeting area, and kitchen and dining alcove. The Espace 108 offers both a centrally located base camp from which to discover the Loire Valley and a socially inviting atmosphere for travelers to meet and mingle with other travelers in the region. Espace 108 also offers a separate seminar/movie viewing room, plus an on-site chef if needed. The Espace 108 was designed to appeal to visitors looking for an alternative lodging option to the traditional hotel or B&B experience. Being centrally located to the region's favorite castles, villages, and activities, it's an excellent choice for small travel or specialty groups, families or groups of friends traveling together, and for company seminars and team-building events in the region. Contact Bernard and Christine Valois at Château des Tertres for complete details. Château des Tertres, 11 bis rue de Meuves, 41150 Onzain, France.

Phone: 02 54 20 83 88.

Bar a Burgers is a charmer—one of the hottest spots for whole, clean food in an unexpected small village. France is known for its fabulous eateries; and in this quiet, charming village of Onzain, across the river from Chaumont, visitors can experience excellent French fare at modest prices. The owners pride themselves on using only the freshest and most wholesome ingredients. Go for the tasty burgers and *pommes frites*! http://www.babburgerbar.fr

La Chancelière is a handy *maison* with B&B charm. http://www.la-chanceliere.com

Château de Cheverny**

> Cheverny is a rare thing within the Loire Valley—a *château* that appears untouched by the Renaissance. This could have a lot to do with the fact that it has remained in the same family, the Huraults, for six centuries... the 17th century *château* is built in pure Louis XIII classical style with a rigid symmetry.
>
> —*http://www.experienceloire.com/cheverny.htm*

What could hunting hounds, Tintin, and legacy DNA have to do with a pure French castle not far from Chambord? Cheverny has all that—and more.

Château de Cheverny was begun in 1604 at the edge of the Sologne Forest. It has remained unchanged since being erected by Henri Hurault, Comte de Cheverny (1575–1648). This pure 17th century *château* made of white Bourré stone and slate is perched "on an ocean of perfectly kept lawns." Its harmonious Louis XIII façade is intact after several centuries. Unlike the rest of the Loire, Cheverny repelled the influence of the Renaissance as if it were a filthy beggar with the plague. Instead, Cheverny remains a sublimely unified Classical French edifice, exact and perfect to this day.

Hurault, Comte de Cheverny, was a famous lieutenant general and military treasurer for Louis XIII. His various descendants still inhabit this remarkable estate in the form of the current Marquis de Vibraye, who is the present owner. Hence, the Comte's DNA still energizes this harmonious castle, 368 years after his death.

The estate has had some brushes with DNA interlopers—no matter that the new DNA was quite attractive. Yes, divine mistress Diane de Poitiers flitted through these corridors too. (She was perhaps the top real estate aggregator of her day.) The Huraults briefly lost the land and the old Cheverny fortress-castle to the state due to fraud allegations. King Henri II then turned around and awarded it to Diane de Poitiers on a platter. She, however, preferred Chenonceau, so she shrewdly sold the property back to the former owner's son, Philippe Hurault. (I assume she used the proceeds to enhance Chenonceau—and yet again show Catherine de' Médici how to be the prettiest girl in the kingdom *and* the richest.)

Happily back in Hurault hands once more, the new *château* was constructed between 1624 and 1630 to designs by the sculptor-architect of Blois, Jacques Bougier. His designs are loosely based on the Palais du Luxembourg in Paris in the Luxembourg Gardens (which I visit regularly in Paris). This is exactly the estate we visit today still regal in its immaculate symmetry.

For the next hundred fifty years, ownership passed along the family line; in 1768 a major interior renovation was undertaken. By the time of the French Revolution in 1789, the family was unfortunately required to forfeit a great portion of the Hurault wealth. But the estate itself was spared any destruction, since it was quite popular with the locals, especially the farmers. It remains as beloved today.

The family finally sold the property in 1802 at the height of the Empire. But miracle of miracles, the family bought it back yet again in 1824, during the Restoration under Charles X. Thus you will sense the fierce pride in this estate that has survived the tides of war, lust, revolution, and near bankruptcy. In 1914 the owners opened the *château* to the public—one of the first to do so in the Loire—and Cheverny has been a fan favorite ever since.

The gorgeous external symmetry makes this a most pleasant estate. But Cheverny is also famed for its fantastic interiors, period furniture, tapestries, and *objets d'art* deemed some of the best in the Loire. As you enter this beautiful *château*, Hurault's heavenly crest of two collars sets the tone. One collar symbolizes the Order of the Holy Ghost, while the other marks the Order of St. Michael.

Touring the interior is a regal endeavor. (And there's a treasure hunt for children as they explore the *château*.) The interior is a living history of the generations of the family. The ground floor Grand Salon was decorated under the orders of the Marquise de Montglas. Among the paintings are a portrait of Jeanne d'Aragon, from the school of

Raphael, and a portrait of Marie Johanne La Saumery, Comtesse de Cheverny, by Pierre Mignard. The furnishings are 17th and 18th century treasures. A Gallery leads to the Petit Salon, which is hung with five Flemish tapestries and a portrait attributed to Maurice-Quentin de La Tour. In the Library are portraits by Jean Clouet and Hyacinthe Rigaud.

The Private Apartments are accessed in the west wing via a splendid main staircase with straight flights of richly decorated steps. The apartments consist of eight rooms, all magnificently furnished. The nursery displays a baby's first crib. The Chambre du Roi (Kings Chamber) is the most splendid room in the *château*. The ceiling is gilded and painted by Mosnier. On the walls are five extraordinary Paris tapestries after 1640 designs by Simon Vouet, representing the story of Ulysses.

The largest room, the Arms Room, contains weapons, tapestry, chests, trunks, and a carved wood chimneypiece painted by Jean Monier in the 17th century. The dining room has decorated wood panels that tell the story of *Don Quichotte* (French for Don Quixote). At the end of the room is a beautiful fireplace and dresser from the 19th century. On the walls hang superb 17th century Flemish tapestries.

By the way, the neighborly viscount and his family still live on the third floor, but their private areas are not open to the public. *Quirky note:* I was getting out of my car in the parking lot one afternoon, when a good looking man in a maroon sweater and casual pants sauntered past. I noticed him for some reason and then observed as he stopped at the end of the lot near some trees to chat with a few locals. It wasn't until later I realized it was the viscount himself—in jeans! He's definitely a down-to-earth kind of guy, despite his titles.

But there's still more at Cheverny that's enticing. In the kennels beyond the castle, you'll get to meet the most delightful pack of over seventy hunting hounds on the planet. They are even YouTube stars. There are more than 7,000 videos of these yapping darlings in their element (mostly eating raw chicken on command). I'd suggest they're the face of Cheverny (although the owners may disagree). You'll find lots of quirky hound souvenirs in the gift shop.

Visitors have access to this pack of handsome hounds, who move around their digs like a swarm of teenagers (when they're not passed out asleep). These dogs are a combination of English foxhound and French Poitou—combining the best of English and French poochology. (Dare I say the sleek coats are probably the French part, while the hunt-and-conquer physiology is British?) Nevertheless, these lively pooches are all flirty fun with their big paws and floppy ears; they'll run toward you ready to bury a wet nose in your, er, hand. (I had a hard time pulling my companion away to see the castle itself; she lingered to take hound pictures—more than a hundred of them!)

During summer months this pack "performs" a feast ritual called *la soupe des chiens* (dog's soup or dinner). At a specific time with the public invited, the dog's lab-coated French trainer hauls out a wheelbarrow of seasoned raw chicken breasts (with a Kibbles 'n Bits chaser). Then he handily dumps it all out in a long row on the newly hosed floor. The dogs are then let in through the upper gate and allowed to line up just in front of the food. But they must pause, voices yapping and tongues dripping with desire— until their trainer gives the French command for them to eat. (I listened carefully, ears pricked up for the "eat now" command. I can definitely reveal it wasn't "*Bon Appetite.*" More like "*Mush!*")

Then the pack leaps into the food, bodies quivering, food flying. It looks like a kids' lunchroom in a food fight. But it's a delight to watch these yapping cuties devour their lunch! My favorite part of hound adoration day, however, was the fact that Cheverny lets visitors name one of the dogs in the pack starting with a chosen letter of the alphabet. The year I visited, the letter was M. I suggested "Mirabeau"

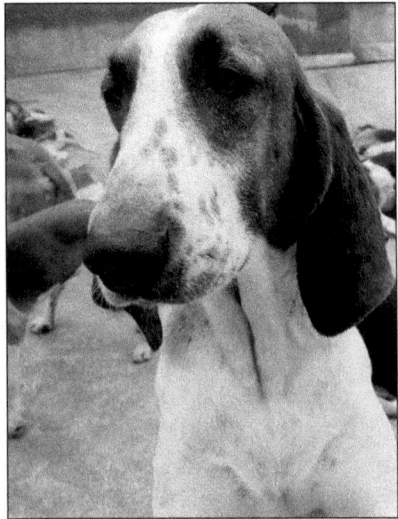

for my favorite rosé wine. (Do you think I could have ordered a little rosé wine for Mirabeau's water bowl?)

The viscount takes this agreeable brood for hunts (called "riding to hounds") twice weekly. For those who don't know, "the hunt" has been the sport of aristocrats all over Europe for centuries. In the past, it consisted of chasing an animal—fox, deer or boar—across open countryside. Fashionable red-coated riders on horseback then follow the pack of baying hounds, jumping fences and ditches. There are no firearms. The dogs are taught to corner the prey. (Sometimes the prey escapes, sometimes not.)

Reluctantly I dragged myself away from these charmers and soon ran into another internet star: Tintin. Tintin is the interstellar adventurer created by Belgian comic book creator Hergé. In *The Adventures of Tintin* books, Hergé used Cheverny as a model for his fictional "Château de Moulinsart" (Marlinspike Hall in English). In these fantasies, Tintin's friend Captain Haddock has a "home" that looks exactly like Cheverny minus the two outermost wings. Cheverny promotes the stories and naturally has a permanent exhibition on Tintin and his travels. (I especially liked Tintin's shiny space suits.)

The grounds of Château de Cheverny with its vast lawns and waterways make for a delightful stroll on foot—although it's two hundred forty-seven acres. A unique feature is the magnificent giant redwoods, cedars, and lime trees that were planted between 1820 and 1860 by Paul de Vibraye. The "Apprentices Garden" was created in 2006. This "Beauty of Eden" stretches all the way from the *château* to the orangery. It was built in a contemporary design between cultivated structures that are placed along a central axis; it wends like a colorful serpent along the borders. In the kitchen garden you'll find flowers that go into arrangements for the castle as well as comestibles.

Visitors—and pooches—of all ages will especially enjoy a tour of the grounds aboard a golf cart; or, for a more leisurely tour, you can even take a boat ride on the canal.

Outbuildings include Cheverny's Orangery, which has a noted past. During World War II, it safeguarded many of the works of art from the Louvre in Paris. Picnicking is encouraged at this pretty spot.

I have a hanging tapestry of Cheverny and the hunt in my living room, by the way. Thus I think of it fondly every single day, since I look at it as I pass through my hub home in the US. And sometimes I check on Mirabeau via pooch-cam on YouTube.

There's ample parking within easy reach of the *château,* plus a lovely village setting giving you a number of eating options. These are very reasonably priced, considering their location. Shuttle vans or buses can take you out to Cheverny from Blois or Amboise. The estate is visitor-ready and provides brochures and guides as needed. Cheverny also has a sparkling website to offer you all the details you need for a visit. http://www.chateau-cheverny.com/en/

Another fun feature of a visit to Cheverny, I might add, is a visit to La Maison des Vins. This wine tasting room that aggregates thirty-two local vintners sits just outside the gates of the estate. It's a superb place to pop in and taste the fruity light wines of the area, including those of the estate. I highly recommend a visit to sample the free tastes or some more serious wine tasting for a few euros per flight of tastes.

Cheverny Accommodations

Chambre de'hôte Le Béguinage is surrounded by a gorgeous wooded lake and park lands. This ivy-covered town house that has wonderful rooms. http://www.lebeguinage.fr
Chambre de'hôte La Raboulière is a Sologne longhouse that makes for a unique stay. http://www.larabouillere.com
Domaine Le clos Bigot is another converted longhouse with rooms and an apartment. http://www.gites-cheverny.com
Hôtel St-Hubert is a comfortable in-town hotel and restaurant. http://www.hotel-sthubert.com

Cheverny Dining & Wine Bars

Le Botte d'Asperges offers a rustic setting for traditional dishes. http://www.labotte-dasperges.com
La Rousselière is beloved by golfers. The terrace overlooks the lake, and nice food is served in a convivial atmosphere. http://www.golf-cheverny.com

Château de Sully-sur-Loire*

 Château de Sully is an unfussy *château-fort*, a true castle, built to control one of the few sites where the Loire can be forded. It retains its medieval fortress profile. In fact, it rises directly from its moat. But instead of floating like delicate Azay-le-Rideau, Sully resembles a wizard's fortress parting the River Sange as it heaves to life.

 Sully is, in fact, two separate castle systems, each with its own defense system. Originally, the site had been a fortified Gallo-Roman locale. In 1218, Philippe Auguste constructed a cylindrical keep to the south of the present structure. Guy de la Trémoille inherited the fortress. With help from the king's architect, Raymond du Temple, he constructed the donjon, flanked by four towers, starting in 1395. It was intended as both a fortification and a fine residence for entertaining.

Workaholic Maximilien de Béthune (1560–1641) was the first Duke of Sully. He bought the fortress-castle in 1602. He strengthened the embankments of the river to protect the town from occasional flooding. He also added the Petit Château to one side as a palatial seigneurial residence where the Duke and his family could live comfortably.

A great soldier and the best artilleryman of his age, the Duke of Sully evolved into a tireless administrator; he became the First Minister of Finance for Henri IV. Together they gave France twenty years of much-needed peace. Following the Wars of Religion, the Edict of Nantes guaranteed religious tolerance.

He began his day at 3 a.m. every morning and kept four secretaries busy writing his memoirs. I'd call him the Loire's first newspaperman, since he smartly set up a printing press in one of the fortress towers and had his minions print his memoirs on the spot to prevent "leaks of information." Sully's castle held Joan of Arc captive for a time until she escaped in 1430.

He had a softer side, however, and created walking gardens to make the castle livable and pleasant. Sully was especially committed to tree planting. He's often credited with starting the French tradition of planting poplars alongside roads—an image which, for many, typifies France.

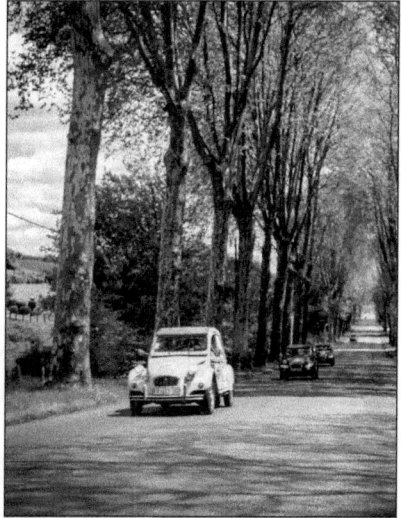

Voltaire spent time here with his 18th century great friend the Duke of Sully, who sheltered him from persecution in Paris in 1716 and again in 1719. Sully was so fond of Voltaire that he built a theatre for him on which to stage performances at the castle.

Sully is another one of the few Loire castles that remained with original descendants. World War II brought some bombing damage (by the Germans *and* by the Allies), but restoration work has been continuous. The family finally sold the estate to the local Loret government in 1962. The state has fortuitously worked on restoring it since that time. It's handsomely floodlit at night and the castle and grounds make for a lovely sunset picture.

Inside, visitors will find some splendid period furnishings, tapestries, and artwork; it definitely resembles Chaumont in style. The Louis XI wing is particularly arresting, with sumptuous 17th century stylings. Six centuries after its construction, the roof of the Great Hall is still an impressive structure. The *château* hosts a classical music festival every year as part of the Music Festival De Sully & Du Loiret. http://www.chateausully.fr

The popular town of Sully-sur-Loire is popular with holiday makers as a riverside resort offering fishing, walking, and river trips near the rest of the Orléans and Sologne. The town also boasts the Loire Navy Museum and the Abbey of Saint Benoit.

Sully-sur-Loire Accommodations/Dining & Wine Bars

Hôtel de la Poste is a long-established, family-run inn with eatery that's very popular with locals. Ask for a river view. http://www.hotel-la-poste-loire.com

To summarize this unique region, Orléans and Blésois have some of the most beautiful and stunning scenes in all of the valley. More eccentric than feminine Touraine and less equestrian than Anjou, this whimsical domain is raw, gorgeous, and unconventional. The site of the gorgeous gardens, the regal power of Blois, Chaumont, and Chambord, plus the earthy aroma of princely wines and happy hounds make this another of the unique enchantments in the Valley of the Kings.

CHAPTER NINE

Berry
(Bourges, Sancerre, and Valençay)

Berry lies in the very center of France, south of the
Paris Basin and just north of the Massif Central. It is
a varied land of wheat fields, pastures and vineyards,
and elegant manor houses. Mainly off the beaten
tourist track, the region gives visitors an opportunity
to experience the rural heart of France.

—*Eyewitness Travel: Loire Valley,* Duncan Baird
Publishers/DK Publishing

Yes, the province of Berry may be the wildest part of
the Loire with only a few notable *châteaux*. But it's a
uniquely eco-friendly environment that offers much for
visitors who love the vast outdoors and the quirky corners
of rural France. This is a land that smells fresh and earthy

as soon as you drive or cycle into it. No wonder it produces Sancerre, some of the best-loved wines in France.

Many first time Loire visitors bypass Berry. It's a bit off the beaten path and has very few famous castles. In fact, some say, "Berry does a good job of hiding its assets." But those who venture here will find winding country roads that pass along mile after mile of lush vineyards and fields loaded with vegetables. The well-tended forests make for fine hiking. Fishing and bird watching delight many fans in La Brenne. Sailing and canoeing on Berry's rivers and lakes is an idyllic pastime for many. Below the town of Bourges is the Champagne Berrichonne, an immense agricultural region producing wheat, barley, and oil-rich crops like rapeseed and sunflowers. The Loire River makes the natural boundary between Berry and Burgundy to the east as it flows through the fabulous Sancerre hills.

Thus this uncrowded locale is a natural habitat for that most unique of humans, the cyclist. This is, of course, why the world-famous cyclists of the Tour de France regularly wend through Berry. It offers miles of mostly auto-free roads where the only companions may be a harvester, an occasional white delivery van, or rabbits skittering over the road.

The culinary tastes of Berry include flavorful dishes made from local game and mushrooms. And of course there is exceptionally good goat's cheese—Crottin de Chavignol, to name just one. They find their way onto the plates of the wealthiest diners in the world. In northeast Sancerre, one of the most cherished wine regions in France spreads across the valley.

Still, favorite son Alain-Fournier (Henri-Alban Fournier), who penned the beloved novel *Le Grand Meaulnes* (The Lost Domain) in 1913, wrote, "You need to part the branches to get to know the area." He wrote movingly of his childhood memories in the Sologne in Berry north and the sunny countryside in the south. He illuminated the delights of this less-traveled area for many readers who still love his Berry ruminations today.

Interestingly, wild Berry attracted and still attracts a number of famous people who thrive on the clean air, hearty food, and soul-inspiring vistas. Among them are George Sand, the female French novelist of *Consuelo*, *La Mare au Diable*, and *Le Meunier d'Angibault*, who lived near Bourges and had many famous lovers, including Frédéric Chopin; Honoré de Balzac, novelist, playwright, and coffee lover; and contemporary actor and bad boy Gerard Depardieu—who clearly marches to his own drummer in his roles as well as in his private life. (He recently took up residence over the border in Belgium to evade paying taxes.)

Taxes aside, in this section we'll explore this pastoral Berry countryside and my not-too-expensive favorite haunts: 1–the historical town of Bourges; 2–Sancerre, the wine queen of Berry; and 3–Château de Valençay, the famous abode of infamous Talleyrand.

Bourges

Capital of the province of Aquitaine at the end of the Roman Empire, capital of the Kingdom of France in the reign of Charles VII, Bourges carefully maintains its heritage from a glorious past…A city of art and history included on the UNESCO World Heritage list, its old streets and its half-timbered houses [are superb]…A green city, Bourges is one of the greenest cities in France with 135 hectares of marshland in the heart of the city and more than 50 m2 of parks per inhabitant…A city of culture, Bourges is proud of its "Maison de la Culture," the first to be created in France and of its music festival Le Printemps de Bourges, a true national and international event.

—*http://www.ville-bourges.fr*

Bourges is a practical starting point for exploring Berry. This handsome medieval town of half-timbered houses and historical heritage was the original capital of the region. Julius Caesar embraced it as "Avaricum," and he hailed it as "the most beautiful in all of Gaul." Today, this proud enclave, which birthed kings of France and now acts as the economy-friendly capital of the Department of Cher, makes for a happy visit if you want to see few-frills Loire. Large national companies make their home here, however, so you'll find many Parisian-style comforts to infuse this quiet locale with style. But best is the pretty greenness and down-to–earth, rural-France nature you can enjoy within the town's environs.

The Bourges name comes from either the original inhabitants the *Bituriges* tribe or the Germanic name for *Burg* or hill/village. As mentioned above, Caesar overtook the area in the Gallic Wars of 58–50 BC; his "scorched earth" policy caused the destruction of the old city and all but 800 of its inhabitants. But the Romans reconstructed Avaricum to their liking. They added aqueducts, thermal baths, and an amphitheater. Massive walls enclosed the city, fronted by a monumental Roman gate.

In the first and second centuries, Bourges reverted to its original name and came under the rule of counts loyal to the Aquitaine dukes in the south. During the Middle Ages, Bourges acted as the capital of the Viscounty of Bourges. In the 14th century, it became the capital of the duchy of Berry. Charles VII, who reigned from 1422–1461, made Bourges his base camp while he fought for the French crown during the Hundred Years' War. As previously discussed, it was Joan of Arc who helped him muster the confidence to be crowned king. His treasurer and local boy Jacques-Cœur was vital in making his French kingdom financially solvent.

Charles's son, Louis XI, was born in Bourges in 1423. Louis loved Bourges. He supported Jacques Cœur (see his palace above) and his own nobles in developing independent trade. (This was perhaps the beginning of a serious merchant class in France.) Cœur grew into the greatest merchant (and later statesman) in the land; he erected a mighty palace, as well as other religious structures in the town. His son, Jean Cœur, became Archbishop of Bourges.

Even now, Bourges is a stately city with a long tradition of art and culture. Famed sites include the Gothic St-Etienne cathedral built between 1195 and 1255, the Jacques Cœur Palace, the Berry Museum, Hôtel des Echevins and Estève Museum, and the ruins of the Gallic-Roman walls.

Cathédrale St-Etienne is one of France's finest Gothic cathedrals. Built mainly between 1195 and 1255, the unknown architect designed this essentially bullet-shaped structure without transepts—making it much lighter and airier than most Gothic cathedrals. The brilliant medieval stained glass makes the most of the sparkling light play. The double rows of flying buttresses that rise in pyramid-shaped tiers are visually arresting. The Chapelle Jacques-Cœur has a fine Annunciation window. And don't miss the clever astrological clock created by mathematician Cannon Jean Fusoris.

Palais Jacques-Cœur is among the finest Gothic buildings in Europe. This grand *maison* was built by a clever man who nevertheless fell on hard times due to the whims of the monarchy. The son of a furrier, Jacques Cœur (1400–1456) became one of the richest and most powerful men in medieval France. A natural trader with a gift for making money, his merchant fleet sailed to the eastern Mediterranean and the Far East, bringing back fantastic luxury goods: silks, spices, mohair, brocades, exotic woods, and precious metals.

Cœur developed a huge international merchant operation that placed France in a position to compete favorably with the great trading empires of Italy and the Orient. In 1436, he was summoned to Paris by Charles VII and made master of the mint. He succeeded so well that he became steward of the royal expenditure. He even represented the king at the court of Pope Nicholas V. By this time, the oceans were rife with his ships. Three hundred managers were in his employ. He built houses, chapels, and trading centers in many French cities and founded colleges in Paris. In time, he was lending money to needy courtiers and even to the king himself. But the winds were soon to shift.

Cœur's debtors, jealous of his wealth, were keen on arranging his downfall.

When the king's favorite mistress, Agnès Sorel, was poisoned to death, Cœur was fingered for the deed. Despite his protestations, the king ordered Cœur's imprisonment and the forfeiture of his empire. After several years in prison, where he was also tortured, he escaped. Luckily, he was welcomed in Rome by Nicholas V, who put him in charge of an expedition against the Turks. Old and broken, Cœur died during the adventure. After his death, Charles VII apparently felt guilty and allowed Cœur's sons to inherit whatever was left of their father's lands and estate.

Jacques Cœur's great palace, still standing in Bourges today, is a testament to the man's modern sensibilities and cultural acumen. Constructed as early as 1443, it has many remarkable innovations for the period. These include rooms opening off corridors instead of leading into each other (as in Versailles and Chambord), stone lavatories, and room labels that employ a carved identification scene over each doorframe. At the time, Bourges was famous for alchemy and mystical arts. And Jacques-Cœur was a particular devotee. His mystical bent is seen in the abundance of mystery symbols and creatures found in the *façades* and *Trompe l'Oeil* motifs throughout his palace. Of course the heart symbol threads romantically throughout as well; "*cœur*" means "heart" in French, and it is the heart symbol that romantically appears in the great man's coat of arms.

Hôtel des Echevins and Estève Museum (the house of the alderman) is a 1489 building remarkable for its intricate carved octagonal tower. It served as the seat of the Bourges city council for three centuries. In 1987 it was beautifully renovated and became the Musée Estève. Today, this handsome museum displays paintings of local boy Maurice Estève, who became a powerful modern art painter. His and other contemporary exhibitions look serenely elegant in their centuries-old gothic home. The Musée du Berry nearby concentrates on displays of local history and art. These include Gallo-Roman artifacts, Gothic sculptures, and rural Berry arts and crafts.

Bourges has another clever feature: Green Routes. In 2005, the Mayor of Bourges tired of the constant automobile traffic and came up with an innovative plan to limit traffic and make the city green and friendly. He oversaw the construction of a network of "Green Routes" that function as verdant pathways from one place to another without the use of a car. Walkers, runners, cyclists, and roller skaters gleefully use the wide routes that wend their way through the town. And of course lovers enjoy the green bounty for wooing the day away.

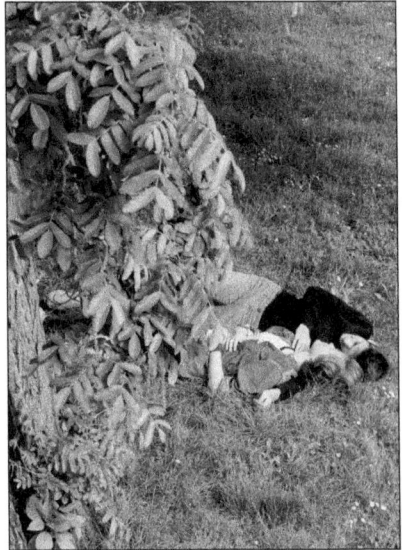

Jardin lovers will especially enjoy the colorful Bourges Gardens. These include the Art Deco Prés Fichaux with its sculpted vegetation, lime trees, and immaculate yews. The cheerful gardens of the Archbishop's Palace at the foot of the cathedral make for a pretty wander, as do the bright Jean de Berry and Édouard André gardens.

A city of light and music, Bourges also puts on three grand annual pageants that will knock your sunglasses off. These include "Springtime in Bourges," "Summer in Bourges," and "Illuminated Nights," a magnificent sound and light circuit that combines culture, tourism, and heritage. The spring pageant is particularly loved by young people as a world-class rock and roll festival.

Bourges Accommodations

Hôtel d'Angleterre is located in the middle of the old town center. It's an elegant 19th century hotel with a pleasant dining establishment that meets most travelers' needs. http://www.bestwestern-angleterre-bourges.com/English.phtml
Hôtel de Bourbon, a Mercure property, the accommodation incorporates the remains of the Abbaye Saint-Ambroix. Located within walking distance of the old town, it has a terrific restaurant. http://www.mercure.com

Bourges Dining & Wine Bars

Restaurant Le Beauvoir is a modern-*décor* eatery with good food at reasonable prices. Locals particularly love it. http://restaurant-lebeauvoir.com
Abbaye Saint-Ambroix is an award-wining gastronomic restaurant and wine cellar located in the Hôtel de Bourbon. It's fabulous, but pricey. http://www.abbayesaintambroix.fr/abbaye/

Sancerre*

> Just say "Sancerre" quietly and you'll get an initial sense of the built-in appeal of this white wine from the Loire Valley. The soft sibilance, the internal alliteration, the smooth completion, whether you give it the clipped French pronunciation or simply ease off the word American-style—it's a beautiful sound, suggestive of beautiful wines.

—Eric Asimov, "Sancerre: Say It with Feeling," *The New York Times*

My California-based French *boulangère* Benoit laughs when I ask him which part of the Loire he loves best. Yes, I know he was born in the Loire. That he trained in Tours and elsewhere. That he opened O Gourmet Bakery in San Juan Capistrano down the hill from my California home. Yes, *that* San Juan Capistrano, where the swallows come home each spring and where I can visit a little bit of the Loire in his sublime bakery anytime I'm not in France.

"Skip the *châteaux*," Benoit begins, as I sit at my usual table near his warm ovens. The smell of baking *brioche* and cooling *macarons* wafts past my laptop as I listen to his advice. "Skip Fontevraud. Skip Tours and Chambord and Chenonceau. Go straight to Sancerre for the heavenly wine route. Spend an entire week there, going from vineyard to vineyard, tasting the best wine on the planet."

I do think he's bit biased, of course. But as a Loire native who knows every inch of the valley by its smells and tastes and flavors, I find it amusing he's so certain Sancerre is the finest locale in the Loire. Yet he isn't alone in his adoration. This grape-rich region with its medieval hilltop town of the same name is noted for several things, including heaven-sent wine and legendary goat's cheese.

Sancerre has quite a history. Founded by the powerful Celtic tribe called the Bituriges (the "Kings of the World") after their defeat at Bourges by the Romans, they settled in Sancerre to rebuild their tribe, make wine, and eventually commingle with Roman blood. By the time of the Carolingian period there was a small village on the hillside, clustered around the Saint Romble Church. An Augustinian abbey was founded in "Saint Satur" in 1034. By the 1100s, Sancerre was a feudal possession of the Counts of Champagne. They built a *château* on the hill and ramparts to protect the city. The clever merchants of Sancerre were considered the most progressive in the Capetian kingdom.

The now-fortified city repelled the English forces twice during the Hundred Years' War. But much of the surrounding area, including Saint Satur and Saint Romble, was eventually destroyed by the forces of Edward, the Black Prince. Still later, Sancerre was again the site of a vicious attack called the Siege of Sancerre (1572–1573) during the Wars of Religion. The siege was one of the last times in European history where *trebuchets*, the "Arquebuses of Sancerre," were used in warfare. The stalwart Huguenot population held out for nearly eight months against the king's Catholic forces before being defeated. In 1621 much of the feudal *château* and city walls were destroyed by orders of the king to prevent further resistance.

The Sancerre countryside was devastated by the mass exodus of Protestant merchants and tradesmen in the 17th century after the revocation of the Edict of Nantes

(1685) by the "Sun King" Louis XIV. The area suffered considerably for at least a century afterward. Sancerre became more attractive, however, by the construction of a suspension bridge at Saint Thibault (1834), the Lateral Canal of the Loire (1838), and decades later, the Bourges-Sancerre railroad line (1885). Life flowed back into the region.

In 1874, the Crussol d'Uzès family (of the duchy of Uzès, often called the First Duchy of France) built a notable mansion on the ruins of the original Château de Sancerre. In 1919, Louis-Alexandre Marnier-Lapostolle, creator of the Grand Marnier liqueur, purchased this Louis XII–style mansion and vineyards. During World War II, Sancerre was a regional command center for the French Resistance.

Sancerre grapes have a history as well. Until the late 19th century, Sancerre produced mainly fine red wines from the Pinot Noir grape. The region's link to the duchy of Burgundy (red wine country) may explain why Pinot Noir was grown here in abundance. But tragedy struck. In the late 19th century, the phylloxera epidemic devastated the area, wiping out the majority of the region's vines. These destroying aphids killed much of the wine crops, though some Pinot Noir vines were retained while most of the Gamay was lost. Locals wept as they cleared the decimated fields. The acreage was ultimately replanted with

Sauvignon Blanc vines, partly because they grafted better onto American rootstocks, which were used due to their resistance to the pests.

The vines flourished once again—and white wine predominated. In 1936 Sancerre white was given AOC status; reds were AOC classified in 1959. Today, the following communes fall inside the "Sancerre" and "Sancerre-Loire Valley" controlled wine label of origin region: Bannay, Bué, Crézancy-en-Sancerre, Menetou-Râtel, Ménétréol, Montigny, Saint Satur, Sainte-Gemme, Sancerre, Sury-en-Vaux, Thauvenay, Veaugues, and Verdigny et Vinon.

During the 20th century, the wines became especially popular in Paris as a flavorful equivalent to Beaujolais. In the 1970s and 1980s, Sancerre had evolved into an elegant and food-friendly wine with a stellar reputation. The area now produces superb white, red, and rosé wine.

But Sancerre is not just all wine flash. The earthy smell of happy goats tells visitors immediately that Sancerre is a haven for goat's-cheese making. The nearby village of Chavignol, which gave its name to the Crottin de Chavignol cheese, is located here. And other cheesy favorites that melt in your mouth hail from this locale as well.

Wine tasting first is *de rigueur* in Sancerre, however. A visit to the Maison des Sancerre is helpful if you hope to get an understanding of superlative local vintages. A very good film in the lobby explains the evolution of Sancerre wines—plus you can taste these succulent beauties in the tasting room. I particularly relish wonderful Sancerres. Unlike the Sauvignon Blancs of New Zealand or America, Sancerres are restrained with notes of citrus and chalk, rather than ripe fruit. As you drink, you're reminded of lime, grapefruit, and lemon, as well as herbs. In a pinch, you can enjoy a Sancerre with any type of meal since its composition fits with most any flavor.

After your tastings, you'll want to visit the sensory garden within the grounds of the Maison. Here, you can practice identifying the aromas that you find in the wines. The boutique at the entrance of the Maison offers a great range of gifts and resources too.

A visit to the nearby Sancerre Tourist Office offers some wonderful ideas for exploring the area. One of these is the Sancerre Past and Present walking tour. This self-guided tour of about 1.5 hours sets out from the tourist office. All you need do is follow the burgundy line as it leads you through the picturesque medieval streets of the village with its pretty blue shutters and ancient doorways interspersed with artisanal boutiques. Along the way, you'll see the spectacular Tour des Fiefs. Built in 1380, this last remaining tower was once one of six that formed Sancerre's original fortifications. For a small donation you can climb the tower. Up top, you'll be rewarded with a spectacular view, which takes in the Loire River, the nearby viaducts, vineyards, and local *château*.

Sancerre Accommodations

Le Panoramic Hôtel has rooms with magnificent views.
http://www.panoramicotel.com
Château de Beaujeu is a stunning location with much to offer. Think of it as a French version of Downtown Abbey.

http://www.chateau-de-beaujeu.com

Sancerre Dining & Wine Bars

La Tour, intimate but not at all stuffy, uses local produce and offers the quality and service you'd expect from a starred restaurant. If you happen to be visiting at lunchtime, I can highly recommend the reasonably priced three-course lunch special, which, as in typical high-end French dining, are actually six courses. Reservations are recommended. http://latoursancerre.fr
Auberge Joseph Mellot, a restaurant founded in 1882, provides friendly service, fine food, and noted wines. See the amazing copper still, originally used for making Eau de Vie in the 1800s. And don't miss the enticing boutique. http://www.josephmellot.com/index.html
La Tasse d'Argent (Les Augustins) is where you'll get a fantastic dinner overlooking the vines. http://www.restaurant-traiteur-lesaugustins.com/en/
Picnicking is an absolute must-try in this verdant Heaven on earth. Pick up a couple of small white discs of Crottin de Chavignol, buy some of the delectable local ham called Jambon de Sancerre, acquire a baguette or two, plus some wine and paper cups, and you're off on the most marvelous dining adventure on the lovely Sancerre hillsides.

Wine and Cheese Tour**

The Sancerrois region in eastern Berry is famous for its luscious wines and tasty cheeses. Anyone—from gourmets to run-of-the-mill fans—can enjoy a most unique opportunity to sample the fabulous tastes of Sancerre by taking the self-led wine and cheese route here.

This approximately 20-mile meander makes for a perfect day of noshing and wine tasting, with just a little driving, and some of the most gorgeous scenery on the planet. Here are the details of the route from point to point:

1. *Sancerre.* Start at the Maison des Sancerre for an orientation. http://maison-des-sancerre.com/mds/en/
2. *Ménétréol-sous-Sancerre (less than 2 miles).* At Chèvrerie de Chamons, see how Crottins de Chavignol are made and taste your way to the gift shop. (See the frisky ponies nearby as well.) http://www.chevrerie-les-chamons.com
3. *Vinon (about 5 miles).* Wine growers in this charming village offer guided tours and wine tastings (plus wine to purchase).
4. *Bué (about 1.5 miles).* Nestled here are such famous vintners as Crochet, Balland, and Roger. Wine tours and tastings are available.
5. *Chavignol (about 6 miles).* You'll find quaint village charm with a marvelous exhibition at the cheese shop Dubois-Boulay, which tells the story of the famous goat's cheese.

http://www.dubois-boulay.fr

6. *Verdigny (1 mile)*. By appointment only, pay a visit to the Musée de la Vigne et du Vin that charts the history of the winemaking area. It has some stellar historical pieces, such as centuries-old ancient wooden wine press. http://tourisme-sancerre.com

I can highly recommend this wonderful tasting route that is both sumptuous and romantic. The exquisite Sancerre area beauties and tastes will linger in your memory for a lifetime.

Château de Valençay***

The renaissance *château* of Valençay is a massive luxuriously furnished structure with echoes of its former owner Talleyrand (a famous French diplomat who helped broker the Louisiana Purchase). It has a killer kitchen, lovely gardens, kid-friendly activities, elaborate big toys, and lots of summer events such as fencing demonstrations and candlelit visits.

—Rick Steves, *Snapshot Loire Valley*

Château de Valençay is among the most splendid *châteaux* in the Loire. Located in a quiet corner to the southeast of the Loire valley, it's slightly removed from the grand estates of Chambord and Chenonceau, but it's one of the most beautiful, with its romantic spires, intricate decorations, and Renaissance symmetry—in addition to its breathtaking grounds where peacocks and llamas roam in regal splendor.

The castle was originally built on the remains of a 13th century domain in Valençay in the 15th century. The fiefdom was acquired by Robert II d'Estampes in 1451; he then extended the property. It was substantially rebuilt in the first half of the 16th century by great-grandson Jacques d'Estampes, using predominantly the Renaissance style that was fashionable at the time. He notably finished the large tower, adding an uncommon imperial roof. The marriage of his son, Jean. to heiress Sara d'Applaincourt relaunched construction with the building of a remarkable keep in the style of Chambord.

It was under the reign of Louis XIV, when the title of second Marquis de Valençay was given to Jacques II, and then to his son, Dominique, that the d'Estampes family reached its peak. Dominique made a prestigious alliance in marrying Marie-Louise de Montmorency and had a particularly favorable position in the king's court. Thanks to him, the buildings surrounding the Cour d'Honneur were completed, including the west wing, coupled with a gallery, plus construction of a symmetrical wing to the east, and a stone arcade wall to the south enclosing the courtyard.

As is sometimes the case with history, the d'Estampes died out with no direct heirs. Continued conflicts arose related to the heritage of the estate and *château*. The *château* was sold several times before becoming the property of farmer-general Philippe-Charles de Villemorien in 1766. Villemorien cleared some of the old wing structure and had a new *façade*, courtyard, and roof added to the main building.

In 1803 the influential (some say manipulative) diplomat Charles Maurice de Talleyrand (1754–1838) purchased the estate. Cultivated and highly intelligent (though hobbled by a clubfoot which he grew artful at hiding), Prince de Talleyrand was one of Napoleon's most important ministers.

Talleyrand, however, is a controversial figure. His career spanned the regimes of Louis XVI, the years of the French Revolution, and the reigns of Napoleon, Louis XVIII, and Louis-Philippe. Those he served often distrusted Talleyrand; but many, like Napoleon, found him extremely useful. Talleyrand artfully supported the aristocracy, then the Revolution, then the Restoration—seldom misstepping the political terrain.

He may have been the most political statesman of his era—especially because he had a cat-like ability to land on his feet no matter who was in charge of France. The name "Talleyrand" has become synonymous for crafty, cynical diplomacy. Even the estate of Valençay has this to say:

Distancing himself from those in power as soon as he thought the worst hit, he willingly supported the monarchy, Revolution, Directory, Consultate, the first Restoration and the July Monarchy. This man also had a wonderful sense of humor, for he once said: "I have not abandoned any government before it abandoned itself."

An entrepreneur at heart, Talleyrand became a great businessman who never hesitated to invest in companies or take chances on real estate. He served as Foreign Minister under several regimes; he was famed for practicing the "art of diplomacy" which today we would call the "art of bribery."

At Napoleon Bonaparte's insistence, Talleyrand (with additional cash from Napoleon's coffers) purchased Valençay. Talleyrand seldom visited, but he continued to renovate as well as to build servants' quarters and rearrange the gardens. Napoleon wanted to have a grand estate in which to entertain foreign dignitaries.

At one point, Napoleon had Talleyrand "host" King Ferdinand VII of Spain and his family after Napoleon's invasion of Spain. The problem was, Napoleon wouldn't allow the family to leave for six years (1808–1813). Talleyrand fumed at having to serve as "jailor," but he apparently fussed over the King's comfort and built a theatre for him and his family. He also took great pains to school the servants on the proper etiquette when serving a king and his progeny. Later, Talleyrand resigned from Napoleon's ministry—and then took bribes from foreign powers to divulge Napoleon's secrets.

Among some of Talleyrand's other notable accomplishments before he retired in 1834 were helping to restore the House of Bourbon to the throne of France, being ambassador to Britain, and negotiating the sale of the Louisiana Territory to America (under President Thomas

Jefferson) for $11,250,000.

When Talleyrand expired in 1838, he had no legitimate heirs (but plenty of illegitimate offspring, since he was a man of considerable sexual appetites). His collateral descendants retained ownership of the state until 1952 when the male line ended. The last prince bequeathed the property to his stepson, who sold it at auction in 1979.

Interestingly, Valençay escaped World War II unscathed, since the princes of Talleyrand-Périgord were linked to German nobility by virtue of their nominal control of a duchy in Prussia. On this technicality, Valençay was spared German occupation; and thus, the French were able to store some of the finest Louvre pieces here unmolested, including the Winged Victory and Venus de Milo.

Today, the royals and politicians are gone, and the public has wonderful access to this mighty estate. A visit to Valençay is definitely a treat. But the estate operates within strict windows of visitation, so check the website for details before you visit.

The estate itself is all magnificent glamour. The entrance pavilion, designed like a feudal keep but for show only, looks like the entrance to a magic castle. The west wing includes a dramatic gallery devoted to the Talleyrand family and the elegant Grand and Blue Salons brimming with sumptuous Empire furnishings. Upstairs are the fantastic apartments of the King of Spain and his family.

Outside, black swans, ducks, and peacocks strut majestically through the splendid gardens. In the great English Park beyond, deer, llama, camels, and kangaroos live in harmony under the great trees. Château de Valençay is now very much a local attraction with lots of activities and family-friendly entertainment. Here you'll find a substantial labyrinth, children's play areas, an automobile museum, historical re-enactments, and several fantastic light shows and pageants.

On "Gourmet Thursdays," chefs offer gourmet food demonstrations. "Christmas at the Castle" is an absolute highlight of the holidays when visitors can enjoy the Christmas-themed gardens, take a workshop on Christmas cake making, and create wreaths from scratch. Valençay also has its own wine appellation; you can wine and dine at the handy L'Orangerie restaurant on the premises situated in the gardens (although service can be spotty). The famous pyramid-shaped Valençay goat's cheese with a flat top comes from nearby goat farms—try a taste on a crunchy baguette with the estate's wine. http://www.chateau-Valencay.fr/en/

Valençay Accommodations/Dining & Wine Bars

There are no particular recommendations; stay elsewhere

and drive to the *château*. There are some passable eateries near the *château,* such as La Duchesse de Dino.

In sum, outdoorsy Berry is another unique area in the Loire Valley that offers fine wine, legendary cheese, stunning outdoor experiences, and a glimpse of the royal lifestyle of the past that visitors of today can now enjoy with relish.

CHAPTER TEN

Northern Loire
(Chartres, Le Mans, and Alpes Mancelles)

Chartres, town of light: Built in the middle of stretches of golden wheat swaying in the wind, Chartres has several strings to its bow. Its cathedral, listed as a World Heritage site by UNESCO, will be your lighthouse in this Beauce landscape. With 2,600m² of stained glass lighting up the heart of the nave, this monumental building is a model of gothic architecture.

—*http://www.loirevalleytourism.com*

Chartres, with its spectacular gothic cathedral, is the main draw in this northern corner of the Loire valley called the Eure-et-Loir. But Le Mans has pride of place not only as the home of the world-famous 24-hour auto race, but also as a stellar medieval town with many sites to beguile visitors.

This relatively flat area is named after the two rivers that cross the land, the Eure and the Loir (no *e*). In the eastern portion, the land is all wide-open spaces, ideal for cultivating cereal grains—but you'll also see windmills dotting the land, thanks to Dutch settlers from centuries past. In the western portion, undulating hills and patches of forests form the Perche region. This Northern Loire territory serves as a gateway to the rest of the Loire region. Since Chartres is a short hop by train from Paris, many visitors journey here in a morning and can be back in Paris for a late lunch. Some stop in on their way back from the Loire as they travel to Paris. Still others come for a weekend or a week to discover the delights of this unusual area.

Although not as industrial as Orléans and its surroundings, the Northern Loire has some destination locales for those with specific targets. These include Chartres, for its ethereal cathedral—absolutely the most famous in the Loire; Le Mans, the race car capital of France with a royal history to boot; and the Alpes Mancelles, for its hilly and wooded outdoor beauty primed for outdoor lovers.

But first here's a snapshot of the area's history. The Eure-et-Loir is one of the original 83 regions created during the French Revolution on March 4, 1790, pursuant to the Act of December 22, 1789. It was created mainly from parts of the former provinces of Orléanais (Beauce) and Maine (Perche), but also parts of Île-de-France.

The current *département* corresponds to the central part of the land of the Carnutes (a Gaulish tribe), who had their capital at Autricum (Chartres). The Carnutes were known for their commitment, real or imagined, to the ancient Druidic religion. The Romans came and went, and various forces held sway. In the Middle Ages, the local gentry grew in power and authority, and they fortified their residences and constructed impregnable dungeons to protect themselves during sieges. Due to its proximity to Paris, royals often happened by.

Many stopped at Chartres to pay their respects (or beg for forgiveness) at the extraordinary cathedral.

Le Mans was a favored abode of Geoffrey Plantagenet, Count of Anjou. Geoffrey was the father of Henry II, who became King of England in 1154; young Henry was actually born in Le Mans. Geoffrey was married to Matilda, the granddaughter of William the Conqueror. Geoffrey died and was buried in Le Mans. Like his father before him, Henry II retired in old age to Le Mans—that is until his pesky son Richard the Lionheart expelled him. (Henry ultimately died in Chinon, as I previously mentioned, and was buried in Fontevraud near Eleanor.)

Another royal had troubles here. Madness struck Charles VI in the summer of 1392 when he rode from Le Mans with his troops to the west to defeat the Duke of Brittany. Overtaken by paranoid delusions, Charles rode aimlessly and ultimately had to be tied down in a wagon by his troops in order to be transported back to Le Mans for care. Henry V of England took advantage of Charles's off-and-on bouts with madness and had him name Henry himself as his heir.

In the modern era, Le Mans attracts auto-racing fans, while Chartres and Alpes Mancelles attract lovers of God and nature, not necessarily in that order. Most of the area's population here is rural. More than half of the region is composed of the Beauce plain, one of the most productive plateaus in France. It's a treeless area of isolated grain farms and large villages. The Thimerais portion to the northwest encompasses wooded areas and grasslands. To the southwest is the hilly Perche; the rolling hills of the Hurepoix lie in the northeastern area.

The region is divided into the four *arrondissements* of Chartres, Châteaudun, Dreux, and Nogent-le-Rotrou. Chartres is world famous for its High Gothic cathedral and stained glass industry. Not only is mega-busy Le Mans a thriving provincial capital renowned for good food, but it's the birthplace of the French auto industry. Alpes Mancelles is a pretty paradise for hikers and campers that's located just minutes from the hubbub of Paris.

Eure-et-Loir's products include flour, leather, and agricultural machinery, as well as a sparkling cider made famously from the Reinette apple. It is also a haven for the French cosmetics industry that keeps very busy here. Join me now as we tour the sites in: 1–Chartres; 2–Le Mans; and 3–Alpes Mancelles.

Chartres**

Chartres, very early on, had an influence on French history. Starting with the Neolithic period, it was inhabited by humans and would see a lot of great men pass through who forged the history of France, from Henry IV to Jean Moulin. Today, well anchored in Modernity, it has reinvented itself and become, inside the space of a few decades, the Capital of Light and Perfume.

—*http://www.chartres.fr*

According to art historian Emile Male, "Chartres is the mind of the Middle Ages manifest." The name of Chartres brings to mind the most famous Gothic Cathedral in the world. For more than 700 years, crowds of pilgrims and visitors have been admiring it, praying in it, and sometimes living in it, seeking sustenance and redemption. But the town too is a revelation of sorts as a busy working town with a spiritual vibe. Chartres has a wonderful earthy ambiance that hearkens back to the Druidian period when Mother Nature held sway and formal religion had not begun.

The history of Chartres is varied, yet in many ways miraculous. A natural defensive site where the Eure and Cousnon rivers met, the Chartres location was settled during the Paleolithic Era. The town later became the capital city for the Gaulic Carnutes (from whom it gets its name). Romans later renamed it Autricum. Autricum became an important town and the seat of an important bishopric starting at the end of the 4th century.

The initial centuries saw wars, Norman invasions (in 858 and 911), and then sacking by the Normans. Chartres rapidly acquired the role of a religious, political, and military capital. Around the year 1000, during the time of Bishop Fulbert, Chartres became a center for intellectuals and spiritual reformers. During the 12th century, the population expanded toward the valley.

Chartres was ultimately separated into two sections that have a 30-meter difference in height: the high part of town, with the *château* and the cathedral, and the low part, where activities that depend on the river are carried out: tanneries, curriers, mills, etc. In 1328, the Chartres region, which had been under the control of the Counts of Blois and of

PJ Adams   365

Champagne, became part of the French royal domain. In 1584, the town served as the coronation locale for Henry of Navarre, who was crowned Henri IV in the cathedral.

Thanks to the moderate stance exercised by the inhabitants of Chartres during the Revolution, the Cathedral suffered only limited damage. After the French Revolution, the cathedral was "transformed" into the Temple de la Raison (Temple of Reason), which Antoine-François Sergent-Marceau proposed to avoid its destruction. An accidental fire in1836 destroyed its old framework. The roof was then rebuilt with copper.

By the mid 1800s, the town became a more modern pivot point when the railway system reached it, a splendid train station was built, and a tramway was created in 1849. In 1909 an airfield was laid. More than three thousand pilots got their training during the 1900s at Chartres.

The city suffered its first bombing on August 15, 1918, during WW I; later it was bombed again in WW II in June 1940 and May 1944. On June 17, 1940, the *prefect*, Jean Moulin, courageously opposed the demands of the occupying German troops; he unified the French Resistance at Charles de Gaulle's request. He was arrested in 1943 by the Nazis and died near Metz, while being transported to Germany. He is considered the first member of the French Resistance movement. Sadly, in 1944, prior to liberation by the 20th US Army Corps and by local patriots, the city's Porte Guillaume and its library, which had one of the largest collections of materials in France, were destroyed.

Starting in the 1950s, Chartres experienced true economic and social transformation as a result of industrial decentralization: Twenty thousand jobs were created in the town, and it ballooned from 27,000 inhabitants to 42,000 in just four decades. Today, Chartres is a haven for cosmetic manufacturing and as such has been dubbed "the Capital of Light and Perfume."

In the modern age, Chartres Cathedral remains one of the most visited pilgrimage destinations for religious and nonreligious visitors. I will explore it here in some detail.

The Chartres Cathedral is one of the great buildings of the world—and it is now a cherished UNESCO World Heritage site. Vast and beautiful, it stuns by its sure size and grandeur. (Photos don't do it justice at all.) The cathedral was constructed quickly by medieval standards in just 25 years, starting in 1020. It has curiously mismatched spires, one simple from the 1100s and one elegant from the 16th century Gothic period. The structure incorporates the west front and the crypt of its late Romanesque predecessor, which had been destroyed by fire in 1194.

The "new" building incorporated Gothic ideas to create a masterpiece of craftsmanship. The most striking features upon entering the cathedral are its massive dimensions; it has the widest nave of any church in France. The second most striking feature is the extraordinary quantity and richness of the multi-hued stained glass. Finally, it has an amazing floor labyrinth that exists within the cathedral itself. This is quite unusual and has a religious significance I'll explain presently.

If you enter the structure on a sunny day, you may feel like you are on the inside of a great kaleidoscope. This is because the light is streaming through the cathedral's 150 dazzling stained glass widows. (All totaled, their combined glass surface adds up to 2600 square meters.) The color and craftsmanship, depicting Bible stories, is simply awe-inspiring.

According to tradition, Chartres Cathedral has housed the tunic of the Blessed Virgin Mary, the Sancta Camisia, since 876. This delicate relic was said to have been given to the cathedral by Charlemagne; Charlemagne allegedly received it as a gift during a trip to Jerusalem.

Because of this relic, Chartres has been a very important pilgrimage center—and the faithful still come from the world over to honor it.

During the Middle Ages, the building was often filled with overnight guests, many of them sick and hoping for a miracle cure. An unusual 13th century labyrinth is inlaid on the floor of the nave (interior labyrinths were a feature of many medieval cathedrals, but this one is quite extraordinary). As penance, pilgrims would get on their knees and "walk" the labyrinth, symbolizing the Way of the Cross. The journey of 860 feet typically took them about an hour to complete.

Notably, the stained glass of Chartres is studied endlessly by scholars today. (Visitors are encouraged to bring binoculars to view the panels fully. In a pinch, I use my camera to zoom in to see the detail, particularly of the

West and North Rose Windows, as well as the Tree of Jessee.) This is arguably one of the best collections of stained glass in the entire world.

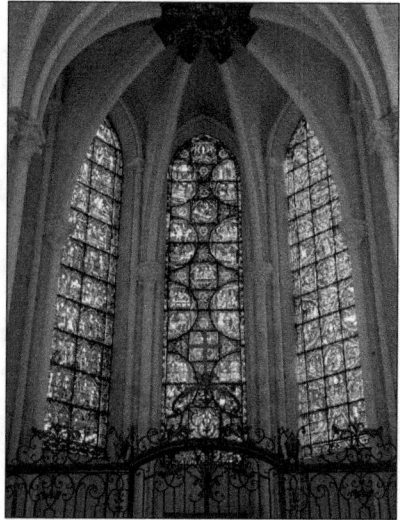

Understandably, during both World Wars, each window was dismantled piece by piece and moved to safety. Not a shard was lost. Some windows have been restored and re-leaded in recent decades, but much restoration continues.

The Chartres labyrinth is the subject of continual research and speculation as to its significance and power. There are more than 177,000 articles about it on the internet, and numerous books and essays have explored its origins and modern-day applications. This particular article by Jeff Saward provides some fascinating detail about it: http://www.labyrinthos.net/chartresfaq.html

Explanatory signs in English and French explain the various exhibits and areas within the cathedral. Tours are offered in English starting at the gift shop. Tours of the crypt (the largest in France) are also offered. When you visit, I would highly recommend a walk through the famous labyrinth, as well taking time to sit down in the cathedral and contemplate the beauty around you. It's truly a life-affirming experience.

Near the cathedral is the exceptional Centre International du Vitrail. This organization is committed to the preservation, research, and education of stained glasswork. You can watch skilled artists at work, take classes, and learn the secrets of stained glass design. Nearby are two additional sites. First is the Maison Picassiette, home of eccentric train conductor Raymond Isidore (1900–1964). On the way home from work each day, Isidore would collect bits of broken glass and pottery. He then spent his lifetime making them into sculpture, mosaics, and murals that appear all over his house and garden (even covering some of the furniture). Second is the Musée des Beaux-Arts, the Fine Arts Museum housed in the Bishop's Palace that displays an important collection of art, tapestries, and enamels.

The town itself is also worth a wander for its quirky streets, ancient half-timbered houses, and old bridges. Shops, crafts work shops and restaurants punctuate the town, as well as consortiums of glassblowers, perfumers, and cabinet makers, to name just a few. When you dine, try the local *foie gras, Pâté de Chartres*, and zesty Perche cider. Chartres is also famous for *Le Miel de Chartres* (its own honey), as well as *cochelin,* a puff pastry in the shape of a man and filled with chocolate cream or almond paste.

Chartres is an easy and popular day trip from Paris—but it's also the spiritual gateway to those who enter or leave the Loire Valley. A scant 100 km drive from Paris (or minutes on the TGV), Chartres is well worth a visit. Tours of the Old Town are available through the tourist office, either with a guide or with a one-hour audiocassette (although a wander by yourself works too). For sure pleasure, take a horse-drawn carriage or little white train ride to view the town from a comfortable seat.

A number of festivals are held in and around Chartres. Among them are Musical Saturdays and Lyrical Days, where music is presented in a variety of formats. The Festival de Jazz is held in March, while the Harpsichord Festival kicks off in May. The International Organ Festival is held July to August.

Near Chartres is the much-loved village called Illiers-

Combray. This is where beloved novelist Marcel Proust (1871–1922) spent his childhood. Proust, arguably the finest French novelist of the 20th century, drew inspiration for his great work, *À la Recherche du Temps Perdu* (*In Search of Lost Time*) here. The Musée Marcel Proust is located in the home where the author spent time with his aunt; it displays family memorabilia and artifacts of the author. Though depicted in his works, the town of Illiers was disguised in Proust's works as "Combray." In honor of the hundredth anniversary of Proust's birth in 1971, the town changed its name from Illiers to Illiers-Combray.

Chartres Accommodations

Le Grand Monarque is a fantastic Best Western property in an 18th century building, with wonderful rooms and a fine restaurant with a noted wine cellar.
http://www.bw-grand-monarque.com/uk/index.php
Hôtel Jehan de Beauce has elegant rooms in a fine location. http://www.jehandebeauce.fr

Chartres Dining & Wine Bars

St. Hilaire is a lovely bistro with great prices, great dishes, and great wines, as well as a convivial atmosphere. http://www.restaurant-saint-hilaire.fr
Le Café Serpente is a place I adore for breakfast or lunch. It's right across from the cathedral; it's friendly and not too expensive or fussy. http://leserpente.fr/en

Le Mans**

Located just under an hour southwest of Paris via the high-speed TGV train, Le Mans sits on the banks of the Sarthe River at its confluence with the Huisne. It's a thriving municipality with a medieval core, famous for tasty cuisine like potted pork *rillettes*, thirst-quenching sparkling cider, and the granddaddy of all 24-hour auto-racing events, Le Mans.

The Old Town (Le Vieux Mans) is built on a pretty hill overlooking the rushing river. It can be explored easily on foot. Perky restaurants and craft shops brimming with goodies anchor its winding, cobbled streets with half-timbered houses. Nearby are 18th century Renaissance town houses finished with handsome wrought iron balconies and ornate *façades*. Along the Sarthe quay, the finely restored Gallo-Roman ramparts with their pinkish hues make for a stunning landmark. The lengthy military-crisp ramparts are punctuated by eleven towers and make for one of the longest remaining ramparts seen in France today.

The local Cathedrale St.-Julien sits in a bustling square called Place des Jacobins; this grand Romanesque church is worth a visit for its Y-shaped, two-tiered flying buttresses, finely carved stone capitals, and intricate interior. At the entrance to the Wilbur Wright tunnel that cuts through the town stands a monument to the famous American aviator who came to Le Mans for airplane trials.

Nearby is the captivating but listing Maison Adam et Ève. This is the superb Renaissance mansion and former home of Jean de l'Épine, a noted astrologer and physician. A bit further, the Musée de Tessé is housed in the old bishop's palace built in the 19th century; it features a particularly good collection of Egyptian artifacts, Plantagenet memorabilia, and Renaissance artwork. In spring you can view the amiable town plus visit the exceptional Spring Festival welcoming in the glories of the season to Le Mans. In September, you can enjoy the much-loved Onion Festival, and the list of fun and frolic goes on and on.

Le Mans is most famous, of course, as the birthplace of the French motor-car industry and, later, the grueling 24-hour motor race beloved the world over. In the latter half of the 19th century, Amédée Bollée (1844–1917) became interested in the newfangled contraption called the automobile. A bell-founder by trade, Bollée built his first car, called *L'Obélissante,* in 1873. He later built the *Mancelle,* the first car to have a front-end engine under a "bonnet" as well as a transmission shaft. Austria's longest running emperor, Franz-Joseph, even went for a ride in it.

Bollée's son Amédée (1867–1926) spent much of his life racing cars; these were fitted with Michelin tires and reached 62 mph. After WW I, he began to produce an early form of piston rings, which became the main line of manufacture at his factory.

The idea of a French Grand Prix "race" originated from the Gordon Bennett races, established by American millionaire James Gordon Bennett, Jr. in 1900 and intended to encourage automobile industries through sport. By 1903 the Gordon Bennett races had become some of the most prestigious in Europe. The idea of closed-road racing among similar cars replaced the previous model of unregulated vehicles racing between distant towns, over open roads. Entries into the Gordon Bennett races were by country. The winning country earned the right to organize the next race.

On June 27, 1906, the first prize on the 12-hour Sarthe circuit in France, dubbed the "French Grand Prix," was won by Ferenc Szisz, a Hungarian driving a Renault with detachable Michelin rims. In 1908 Amédée's brother Léon invited Wilbur Wright to attempt one of his first flights in an "aeroplane" at Les Hunaudières. In 1936 Louis Renault set his first decentralized factory south of Le Mans.

Over the years, the idea percolated for a longer and longer race, testing the stamina of man and car, while the auto industry expanded around Le Mans. In 1923, Gustave Singher and Georges Durand launched the first Le Mans endurance test. It was to become a universal sporting event held in June each year, but also a testing ground for car manufacturers. The difficulties of the circuit, coupled with the day-long length of the race, were designed to be a severe test of the endurance of the auto as well as its driver and crew. Nearly a hundred years later, this mega-popular event is still known as the "Grand Prix of Endurance and Efficiency."

Today's spectacular race represents one leg of the Triple Crown of Motorsport; the other events are the Indianapolis 500 and the Monaco Grand Prix. The 24-hour Le Mans circuit is 8.5 miles long and runs a mix of public roads and special racing circuit. It begins with a roar at the Tertre Rouge bend on N 138. Drivers make the journey over and over for the full 24 hours, engines revving, petrol flaming the air, the squeal of brakes punctuating the turns as the vehicles hurtle up the Hunaudières at 200 mpg, as roars heave up from the crowds every few minutes.

Modern Le Mans is such a draw that a gigantic racetrack

complex accommodates the legion of fans (nearly 200,000, plus 2500 journalists) who come from all over the world to watch the race. Scattered in the pinewoods or fields are additional spectators who love to view the day long, ear-splitting spectacle from a picnic blanket spread with wine and cheese and a baguette—or from the top of a tree! Note:

the track and views have been much improved since the tragedy of 1955 when driver Pierre Levegh and 83 spectators died in a horrific crash. For full safety, however, you can also watch it on satellite TV these days.

Le Mans has become not only a world-famous race, it's the basis of an entire culture built up around the race, the people, and, of course, the legendary cars. The race is the basis of numerous video games for armchair race drivers. And most readers will be familiar with movies related to Le Mans, including Steve McQueen's 1971 cult favorite *Le Mans* and the 2008 documentary *Truth in 24* narrated by Jason Statham about Audi's attempt to win a fifth straight title. A recent documentary called *Steve McQueen: The Man & Le Mans* details McQueen's time at Le Mans and the arduous making of the movie. (This is a raw depiction of the Hollywood star who comes across as a narcissistic meddler with addiction problems; McQueen nearly torpedoed the movie due to his incessant demands. But it's interesting to learn the backstory as well as hear from some of the original actors and crew who yet live to tell the dramatic tale.)

There are other versions of the 24-hour race for motorcycles, karts, and trucks. There's also a cheeky parody race called the "24 Hours of LeMons" that pits cars that are "lemons" against each other in races across the US, Australia, and New Zealand. To learn about the actual 24 hours of Le Mans races (or to become a social media fan), go to http://www.lemans.org/en/24-hours-of-le-mans/.

After the big race is over and all the champagne is gone, fans can extend their pleasure with a nostalgic wander through the Musée de l'Automobile de la Sarthe (Musée de 24 Hours). This extensive car museum with more than 115 vehicles details the race, shows the cars that have run them, and presents a superb collection of vintage wheels, including a 1924 Bentley, a 1949 Ferrari, a 1992 Peugeot, and a 1998 Jaguar—all in mint condition. http://musee24h.sarthe.com

Le Mans Accommodations

Mercure Le Mans Centre Hôtel is a mid-scale hotel for business or pleasure, within walking distance of the old town; it's elegant, yet affordable. http://www.mercure.com
Inter Hôtel Chantecler offers comfortable and classic accommodations near old town. Books up fast in season. http://www.hotelchantecler.fr

Le Mans Dining & Wine Bars

Le Grenier à Sel is a bright restaurant in a period building, and it offers a delicious, traditional menu and good wine list. http://www.restaurant-le-grenier-a-sel.fr/restaurant-le-mans
La Ciboulette is a gourmet address that offers consistently good food. http://laciboulettelemans.com

Alpes Mancelles

When you reach castle and racecar overload, you may yearn for the great outdoors to reground in nature. This area of the Loire will not disappoint. The Alpes Mancelles is the French term for the "Alps of Le Mans." Although an exaggeration, these winsome hills and green meadows that stretch between Fresnay-sur-Sarthe and Alençon form a kind of lowland alpine experience for nature lovers. Streams wind through deep gorges, sheep and fruit trees dot the hillsides, and heather carpets the land as far as the eye can see.

Now incorporated in the regional park of Normandie-Maine, the prettiest villages are St-Céneri-le-Gérel and St-Léonard-des-Bois. Sports abound here, of course, including walking, hiking, zip lining, camping, cycling, and fishing. This area makes for great family vacations in camping or *gîte* venues, as well as holiday hotels and cottages. Check this website for accommodation ideas and dining offerings.

http://www.tourisme-alpesmancelles.fr/en/

Keep in mind that this off-the-beaten path area makes for a quick sojourn in a rental car from Paris. Or it can cap off your visit to the Loire in the lap of auto royalty—or the arms of Mother Nature or the ethereal heart of Chartres. Whichever you choose, you'll find the Northern Loire yet another stunning area of the Valley of the Kings to enjoy for its unique beauties.

Conclusion

The Loire Valley is the biggest area in France ever to be included in UNESCO's World Heritage list.... Kings, artists and famous authors have fallen under the spell of the Loire and taken up residence on its banks in droves. Here the local stone and slate are reflected in the water of the river. On foot, by bicycle or on board a barge...(one can) enjoy the harmonious landscape at the heart of the unspoiled natural world. The wines of the Loire and the renowned gastronomy can be savored in a troglodytic cave dug out of the rock, at the table of a restaurant or at a gourmet village market.

—*http://au.france.fr/en/discover/loire-valley*

Yes, the Valley of the Kings is full of wonderments. "With crenellated towers, soaring cupolas and glittering banquet halls, the *châteaux*, and the villages and vineyards that surround them, [this valley] attests to a thousand years of rich architectural, artistic and agrarian creativity," as *Lonely Planet* describes it. This truly is a paradise on earth.

As we've explored its delights in these pages, we've visited charming **Anjou** with its Plantagenet heart at Angers, its wine and horses enclave at Saumur, and its royal Abbey at Fontevraud. We've visited its storied *châteaux* at Brissac, Plessis-Bourré, Serrant, Montgeoffroy, and sprawling Montreuil Bellay.

We've traveled on to storybook **Touraine**, exploring the ancient streets of Tours and sampling the offerings of stately Amboise. We've followed the royal road of kings, queens, concubines, and creators such as Leonardo da Vinci at Clos-Lucé, the women's castle at Chenonceau, verdant Villandry, jewel box Azay le Rideau, Sleeping Beauty's Ussé, serf-and-seigneur Langeais, and wine-haven Chinon where wine is king and Joan of Arc shaped the history of France.

We've meandered grand **Orléanais and Blésois**, exploring the towns of historic Orléans where Joan of Arc defeated the English, troglodyte haven Vendôme, and Renaissance Blois. We scaled the heights of granddaddy Chambord with its 400+ rooms and 365 fireplaces. We wandered grandiose Chaumont and the glorious international garden installations. We met the tail-wagging hounds at graceful Cheverny and visited Voltaire's favorite Sully-sur-Loire.

We detoured to **Berry**, where we went on a wine-and-cheese escapade through wine and cheese princess Sancerre, lingered at Bourges, and gaped at the grandeur that is Valençay. Finally, we revved our engines at Le Mans in **Northern Loire**, then grounded in Alpes Mancelles and communed with the All-That-Is at heavenly Chartres.

But there's something else that draws us here. It's an indescribable allure the Loire has, that enchants visitors and brings them back again and again. But what exactly is it? My friend Jeremy Kolbe has an idea. After living in the Loire for over twenty years, he muses:

> Some say the Loire is "*La Face Cachée de Paradise.*" In English this means "the hidden face of Paradise." I would agree the Loire feeds your palette as well as your soul. It's the place where you can live like a king without losing your life *or* your largesse.

Do we glimpse the face of heaven of here? I can't say for sure. But I do know I love this fine valley with its historic sites but accessible pleasures. Despite the fact that I've written an entire book on the area, I'm already planning a month-long sojourn next year.

I feel comfortable, enchanted, and satiated in the Loire—without incurring a heart-stopping drain on my pocketbook. The pleasures can be simple, since the views are so stunning. The wines are sumptuous but affordable. The mouthwatering cuisine and local delicacies make dining an endless pleasure.

You don't need the high vibe of Paris to be happy here. Is that paradise, as Jeremy says?

Paradise lies in the heart of the perceiver I think. I know that when I see the grand *château,* I access some fairytale place in my psyche that feels a lot like heaven. What I think I experience are the magical possibilities that humankind has made real in the Loire. I sense life's sumptuousness as it oozes out of the stone and caves and eggplant and Chinons and cheeses and regal fabrics and uber-green gardens. I stop short of saying this is God's country. But it's definitely a place for those who want to experience the wonder and abundance this most regal locale has to offer.

In all, it has been my pleasure to take you through this extraordinary Loire, the Valley of the Kings. My other books about areas of enchanting France or other topics, include:

- *Intoxicating Paris*
- *Intoxicating Southern France: Uncorking the Magic in the French Riviera, Provence, Languedoc, Dordogne, and Bordeaux*
- *Intoxicating Southern France: Provence & Languedoc Spotlight*
- *Intoxicating Southern France: French Riviera Spotlight*
- *Intoxicating Southern France: Bordeaux & Dordogne Spotlight*

- *Daughter Wisdom*
- *Freud's Revenge*

For more information about my books and travels, see www.meanderingtrailmedia.com. You can also follow me on Facebook or Twitter @PJAdams10. Happy travels!

　　　　　　Intoxicating Greater Paris: Loire, Valley of the Kings

Acknowledgments

I wish to thank a number of individuals who contributed to the creation of this book. Among them are contributor Christy Destremau of France Off the Beaten Path Tours, who provided some superb photographs plus fantastic insight into the Loire as a French local and tour expert; Chef Benoit Jussaume for his insight into his native Loire and cuisine trends; Chef Damien Garanger for teaching me about French cheese; Christophe Cosme for coaching me on *macaron* making; special thanks to Christophe Quantin for his invaluable tips on Loire cuisine (as well his patient assistance when one of my party fell ill); Angelique Quantin for her charming food tips; Jeremy Kolbe for his historical Loire insights and insider stories; Julie Kolbe for her support and Loire savvy; Jean-René and Mary-Lyn Camus, who offered me wonderful support in Saumur; Jean-Pierre Parent, France expert and wine connoisseur; fellow scribe and mentor Tom Leech for his book smarts and unflagging support; Jim Lockard, wine pro and positivity coach; Peter Stewart and Carolyn Boyd at *France Magazine* for insights and tips on France; Maureen Beals, savvy traveler and photographer; Shaun Griffin for her book shepherding; Lynette Smith for her fine editorial support; Rachal Cox for her superb design; Ashley Regan for her support and love of France; and John Birkhead and Meandering Trail Media for great photography and unflagging support.

PJ Adams is a practicing psychotherapist, best-selling author, and former publishing executive who splits her time between Southern California and Europe. Previous books include:

- *Intoxicating Paris*
- *Intoxicating Southern France: Uncorking the Magic in the French Riviera, Provence, Languedoc, Dordogne, and Bordeaux*
- *Intoxicating Southern France: Provence & Languedoc Spotlight*
- *Intoxicating Southern France: French Riviera Spotlight*
- *Intoxicating Southern France: Bordeaux & Dordogne Spotlight*
- *Daughter Wisdom*
- *Freud's Revenge*

For more information see www.meanderingtrailmedia.com, Facebook, or Twitter @PJAdams10.

Contributor Christy Destremau is the Founder and President of **France Off the Beaten Path Tours**, a France travel specialist. She's also a published photographer. As an American with French citizenship, she splits her time between her homes in France and the US. She is an active participant in her tour company's day-to-day operations, and she enjoys travel, photography, hiking/walking, writing, exploring new places, and making friends around the world. For more information go to this website: https://www.traveloffthebeatenpath.com

Index

A

B

greengage plum 71

H

Louis XIV ("the Sun King") 50

M

N

poulet 77
primogeniture 270
pyramid of fromage 82

Q

Queen of Abbeys 185
Queen's cloth 231

R

Renaissance 44
René Descartes 60
Restaurant La Maison d'a Cote 317
Richard the Lionheart 41
riding to hounds 331
rillauds 79
rillettes 79
rillons 79
Rillons 80
Ritz Hôtel 172
Rivau 277
Robin Hood 42
Rolling Stone 196
Royal Abbey 184
Royal Château of Blois 296
Russians 168

S

Sainte-Maure de Touraine 83
Saint Martin of Tours 198
Sancerre 118, 120, 345, 349
Sancta Camisia 368
Saracens 81
sardines 77
Saumur 104, 163
Saumur-Champigny 104